Love Me In Color

Bella Pursell, Reba Toledo

Love Me In Color

Cover designed by Kylah Designs

ISBN: 979-8-9900626-2-7

To all the people out there choosing to love every single day.

Note From The Author

Thank you so much for picking up a copy of **Love Me In Color**! This book has been in our brains for a long time, and we are excited to bring it to you. On that note, a few FYIs for this book are noted below.

The main location that this book takes place in is New Windsor, Virginia. Do not be alarmed if you cannot find it on a map. It did not disappear from the face of the earth. This place does not exist. The city is a figment of our imagination.

This is a closed-door romance, meaning you will not find explicit sexual scenes – commonly called 'smut.' However, there is the use of profanity and sexual references within these pages. These might not be everyone's cup of tea, and that's okay!

The potential triggers in this book are mentioned below. These may be sensitive topics for some readers. Please remember that these experiences vary from person to person, and one depiction does not represent everyone.

- Anxiety
- Anger issues
- Panic attacks
- Divorce (not by main characters)

That being said, we hope you enjoy Blake's story!

Playlist

"Chronically Cautious" by Braden Bales

"Selfish" by Madison Beer

"Easy For You To Say" by 5 Seconds Of Summer

"2AM" by Landon Conrath

"Love You Anyway" by Luke Combs

"Float" by Harbour

"Best Friends" by 5 Seconds Of Summer

"Wandering Lies" by Busty And The Bass

"Life In Color" by One Republic

Prologue

Friday afternoon.

One thousand nine hundred and eighteen days left.

I stared at my best friend from the upholstered grey couch. The itchy fabric bothered my thighs, but it was the most comfortable place to sit in the house. He paced between me and the weathered coffee table, waiting for my phone to ring. The sun started hiding behind a cloud, so the living room progressively darkened.

Connor, the CEO of Capital Media, said he would be making final decisions on staffing today. Any minute, we would hear back about whether or not I had a job waiting for me after graduation. Erik had received his call earlier.

My phone sat face up on the table, and the house was eerily quiet. We were at his house since my roommates and their boyfriends crowded our apartment. I didn't mind, but the noise just added to my nervousness. His two roommates were out of town on a camping trip, and the place smelled the best it ever had in the year he had lived here. I stared at Erik, his dark eyes comforting me at a time of uncertainty.

Time stopped when my phone rang. I stared at the unknown number on my screen.

"Pick it up!" Erik urged.

"Hello?" my hands trembled as I put the phone to my ear.

Erik sat beside me, sinking the couch and tilting me toward him. He set his comforting hand on my thigh. It was warm and sent goosebumps down my leg.

"Hello. Is this Blake Johnson?" the male voice on the other end said. "This is Connor Phillips from Capital Media."

"Yes, this is she."

"Good afternoon, Ms. Johnson. I don't want to take much time from your evening, so I'll get right into it. As we discussed, I was thoroughly impressed by your presentation on Wednesday and enjoyed our subsequent interview. I want to offer you a full-time position within Capital Media starting in July. I think you have a very bright future ahead of you, and I know I could use someone with your drive and creativity on my growing team."

"Oh, wow! Thank you so much, Mr. Phillips!"

"I understand that you cannot give me a certain answer until you see the offer, so I'm emailing that to you now. I would appreciate an answer by Monday evening."

"Yes, yes, of course. I look forward to reviewing it."

"I look forward to your response and hopefully working with you."

"Thank you," my smile was hard to contain as I hung up the phone.

Erik stared at me with a broad smile on his face, expectant. His thumb caressed my thigh as he waited for me to say something.

"I got the job!" I exclaimed, throwing my arms around my best friend as he wrapped his tightly around my waist.

"I'm so proud of you, Button!" he squeezed me, his hot breath in my ear. "It's so cool. We're going to be working together!"

"Our lives are changing, Erik," I shook him. "I'm proud of both of us." I brought him back into a hug.

Suddenly, his mood dampened. His smile was replaced with a pensive frown. "Our lives are changing," he whispered.

"Yes! It's going to be great!"

I pulled away from him and tried to coax back his smile with my own. I was successful as his dark eyes crinkled at the corners.

"Our lives are changing, Button," he repeated, bringing his hand to my cheek.

I could do nothing but stare at him as the unexpected happened. His pull was magnetic and haste, like two opposing magnets being hurled at each other. I felt his lips against mine as fireworks consumed my mind.

I sat frozen in his grasp for a second before finding the previously suppressed desire to kiss him. For a few seconds, the world was still. Then, a strange force overwhelmed me, and I pushed away from him.

"Woah, woah," I chuckled nervously. "This...this is not a good idea, Erik."

"Our lives are changing, Button," he broke away from me and stood up again. He was never good at dealing with emotions sitting down.

"Our lives are changing. We have jobs. We're graduating. Things are going to be different now."

"That's kind of the whole point of growing up," my heart rate rose.

He knelt before me, both hands firmly grasping my outer thighs. My hands went clammy at his touch. I would be lying if I claimed that the thoughts crossing his mind had not crossed mine, but the idea of putting them into action terrified me.

"Let's give us a shot," he stated, not asked.

"I'm sorry?" I muttered. My voice failed me.

"Let's give us a shot, Button. We're lying to ourselves and everyone else by pretending this isn't more than a friendship. I've had feelings for you longer than I care to admit, more feelings than I should have for my best friend. You're the only person I want to go on midnight ice cream runs with, the only person in the world who I let talk me into running three miles. Every time I look into your beautiful gray eyes, I feel like I'm looking into my future. A future I only want to have with you."

"Erik," I whispered. "I...I...its..."

His gaze didn't leave mine. He saw past every worry I had, past every objection I could muster, past every fear. I wanted to see what he saw. Yet, all I saw was that if we gave this a shot and failed, I would lose the person who meant the most to me.

"Scary, I know," his grip was now dimpling my legs where his fingers sat. "But we can handle scary. We've handled scary before. I love you, Button, and I know you love me. I think it's time we stop denying this to the world and open ourselves to the possibility of color."

I took a deep breath, and what our future could be like played in front of my eyes. A house in our hometown, a few streets from our parents. Dedicated careers for the same company – or different ones – that we could both be proud of. Maybe a baby or two. Growing old with the person that I grew up with, the person I had grown to love, even if color was not part of the equation.

"I love you too," I whispered.

He cupped my face in his hands and brought me back to him. I kissed my future, feeling the possibilities of what we could be.

Chapter One

Thursday afternoon.
Eleven days before.

DING!

The alert of the new email in my inbox instantly made my heart frantic. I stared at the dark grey bolded notification sitting patiently at the top of my inbox. The words in there called for me to open it and finally know what I was dealing with.

Nathaniel, the east region sales manager, promised to email me how the meeting went immediately after he walked out. I knew that the message in front of me had likely been typed in the elevator or from the parking lot of Amelia's office. His name was proudly bolded in the 'from' line. This was it.

This was the email that the entire company, but especially my team, had been anxiously awaiting.

The solid blinds that covered the glass wall that allowed me to see my team had been shut all day. I didn't want any of them to see me panic if the news was bad. The illusion of privacy for my anxious pacing and finger-tapping was comforting while I waited for Natheniel's email. It had been challenging to focus most of the day, and I found myself refreshing my email every ten minutes.

Lainee, my administrative assistant, knocked on the half-shut glass door of my office. Her long, wavy hair was pulled back behind her ears in a half ponytail, not a single flyaway. Short, lighting-shaped earrings daintily hung from her ears, and her blouse was perfectly tucked into her jeans.

She timidly stepped inside. Her expression portrayed the nervousness I felt. Fiddling with the edge of her light grey and white polka-dotted blouse, she slowly sat on the plush chairs across from my desk. The chair let out a slight hiss of air.

"I heard the chime," she said. "Have you opened it yet?"

"Nope," my eyes met with the unopened email. "If he got the contract signed, which he obviously did because Nathaniel is incredibly persistent, it will be the largest project we've ever handled. I've never been in charge of something like this."

"You're great at your job, Blake. You can do it."

"Honesty moment, Lainee? I'm not sure I can do this. I mean, who am I kidding? I'm definitely not ready for this."

"Honesty moment? I think you're being stupid for thinking that."

I chuckled at her frank statement. I loved the concept of honesty moments and how I was able to implement them within my team.

Nathaniel and I had coined this between us almost five years ago when we started traveling together and working more closely on our presentations. At the time, it helped foster a genuinely open dialogue, an invaluable tool for us. As our friendship inside and outside of work developed, we kept using them as a way to be completely honest with each other.

Lainee and I embraced the honesty moments concept over the last three years that we worked together. It was a few seconds in any conversation where we stepped outside of our boss-employee dynamic. I valued honesty, so these were incredibly helpful as a manager. These moments helped me stay grounded in my job and encouraged Lainee to tell me when things were going wrong, even if I couldn't see what was happening.

My heart pounded a rhythmic beat in my ears, faster with every second that passed. I tapped the tips of my nails on my desk as I tried to find the courage to see if our hard work had paid off. The momentary silence in the room was heavy.

"I really don't know if I can, Lainee."

"Don't be ridiculous, Blake," she spoke honestly. "If anyone here can handle it, it's you."

"You have entirely too much faith in me."

"No, you don't have enough faith in yourself. You're the only one Nathaniel trusts with his accounts, and the man is an absolute control freak, so you know that you must be good at what you do."

Lainee's reassuring smile helped settle my nerves. She stared at me, waiting to hear the news that the email contained, with a mix of joy and suspense in her eyes.

"I need to open it eventually," I hovered my mouse over the email.

Lainee encouragingly leaned forward, setting her elbows on my desk. Trepidation and excitement crowded the room as the email materialized before me. The text was short, typical for Nathaniel.

A loud sigh escaped me as I started to read it out loud.

Blake,

Meeting with Amelia is done. Contract is signed. She'll be @ HQ with her team a week from Monday. Congrats! Project Porcelain is now in your very capable hands. Boarding now. See you tomorrow.

Nathaniel.

"He did it!" Lainee jumped from her seat. "Blake, he did it! This is incredible! I knew he could do it."

"He did it..." I muttered.

Lainee brought her hands to her mouth and held in some of her excitement. She slowly put them down, revealing a smile that could light up the room.

I could hardly believe the words in front of me. The realization of the monumentality of this moment hit me like a freight train at full speed. A cocktail of panic, happiness, fear, relief, and excitement flooded me. I leaned back on my chair, threw my head back, and let myself smile for the first time since waking up this morning. My black office chair creaked as I shifted my weight.

Nathaniel's proactiveness and perseverance, our countless hours poured into developing the perfect pitch, and lots of hope convinced Amelia to award us our most significant contract ever – a one-year deal to completely handle the marketing for Truly You Cosmetics across the entire country. We had been looking for a widespread national opportunity and finally had it.

Even after five years, Capital Media remained a small company, but our dreams were as big as ever. We served various companies across the country from our two small offices but had never handled one company's entire national presence.

I turned to the windows that composed the back wall of my office and stared down at the streets of New Windsor, where our headquarters was established just three years ago. From this office, we served everything east of the Mississippi River.

The only other office was in California, which had been the original birthplace and headquarters of the company. From there, that team served the rest of our customers since they were primarily local to them. Since our contracts were mostly regional, the two locations had never worked on a joint campaign. Our regions required vastly different approaches, so there was little collaboration. Our presence in the South and Midwest was scant due to a lack of resources, which was quickly changing.

I suffered a mixture of dread and anticipation at the prospect of working with the California office.

Amelia's company, Truly You Cosmetics, was a recently founded brand focused on cruelty-free and 'green' cosmetics. When we started working on their presentation, I ordered some of their items and fell in love with them. Their mascara didn't leave gunk behind when I took it off, and their face cream didn't leave a film on my face as many others did. Advertising a product I enjoyed was easier, so putting together the materials was more enjoyable than not.

From what I understood, Amelia herself had been handling most of the marketing since their support team was small. Most of their employees were focused on research and development. However, their brand was taking off, and she wanted her team to continue focusing exclusively on their products and not worry about marketing. That's where my team shined.

Someone in Nathaniel's web of contacts caught wind that they were open to outsourcing their marketing and passed the tip on to Nathaniel. Immediately, he focused most of his efforts on the Truly You contract and started trying to win them over. We were met with hesitancy and skepticism due to our inexperience with a nationwide campaign, but Nathaniel could be awfully persuasive.

We worked day and night for two weeks to develop the perfect pitch to prove to Amelia that we were the best choice. We were young and small but highly motivated to put forth our best efforts. The countless hours spent confined in the conference room amongst mountains of takeout had come to fruition.

Lainee and I walked out of my office, and I looked out at my team sitting at their desks. I watched them finish their days for a few seconds. This was the team that made this opportunity happen.

Jamie, my research genius, poured over a spreadsheet filled with numbers. Her head was down, and her pencil was moving, indicating that she was double-checking some of the math she had been staring at. Sometimes, I swore that she would be better off without a computer.

Stephen, my gifted graphic designer and the only person on my team who could see all the colors, furiously drew in his notebook. His ideas were often perfected on paper before he touched the software that we spent thousands of dollars on. It frustrated Connor sometimes, but he could design it first on sand, for all I cared, as long as the beautiful outcome was the same.

The rest of our portion of the floor was sparse. The only people left on this side of the break area were us and Gordon from IT, who seemed to be fighting with his monitor. There were cables everywhere, and the monitor was on its side.

Between the four of us, we handled seven long-term contracts and over a dozen short-term assignments at any given time. The workload was heavy, the hours sometimes long, and we desperately needed to add headcount, but my team was excellent. Every day, I aimed to make them feel appreciated and ensured they were adequately rewarded for their hard work.

"Hey guys, can I get a few seconds before we head home?" I called out.

Lainee skipped over to her desk. Giddy. Jamie and Stephen swiveled their chairs towards me. Their eyes were trained on me. We had all been waiting for the news, and they had not been spared of the anxious anticipation.

"Nathaniel just informed me that we have officially landed Project Porcelain!"

"OMG!" Jamie bounced with the excitement of a child with a new toy. Her dark, straightened hair moved up and down with her. "OMG! I've never researched a cosmetics campaign. What does that even really entail? What kind of studies am I looking for? I need to expand my research repertoire. I have so many new things to learn!"

"Jamie, take a breath," I chuckled. She was an avid learner and researched everything to a depth that would put moles to shame. "We'll have plenty of time for research. Here's the plan, or at least an idea of how we'll handle this. Tomorrow, we'll review our current projects and deadlines to determine how to mold our workload into something manageable. We will shift much of our attention to this project over the next twelve weeks, but we still need to ensure none of our other clients get left behind. Once we have a plan for that, we'll work on integrating the California team into our typical process."

"Wait," Stephen groaned. "The California team is coming?"

I nodded, much to his dismay. He was our resident pessimist.

"Do I have to share a desk with Desha again?" he asked. He crossed his arms and shook his head. His jacket sleeves rose slightly to reveal the artwork etched on his skin. "She likes to move my stuff around, and I don't like it. I think she does it on purpose now, just to annoy me."

Stephen came with us from the California branch, where we were so short on space for a year that many of us had to share a desk or a communal area. Then, Desha visited while she and Stephen attended a conference on graphic design. We didn't have the office we have now, so they also had to share a desk temporarily.

"There won't be any desk sharing this time," I assured him. "IT is moving to the other side of the floor by accounting. We'll have a few empty cubes that the California team will take."

The typewriter noise that my phone made alerted me to a text from Connor, interrupting Stephen's next complaint. He asked for me to stop by his office before leaving. A small feeling of excitement coursed through me.

I slid my phone back into my pocket and returned to my team. I reiterated that one of Amelia's stipulations in awarding us the contract was that they retain heavy involvement in everything for the first phase of the campaign. For twelve weeks, Connor had graciously accepted to welcome them into our office. They intended to be here three days a week to ensure we could meet our contract's terms easily.

When I was done talking, they packed up their stuff, and I crossed the silent floor to Connor's office on the opposite corner. He was sitting inside, his back turned to the door, staring at the people walking on the street beneath us.

Connor Phillips was the founder and CEO of Capital Media. His entire career had been marketing, and he was successful enough to go out alone. He founded Capital Media a little over five years ago and hired me straight out of college. From the beginning, his interest in my career afforded me more opportunities than I could ever thank him for.

My knock caught his attention as I entered his picture-clad, award-filled office.

"Nathaniel called as he boarded," he turned around. "Congratulations, Blake!"

"Thank you. It's been tough, but it paid off."

"I'll get right to it since I'm ready to go home, and I'm sure you are as well. I wanted to discuss a few things with you before the craziness of all of this starts."

His light eyes studied me. His body shifted in his chair. His spine straightened, his throat cleared, and his smile disappeared. My hands were suddenly clammy.

"As you know, your...California counterpart...and part of his team will be here for the duration of Project Porcelain. You will be the head account manager and in charge, but teamwork will be essential for this to work."

He weighed his following words carefully. "I'm not oblivious to how things between you and Erik ended when I brought you out here, so I want to ensure that your tumultuous personal history will not pose an issue. More specifically, I want you to promise me that it will not be because, as we all know, Blake never breaks a promise."

I swallowed hard. This discomfort was something I would have to face once Erik arrived and for the next twelve weeks. But I thought I would have more time before I had to think about it.

"I promise that my past relationship with Erik will not be a problem," I did my best to assure him confidently. My voice came out more stable than I expected. I almost believed myself. "We are professionals and have demonstrated that we can work together effectively. It's been three years, Connor. What happened is firmly in the past."

"Great," Connor smiled. "You continue to prove that my confidence in you is well-placed, Blake."

"I'm happy to know that you think that of me. I certainly try to be dependable."

"I'm going to let you in on a secret, Blake. Not many people know this because it has yet to be announced, but Capital Media is going to be expanding."

"That's incredible!" I couldn't hide my excitement. "We could definitely use more people, especially as the workload increases."

"Within the next two years, we will be opening two new regional offices, one to focus on the South and one on the Midwest. I want you to oversee all of them. If this project kicks off to a good start, then I will be bringing you on board the expansion as my National Account Management Director."

I was speechless. My jaw dropped slightly as I stared at him.

"Now," he continued, ignoring my shock at his revelation. "I want Richard to oversee the financials aspect. He's in line for Director of Finance, so this is a perfect opportunity for you guys to work together."

I nodded, playing off the discomfort of his mention of Richard's name and still trying to process the news. His tone left no room for argument as to who would be the financial contact for the project, even though I had planned on having Braeden do it.

"I'll make it happen," I swallowed my thoughts. "Thank you so much for the opportunity to prove myself for this role."

"You've earned it, Blake. You're the best we've got."

"Thank you, Connor," I got up from the chair. "Before I forget, I was wondering if it would be okay for me to let my team go at lunch tomorrow. They've put in a lot of extra hours the last couple of weeks, and I feel like they deserve some back."

"Absolutely. Please take the afternoon off as well. You've all earned it."

I shook his hand across his desk and mentally patted myself on the back as I walked out of his office. Tomorrow, I would devise a plan to juggle Connor's expectations, Amelia's goals, and my workload.

Chapter Two

FRIDAY MORNING.
Ten days before.

The metal elevator doors reflected my worn-down image, and I stared at my tired eyes. I tossed and turned all night, my brain filled with ideas for the campaign, unease about the workload, and worries over Richard and Erik. The shiny doors opened to a dark and desolate office. It was incredibly early, but I loved the silence and peace of working on an empty floor before the day started. I flipped on the lights.

I intended to take the afternoon off for the first time in almost three years, but I had much to do.

I pulled up my team's calendars, opened our shared documents folder, and formulated a complete picture of our workload. My confidence in our ability to effectively handle Project Porcelain and the rest of our projects simultaneously was rattled. I worried that we had bitten off more than we could chew, but at this point, we had no choice but to swallow.

My commitment to the company was as big as it had ever been. I had found incredible success and a career I could not have imagined. I loved what I did and had to make it work to keep growing. Nathaniel and I had proven to be an extremely effective team contributing to the company's growth. We brought in three long-term contracts and eight short-term agreements just this year. It was only May.

If we had the backing of a national portfolio of accounts, we could pursue larger and longer-lasting deals. With the appropriate resources, we would be unstoppable.

The day I graduated college, my wildest dreams wouldn't have taken me to imagine this lifestyle. My goal growing up had always been to get a job that allowed me to settle in back in my hometown and, eventually, raise a family with a white picket fence. But then Connor offered me a career and changed the course of my life.

At the end of my senior year of college, our department head had us present a project that involved developing a fake product and formulating a complete marketing campaign for it. We presented it to industry professionals looking to fill positions within their marketing teams. Connor eagerly listened to every one of our presentations. I distinctly remember him filling up pages upon pages of notes. He had a new company and was looking to hire new ideas.

Erik and I were both hired directly after that project.

We worked side by side for two years, helping Connor build Capital Media from an idea to a growing marketing company. Erik focused on market analytics, developing our research methods, and formulating key strategies. I expanded into working closely with sales. Nathaniel and I were so successful locally that we started traveling and pulling in small and medium-sized customers nationwide.

It quickly became necessary for Capital Media to have a presence on both coasts due to the breadth of our customer base. Connor was from the East Coast, so he relocated our headquarters closer to where his family and many of our clients were. Virginia was the perfect place. It was a midpoint between our customers on this side of the country.

He asked Nathaniel and me to move with him and the company. He wanted our help in building the new office. The opportunity would be life-changing and precisely the next step I needed to take in my career. The only hitch in the plan was that New Windsor was over two thousand miles away from our office in California, from my home, and from Erik. It was two thousand miles away from the life I always thought I would live.

New Windsor represented an incredible opportunity for a new life and a stepping-stone to becoming the person I wanted to be. Despite Erik's vehement objections, I jumped at the opportunity headfirst and moved.

I stared at my name on my locked office door. I fixed the tag that displayed it since it was slightly crooked, and the paper always threatened to slide out. I kept my door closed the entire morning, except when I poked my head out to let my team know they were free to go home at lunch. Putting together the draft of what I thought the timeline for Project Porcelain should be while trying to address my outstanding emails was a bigger challenge than expected.

After noon, my stomach called for my usual Friday lunch at Gabby's Café. I packed up my bag and locked the door behind me. Lainee, Jamie, and Stephen were already gone for the day. I crossed the floor toward the finance department.

Our accounting manager, Barry, inhaled his lunch in the break area while everyone else seemed to have gone out. It was just another typical Friday around here.

Hidden behind the textured light walls of his cubicle, Richard seemed to be having a staring contest with a spreadsheet. He was losing.

"Lunch?" I tapped his shoulder.

"Perfect timing!" he broke out of the fight with the spreadsheet and spun out of his chair. He stretched and groaned like he hadn't moved in hours. I suspected that was precisely the case.

"How long have you been staring at the computer?"

"Too long," he forced a laugh.

He led the way to the elevator and held the lobby door as we walked into the temperate air. Humidity was low, and the sun was shining intently. It felt incredible outside.

The trees and flowers had revived after a long and bitterly cold winter. Three years here, and I still was not used to nor a fan of the several inches of snow or the plummeting temperatures. I stared at the potted flowers at the entrance of the building while Richard tied his shoe. I wondered what color the flowers were.

A few blocks down from our building was Gabby's Café. We walked into a louder-than-usual dining room. Most booths and tables were packed with what looked to be amped-up mothers and daughters and some bored fathers and brothers.

The smell of freshly baked bread spread along the dining room. A frantic Jeremy ran around, making sure everyone had water and what they needed. Richard and I slid across from each other in the last booth by the door to the kitchen. I looked around the white walls, each decorated with what I assumed to be colorful paintings of scenery from around the world. They were just in black and white to me.

"So, did you hear the good news?" I asked him.

"You can see all the colors of the rainbow now because you've fallen hopelessly in love with me?'"

"No," I rolled my eyes. Unfortunately, my world remained greyscale. "Project Porcelain is official. And... you get to be our financial manager!"

His upturned eyes widened, and a smile slowly spread across his face. Richard was an intelligent and dedicated man; I was sure he knew what this meant for him and his career within the company.

Before he could react, a glowing Gabby stepped in front of our table and set two cups of ice water down. Her smile radiated the happiness of seeing her café completely packed. Her crinkled eyes landed on my outfit, inspecting every aspect of it, and she even bent over to peek at my shoes under the table. She left the apartment before me this morning, so I didn't get her routine stamp of approval to ensure everything matched before heading out.

"You did a great job, Blake!" she handed us straws. Her eyes and smile fell when they landed on Richard. Her expression soured. "Richie."

"Gabriella."

They rolled their eyes at each other with disdain. She abhorred being called by her full name; he despised being called a nickname. They were a match made in hell.

She didn't need to ask what we were getting and just confirmed our orders in case Richard had changed his mind. I ordered a grilled cheese sandwich, bacon, and a small salad without tomatoes every Friday. I hated tomatoes. Then, to-go was a blueberry muffin. Richard's go-to order was the club sandwich with a lemon muffin on the side.

While we waited for our food, I glimpsed at my phone. The steady string of emails continued, reminding me of my never-ending to-do list. I complained to Richard about the number of emails in my inbox. He chuckled and shared in my dramatic misery.

Gabby brought our food out a short while later. I tapped the back of my butter knife on the crusted top of the bread and enjoyed the slight cracking sound. Perfectly toasted, as always. A small drop of gooey cheese spilled down the side, and my mouth watered as I took a bite.

"Okay, wait, as stoked as I am to be on that project...last time we talked about it, you were choosing Braeden. He's like your right-hand man in the department," Richard continued.

"Honestly, I was. The idea of breaking in someone new to my working style on a super important project was not exactly in my plans. Connor wants you on it, but I think you know me well enough that my...intensity...won't surprise you."

"I am so excited that Connor wanted me on this! Plus, it'll be great to work with you."

He reached out for my hand as I slithered it away from him. I felt uneasy about us working closely on a project together. My response was clearly not enthusiastic enough for him. He swallowed the last bite of his sandwich, cocking his head and narrowing his eyes.

"Okay..." he tossed the dirty napkin onto his plate. "What's going on in that head of yours?"

"What? Nothing."

"Don't insult me, Blake. As you said, I know you well enough."

"I'm just a bit...apprehensive...about working together. I don't want anyone to know we've been seeing each other. Plus, a lot is happening in my head with the California team coming. I don't know...it's hard to explain."

"Try."

"All right...well...there's history between Erik and me... a lot of it."

"You and the California manager? That Erik?" Richard straightened up and scratched the back of his head. I scratched at my arms. This was uncomfortable for both of us. "What kind of ...history?"

I didn't stop talking for the next few minutes as I told Richard everything. Our history was not a secret at work, given that we had worked in the same office for two years. Everyone in California knew what we were and, to some extent, what happened between us. But the people hired specifically for the New Windsor office, which was everyone except Connor, Nathaniel, Stephen, and me, only knew us separately.

That included Richard.

Erik Walker was the California Accounts Manager and my counterpart in that office. While I was still in California, working side-by-side with him, we had different roles. Yet we often worked together due to the many hats we all wore. However, our relationship didn't start at work.

Erik and I had grown up almost next door to each other in our hometown. Our mothers were best friends, so we spent a lot of time together from the time we were babies. We developed the same interests and quickly became good friends. By the time we were in high school, we were best friends. We were the kind of friends that no one believed were just friends.

We ended up attending the same university about an hour and a half from home, and our relationship dynamic immediately shifted once we were no longer under my dad's watchful eyes and our mother's hopeful wishes. Things between us got...complicated. Every touch started to carry meaning. Every glance held a certain heat to it.

At the end of our senior year of college, even though neither of us could see color, we gave up fighting against our feelings. Everything moved quickly, and we moved in together a few months after our college leases expired. We made a home in a small apartment about ten minutes from our office and thirty minutes from the street we had grown up on.

For years, I was convinced Erik was the one. The one to make me see color. The man I would marry. My crush on him had followed me my entire life, and I had eyes for no one else. I saw nothing but the grey world in front of me, but my heart was convinced I could live a happily ever after with him in a colorless world.

However, the more decisions I made in the interest of my career, the more we started to fight. Our friendship and relationship had always been volatile, but it became even more so in our last few months together. Doors would slam, things would be thrown, and Erik would storm off angrily to the couch while I surrounded myself in the shower's hot water to cry. I wasn't willing to give up on us yet; we had too much history and too many dreams, but my passion was intertwined with my job, so when the opportunity to move came up, I jumped on it. I begged Erik to come with me, but he refused.

Regardless of the decades of friendship, the memories we had made together, and the love I thought we shared, things between us ended horribly and loudly. Erik's eyes and attitude silently betrayed his valiant effort to hide his anger at Connor for choosing me over him until he spat it at me during our last argument. I left him and our home behind three years ago, and we never even said goodbye. The world I thought I knew and the future I thought I would have disappeared in my rearview mirror.

Since then, we have only interacted professionally. We never discussed what happened, and I never intended to talk to him about it. Our working relationship was productive enough and mostly confined to email and the occasional group meeting. We both loved our jobs, so I believed this would all work out. It was only twelve weeks.

"But he didn't give you any colors...right?" Richard begged for confirmation. After two years of dating, I never even got to see the color of the sky.

I nodded.

"I'm probably worrying over nothing," my tone exposed my lack of confidence. "It's been three years. I don't care about him beyond doing good work. It's just a lot."

"You're both professionals, and this is a great opportunity for all of us. I'm sure it'll be fine. As far as you and me, don't worry, I won't say anything, but what we're doing isn't wrong or forbidden."

"I know, but I don't like people in the office knowing my business too much after what happened. Outside of you and Nathaniel, I don't think anyone even knows my phone number."

Richard nodded and gave me an unconvinced smile. We had been casually seeing each other for a few months here and there, and I mostly enjoyed myself, but there were no signs of color. Between him and Erik, I was starting to convince myself that the greyscale was here to stay.

Chapter Three

SATURDAY AFTERNOON.
Nine days before.

Gabby crashed on the fluffy chair next to the couch with the loudest sigh I had ever heard from her. She was drained from the week and dealing with the intense crowds from a bridal expo down the street from the café. Thankfully, she had finally hired enough people she trusted to run the café on the weekends without her.

Her long, curly hair was pulled into a messy bun, and some ringlets hadn't managed to stay pulled back. She grabbed one of the three glasses of wine on the coffee table and one of the muffins she reheated from yesterday's batch. There were bags under her eyes, and she had been stressed, so the nail polish on her fingers was chipped.

Our friend Mason sat on the opposite edge of our upholstered couch. His lanky frame hunched over a lap desk with a mess of papers strewn on it. Occasionally, he would mutter curses at having assigned his students a two-thousand-word essay about the American Revolution. His grading marker swooshed over the papers every twenty seconds, marking what was most likely spelling errors or wrong information.

Initially, we were going to go out to the movies, but we were all exhausted and wanted to stay in. Gabby and I debated what we were in the mood to watch. She wanted a horror movie, but I wanted a cartoon. Our moods seemed to be very different. Mason was too frustrated to give us a deciding opinion and barely listened to our debate.

Gabby made an executive decision to watch one of her favorite movies. I didn't mind too much since we rarely actually watched or listened to the movie. It was more of background noise to our hours of ranting and conversation.

"So, you and Richie will be working on the project together then? I bet he's excited about that." Gabby said.

"Yeah...Connor is testing him for the promotion to the national level once we expand."

"Gross."

"Be nice."

"I don't know what you see in him. Just being around him sucks the life out of me."

"Why do you hate him so much?" I laughed.

From the minute they saw each other at a company Christmas party that Nathaniel and I dragged Gabby to, she and Richard hated each other. It was the opposite of love at first sight. Gabby was a vibes-and-energy person, so I always chalked it up to something related to that. I had no idea why Richard returned her hate.

"He's just gross and gives me the creeps. Plus, I think it's super unfair to you that he gets to screw around and see other people while you guys are sort of together."

"Gabby, our agreement isn't one-sided. I'm also free to see other people. I just don't have time to, nor am I sure I actually want to."

I wasn't committed to Richard, but I liked him well enough over the last few months that we had been going on dates. It had moved from small flirts on the rare occasions we worked together to him asking me for lunch on a random Friday. He had made it clear that he wasn't looking for anything exclusive up front, which didn't bother me. I was dedicated to my job. My life was typically consumed anyway. Richard understood that, so it worked well between us.

"Yeah, sure. Whatever," Gabby rolled her eyes. "Sucks that Connor forced him on your project though. Braeden is so much better."

"Gabby, Richard is brilliant and incredible at his job. That's all I care about when it comes to the project. As long as he doesn't flirt with me in the office when we work together, it doesn't matter who is on my team."

"Gross."

She started acting like a petulant child about him, so I dropped the conversation.

"I'm not worried about Richard. Honesty moment? I'm terrified of Erik being here in nine days."

"I'm sorry. I think I misheard you. What?!" Gabby's eyes widened. It occurred to me that I had omitted that small detail from them.

"Your ex?!" Mason perked up from his papers immediately. I guess my laughable love life was more interesting than the Founding Fathers. "The former love of your life? The one that you left to move here? That Erik?!"

"The one and only," I sighed.

My feelings were highly conflicted about seeing Erik again, especially in person. I unloaded my thoughts on Gabby and Mason.

On the one hand, the nerves of seeing my ex-boyfriend again threatened to be enough to knock me off my game, so I panicked over how I would react when I had to work and talk to him. I had no room for error on this project, so having him in the office with me made me want to vomit. He was good at his job, but this was the one person I dreaded having on my team.

On the other hand, three years is a long time, and there was the possibility that seeing him wouldn't do anything to me. I had moved on. But I knew I missed my best friend and sometimes found myself craving the close friendship we used to share. There were a lot of good memories of growing up with him by my side that I could channel while he was here to overshadow how things ended.

Unfortunately, my brain couldn't decide how to handle it right now and would have to wait until he stood in front of me.

"Honesty moment?" I said. "For a brief moment, the day before Connor sprung up the opportunity to move, I thought I saw a faint glimpse of color in the river behind his mom's house during family dinner. We had been celebrating her birthday, and Erik was playing with his niece. I stared at him for a while, watching him with that little girl, and then I thought I saw the color. I never saw it again, so I think I just hallucinated, or the water caught the light in a weird way that I hadn't seen before."

"Oh...my...goodness!" Mason put the papers he was grading on the coffee table before he had the urge to throw them across the room in excitement. "Maybe...maybe...maybe you were finally truly falling in love with him! Your heart and brain were finally on the same page that you had chosen to be with him. But the next day, you already had one foot out the door, so the colors stopped! Especially if it was the day before Connor pulled you away from him!"

"Mason, I don't think –" Gabby tried to bring him back from his romantic idealism and speculation.

"Maybe this is your chance to rekindle your love like one of those second-chance romance books or a Hallmark movie!"

Mason's hopeless romantic nature was typically wasted on Gabby and me. Sometimes, hearing his unyielding positivity was a breath of fresh air. Gabby stopped him from continuing his rambling and interjected with her theory and belief of how the colors developed. It was a wildly accepted one that Mason never wanted to give any credence to.

Gabby preached her viewpoint every time the conversation came up. She believed that love was exclusively a choice and you had to be fully committed to someone to see in color. Many people thought the same thing, but no one could precisely determine what was true. Those same people insisted that you had to continually decide to love someone for colors to develop, regardless of any feeling.

Mason was on the opposite school of thought. He believed that love was closer to a magical feeling. He argued that once you met the right person, it would make sense why it didn't work out with anyone else. Yes, there was a level of choice in being with someone, but he focused on the feelings.

My view on the subject was not as rigid as either of theirs. I believed it could be a perfect mixture of choosing someone and feeling love for someone. But as more time passed and my world continued to be muted in color, the less I knew what to believe.

"If you're so right, then how come Blake didn't see color when she chose Erik?" Mason taunted.

That was the question I always pondered when the topic came up and one that I asked Gabby often. I chose to love Erik for the two years we were together and had always felt different toward him than anyone else when we were growing up. I tried to fight for us; I tried to choose him.

"That's an easy one," Gabby scoffed. "Her passion for her job and career always outweighed Erik, so she never truly chose him. Then, you chose to stop being with him, so the colors didn't develop. I don't think you chose him. I think you settled for him."

"This is all so easy for you to say!" Mason rolled his eyes. "You've always been able to see color. You've never had to wonder if the man you're dating is just another loser or if your eyes will tell you he's the one for you."

I was always jealous of the people that were born seeing color. Although no one knew why it worked like that, most people thought it was genetics. Then, there were people that never got to see in color regardless of love. Most people were people like Mason and me who daydream of seeing what the world looks like with all of our senses.

"Being able to see color doesn't mean it's easy," Gabby defended herself. "It means I have one less...check...when choosing who to love. I trusted my feelings before, and it still crashed and burned. My choice is based on various factors since it can't be just based on my eyes."

"That sounds almost too...logical...for you," I eyed her skeptically.

"Choosing who you're going to spend the rest of your life with should be a logical decision," Gabby stood her ground.

"Whatever," Mason sipped his drink. "I, for one, can't wait to meet the man of my dreams and have my world erupt in color immediately."

"Unfortunately, I do think love at first sight only exists in movies," I sipped my wine.

"Maybe," Mason laughed.

He pushed aside his papers and decided to change the movie. The topic of love had put him in a cheesy mood, so we ended up watching A Cinderella Story.

I tried to concentrate on the movie, but my thoughts were elsewhere. I didn't want to think that Gabby was right, and I had settled for Erik. Back then, I thought he would be the person I wanted to spend the rest of my life with. I wanted to believe that I had been convinced.

We hadn't been a perfect pair, but we had been comfortable together. If we put aside our arguing, we had a good relationship most of the time. Explosive, but familiar. I called it passionate.

The time that we had been together was predictably unpredictable.

I had an honesty moment with myself. Sometimes, I missed the excitement and the rollercoaster of emotions that accompanied our life. However, I thrived in routine and predictability. I had built my new life around it, and I would be dammed if I let him come here and destroy the walls I had built.

Chapter Four

MIDDAY WEDNESDAY.

Five days before.

Nathaniel eyed me warily across his wooden desk. Almost like he didn't believe a word I was saying. It seemed like everyone had brought their lunch today, and all the tables had been taken when we walked over to heat up our food. So, we retreated into his office to eat.

"I promise. I'm fine!" I reiterated. I slammed my napkin against his desk, which did nothing to help ease his worries that I was losing it. "Let me ask you this. Are you worried about me as the sales contact on the project or as my friend? Really think through your answer because that's what my level of annoyance with you hinges on."

"I'm worried about you as your friend," he said. "You're like my little sister, Blake. It's about to be a few emotional months, and I'm concerned about how you're taking this. I just don't want a repeat of when we moved."

I refused to meet his brotherly gaze. I knew his eyes were pinned on me, trying to decipher what was going through my head. The mound of muscles in front of me had an uncanny ability to read my face and see through me, even when I tried to hide my thoughts from him.

"Should I be worried about you on the professional front too? I hadn't thought about it because I know you would sacrifice yourself to make this project work perfectly, which brings us back to why I'm worried about you as a friend."

"Of course not!" I insisted. "You shouldn't worry about it either way."

My tone was more of a complaining child than a confident adult who could handle herself.

"You're a terrible liar, Blake. Look, I know you. You tapped your fingers the entire meeting with Connor. You held your breath when he brought up Erik and his team. You're nervous, and I need to know what I'm dealing with here to help. I can't have you shutting down on me, kid."

"There's a lot of feelings, okay? It's been three years since I felt so many feelings. I'm incredibly nervous. Terrified. Excited. I don't know if you've noticed, but I don't handle an ocean of feelings super well anymore."

"Trust me, I know," he nodded. "It's going to be hard, kid, okay? I know that. You know that. But I want you to know that you can always count on me to help you calm down. We'll get through this together and earn our promotions on the other side."

I gave him as confident of a smile as I could. Nathaniel was the brother I never got to have. He wore that title proudly and took that responsibility seriously. Over the five years that we had worked together, we had grown incredibly close. He was the only person in New Windsor, outside of Gabby, that I could trust with anything and everything. He knew me, not just the work version of me, but all of who I was.

At work, I prided myself in being friendly but professional and all about my job. That last part wasn't hard since it's who I was anyway. I had forced myself to be this version of myself for the last three years. Not a toe out of line, not a mistake made, not a feeling in sight. If it wasn't about my job, you wouldn't hear me talk about it in the office.

I chewed on my sandwich and thought about what I was facing come Monday. I didn't want to believe that Nathaniel was right to be worried. It had been three years since I had seen Erik. I avoided talking to him as much as possible. It wasn't always easy since we were colleagues, but it had worked so far. Hearing his voice over my laptop's speaker no longer elicited any feelings in me. The walls I had built were thick and impenetrable.

Nathaniel was almost just like me. A big part of his life revolved around his job, and he was always looking for the next opportunity. As I stewed across from him, he alternated between typing on his typewriter-like keyboard, making clicking sounds with every letter, and drinking his protein shake. He had just landed the biggest deal of his career and was already researching his next target.

I got up from the chair across his desk and paced. The blinds to the bullpen were drawn, so I was glad no one could see me.

"Honesty moment, Blake?" he asked. This was his equivalent of asking me for a penny for my thoughts.

I stopped pacing and leaned back against the wall. Slowly, I lowered myself to the floor in frustration. He walked around his desk to look at me. A mixture of concern and pity showed on his face.

"I've moved on," I said, looking up at him. "It's been three years. I don't feel anything for him anymore. Not the way I did before, anyway."

"Are you trying to convince me or you?"

"I know I've moved on. But I'm still scared of seeing him. Why? Why am I so scared?" my voice had transformed into a meager plea.

"Do you want me to comfort you or give you an answer?" he crouched in front of me.

"Both."

He groaned as he sat next to me on the wall. Just his presence was comforting.

"I remember how hard it was for you to make the choices you made when we left California. I remember how hard it was for you to heal. If you ask for my unprofessional psychological opinion with a dash of expertise in Blake-ology, it's not because you still love him. I think... It's because of the way you left all of your history behind. What were the last words you said to him that weren't work-related?"

I thought back to when I stormed out of our apartment in California. Erik and I had been arguing for almost three hours, and my voice was getting tired. Our last interaction haunted me for months after I left. The words played in my mind at full volume.

•••••••••••

"I am such an idiot!" I screamed at Erik. "I'm basically on my knees begging you to come with me because the thought of leaving you behind feels like ripping myself in two, and then you have the audacity to say that to me?!"

"How's that for one of your stupid honesty moments?!" he matched my volume. I was sure the neighbors could hear every word we screamed at each other.

"Screw our history! Screw this. Screw you, Erik! I'm leaving on Sunday. I'm going to Virginia with or without you!"

I turned around and slammed our front door. My car was just outside. I got in it and drove to my mom's house a few streets down. I cried on my childhood twin bed while my mom held me for an hour. I knew it was over.

•••••••••••

The next time I talked to Erik, I was thousands of miles away and through a computer screen. We were meeting with Connor about new dynamics.

"I think you're missing closure," Nathaniel sighed. "Maybe it would be helpful to get some while he's here so you can put this behind you."

"This isn't going to be as easy as I want to pretend it's going to be, is it?"

"No."

Nathaniel threw his arm around me as I buried my face in my hands. Erik wasn't even here and was already messing with my head. The fact that he captured this much control over my thoughts was alarming.

Nathaniel was right. I needed closure. I just wasn't sure how I would get it without subjecting myself to another rollercoaster of emotions.

I was scared of many things. Feelings were number one on my list.

Chapter Five

Friday afternoon.

Three days before.

Gabby dragged her feet while getting ready to go to the gym. Yesterday, she begged me to go dancing with her at a country dance hall in Wimberly, but I wasn't big into dancing. After two hours of going back and forth, I caved, but only if she came to the gym with me since I always found it more inspiring to run with someone. I didn't think she would agree, and now I was trapped with going to the gym and then dancing.

While she got ready, I sat on her bed, listening to another of the repetitive speeches about how I needed to work less and enjoy life more. She preached that running shouldn't be the only thing I do for fun. She swore to me that I would see what I was missing out on tonight.

We walked a few blocks to the gym in the opposite direction of my office. I loved living downtown because everything was close, and I could walk everywhere. Most of the year, the weather was pleasant enough. We weren't south enough that it got boiling outside; we weren't near water, so humidity remained relatively low; we weren't so far north to the point where we got buried in the snow into the spring.

The noise of the crowded gym, combined with the fluorescent overhead lighting, reignited my energy. Squeaking sneakers against the floor and the slamming of weights on the ground was soothing to me. The guy at the counter scanned our QR codes, and we took the stairs to the second floor, where the full-sized track awaited us.

Gabby barely held up her end of the bargain and only ran two of the twelve laps she promised before opting for the treadmill. She was more of a walk-while-watching-TV kind of person.

I continued running without her, feeling some of the stress of the week melt away every time my feet connected with the soft ground.

Come Monday, the pressure to perform would be intense, and the commotion of feelings would ramp up, so I intended to take the weekend to relax my brain and try to put any thoughts of Erik out to pasture. I set my own goal to try and not do any work for the weekend, which would be quite a feat for me.

Sweat dripped off my face as I stretched on the edge of the track, so I made a pit stop in the bathroom to wash my face before heading back downstairs. My cheeks were a shade darker than the rest of my face, and the cold water felt incredible on them. I fixed my ponytail, ensuring it wasn't at that half-fallen awkward spot on my head.

I waved Gabby over as I passed her on my way to the small lockers by the entrance where my keys and wallet were. She held her index finger at me, letting me know her episode wasn't over yet. I opened the locker and grabbed my stuff.

A few lockers down from me, a tall man pressed his forehead to the cold metal. He was defeated trying to open the locker in front of him. I was sure he was new, not because I had never seen him before, but because anyone who had been here before knew to only use specific lockers or bypass them altogether.

"Hi," I tapped him on the shoulder. He tore his head from the metal and slowly turned to me. I took a step back to see the man standing in front of me.

His short hair was a shade of gray I had only seen once before. His eyes were light, almost transparent, as if the sun shone directly on them. A perfectly coordinated Texas-themed tattoo sleeve covered his sculpted left arm, ending at his watch. His right arm was oddly bare, but it made it easier to see the definition of every muscle.

"Would you like some help?" I asked.

"Please!" he groaned in frustration.

"You must be new here," I smiled as he moved away from the locker.

"What gave it away?"

"You're in great shape and work out, so you're a regular at a gym somewhere. Yet, you chose the locker everyone avoids, so it's not here."

"I'm impressed by your inference powers, stranger."

I walked the handsome stranger through each step of opening these metallic monstrosities. He stared at me with an amused smile.

First, the door was finicky, so you wanted to push it in as much as possible while twisting the lock to the first number of the combination. While turning the dial to enter the last number, you push the door toward the hinges and away from the lock while keeping the pressure inward. Last, you jiggled the handle about four times until the click gave it away that it was ready to be opened.

It was a chore to open the lockers, so they were seldom used unless any good ones were available. I became a pro at opening them because I continually forgot which were the good ones and which were the bad ones. If I knew how to open the bad ones, then they were all good ones.

The stranger's door slowly swung open. He pulled out his wallet and keys with lightning speed and a sigh of relief.

"Ta-da!" I laughed.

"That's incredible. How do you know the trick so well? It seems like a lot to remember."

"I always forgot which lockers to avoid, so I learned to open all of them."

"Can't fault logic like that. How can I thank you for rescuing my stuff?"

"Oh, it's nothing. I'm just glad I could help."

I reached for my ponytail and tugged at the tips of my hair, tangling the ends between my fingers. The unexplained nerves in my stomach needed to be reined in.

"How about –" he started.

Gabby's arm landed around me, interrupting the handsome stranger's thought. She visibly eyed the stranger up and down without so much as an attempt to hide that she was sizing him up. Her lips formed into a wide smirk, and she got a wild look in her eye.

"Is this guy bothering you, Blake?" she feigned toughness, even though she was a cinnamon roll in disguise.

"So...your name is Blake?" the handsome stranger extended his hand. I shook it, feeling his warm, calloused hands on mine. "Nice to meet you. I'm Parker. And your bodyguard is..."

"Gabby," she extended her hand.

"Nice to meet you as well, Gabby."

"So, how can we help you on this fine evening, Parker?" she enunciated his name.

"Well...Gabby...your friend Blake here already helped me. She valiantly and heroically rescued my wallet and keys from the evil grasp of the lockers, so I was hoping to thank her by maybe taking her out for a drink tonight. If that's okay with you, of course."

"Well, Parker," Gabby continued to guide the conversation in her usual extroverted way. The glimmer in her eye exposed the lightbulb that went off in her head. I tried to interject, but she shushed me before I opened my mouth. "She already had plans tonight that she, unfortunately, cannot break because she promised, but I have an idea. Do you know how to dance?"

"Dance how? Like twerking in an overcrowded, sweaty nightclub or two-stepping in a dance hall?" Parker asked.

"Dance hall. You know, the one with boots, cowboy hats, and people occasionally screaming yeehaw?"

He chuckled at Gabby's line of descriptions. I knew that if I tried to stop her from doing this, Gabby would just put her sweaty hand over my mouth or potentially beat me into submission. You never knew with her. So, I waited for Parker's answer, but based on the subtle drawl of his deep voice, I expected that the answer was yes.

"I do," he confirmed.

"Great! You can buy her a drink there. We're going dancing in Wimberly tonight, and Blake could use a partner."

The stranger flashed me a coy smile that reached his eyes. "Well, what time and where, Gabby?"

She held her hand out for his phone and keyed in my number. His smile remained wide and entertained. After my phone beeped with a text from Parker, Gabby spun me around and reached into the side pocket of my leggings. She made sure to save his contact.

She texted him the address and the time, utterly unbothered by the fact that this was a complete stranger.

"We'll see you there, cowboy," she winked.

Gabby pulled me away before I could protest or Parker could say anything else. The whole conversation went down so quickly that I was still processing that Gabby landed me a date for tonight when we walked away. She never ceased to amaze me. I aspired to move around the world with half of the amount of confidence that she did.

"What the hell was that about?" I whispered as we walked.

I took a peek behind me and caught Parker still looking at us. He gave me an uncertain wave along with a slightly embarrassed smile. His interaction with Gabby also left him wondering what had just happened.

"I got you a date with a really hot gym guy! Richie doesn't get to have all the fun if I have anything to say about it."

"Yeah, a date with a complete and total stranger!"

"Blake, sweetie, everyone is a stranger until you meet them. Plus, it's not like I gave him our home address."

"Fine, but if I have a date, you'll need one too."

"I don't need a date. There are always plenty of guys willing to dance with me at the hall."

If I had a date, she would have one too. It was one that I was sure would go with her and would do short of commit murder for her. He might even do that if the situation demanded it if I was honest with myself. So, I pressed the name on my speed dial for the perfect dance partner for Gabby.

"Hey, kid. Everything okay?" Nathaniel's gruff voice picked up after the second ring.

"Were you sleeping?" I asked.

"Nah, just relaxing."

"Well, what are you doing tonight?"

"Watching baseball and getting drunk in my apartment since you stole my Gabby from me tonight."

"Don't blame me. She's the one that wanted to go dancing. But what if I told you that you could hang out with Gabby tonight anyway?"

"You're not bailing on her, are you? She's been looking forward to this, and you promised."

"No! But you're coming with us!"

Gabby snickered next to me. She knew what Nathaniel's response would be.

"I'm doing what? Have you lost your mind?" he laughed.

"I have not. You're coming."

"Are you seriously asking me to go dancing with you? Have we not met?"

"Come on! You're a great dancer and already complaining that you miss Gabby. Plus, do you want those drunk strangers putting their wandering hands all over the love of your life on the dance floor?"

I taunted him, knowing how much of a weakness Gabby was for him. I heard the TV turn off in the background. He groaned as he got off the couch.

"Screw you, kid," he scoffed.

"No thanks. Not my job."

"You know me too damn well," he laughed. "I'll be at your apartment in two hours, but Blake, if anyone at work finds out about me dancing, I will murder you."

"Oh, sweet Nathaniel, it's cute that you think you still scare me."

He grumbled a string of curses at me and hung up. I smiled at my smitten roommate next to me.

Chapter Six

FRIDAY NIGHT.

Still three days before.

The rhythmic loud knock on the front door prompted me to look at my phone. It was almost two hours since I talked to Nathaniel, and he was always on time. A few seconds later, he knocked again, rattling the doorknob that was seldom locked before bedtime. He should really have a key to our apartment at this point.

I swung the door open, and a knockoff cowboy stood in front of me.

"Did you raid a cowboy store while you were in Texas?" I chuckled.

"Do you like it?" he asked.

He slightly lifted his jeans and showed off his brand-new dark boots. They had a square toe and made him half an inch taller. His beer-themed shirt fell over his jeans. Apparently, he had drawn the line at getting a stereotypically shiny belt buckle. A black cowboy hat covered his usually messy, curly, dark hair.

"If someone told me I would see Nathaniel Williams in a cowboy hat and boots, I would have called them insane."

"Holy cowboy!" Gabby might as well have screamed behind me. "Hey there, hot stuff."

Gabby walked past me into the landing of the elevator where Nathaniel was standing. His face lit up when she stepped out to him. She wore bell-bottom jeans and a crop top that didn't leave her belly button to the imagination. Her white boots peeked from under the fabric.

He opened his arms for her, and she hopped up and wrapped her legs around his waist. Effortlessly, he hooked his arm under her butt. She took his hat and placed it on her head.

"Hey, muffin," he happily mumbled into her lips.

"You know," I said, grabbing my phone from the entryway table. "This whole dating but not dating thing you have going on isn't healthy."

"Don't worry, little Blake," Gabby hopped off her cowboy and hooked her arm around me. "We'll get your legs wrapped around handsome gym stranger tonight."

Nathaniel's eyes widened at her comment, which prompted Gabby to recount the conversation with Parker at the gym. Through laughter from them and a little bit of secondhand embarrassment for me, he praised her for taking the initiative. Just as Gabby did, Nathaniel knew I probably would have said no if Parker had asked me to get a drink without Gabby there.

"Ah, I get it. You called me to protect both of you in case he's a serial killer?" Nathaniel dramatically flexed his bicep. Gabby's eyes ate him up, and I thought she would faint if he kept that stance up.

"I hadn't even thought about that!" I exclaimed.

We took my car to the dance hall since Gabby didn't have a car, and Nathaniel's car was too fancy for me to feel comfortable driving. Thirty minutes of loud music and laughter in the car went by quickly, and I pulled into the dirt parking lot of the dance hall. It was still relatively early but starting to fill up.

The air conditioning was blasting, and I regretted wearing a sleeveless top. The lights were dimmer than I remembered, and it took my eyes a few steps deeper into the room to adjust. Most of the brightness came from the lit signs on the wooden walls and the dim beer bottle chandelier over the dance floor.

Most people were on the floor, but a growing amount lingered around the bars and the few tables that lined the edge of the dance floor. Some waited for their partners, and some waited for the courage to ask someone standing next to them to dance. Others were more concerned with chugging enough liquid courage to make it onto the dance floor in the first place.

The floor was stocked with people swinging, twirling, and laughing.

"Are you going to be okay by yourself for a little bit?" Gabby bent down to yell in my ear over the music.

"Of course! Go dance!"

It didn't take much egging on my side for Gabby and Nathaniel to disappear into the dancing crowd. I stood at the corner of the bar and watched them for a little bit. Nathaniel pulled her close during the slow song, and she nuzzled her nose into his neck. She was also tall, so they fit together like a puzzle.

They effortlessly swayed to the slow rhythm of the song. A satisfied smile spread across both of their faces. I enjoyed seeing the softer and kinder side of Nathaniel that Gabby managed to pull out of him. He always wore a scowl in the office unless he talked about baseball or Gabby. Many people found him intimidating, and he was cutthroat, but Gabby softened him.

Their relationship was weird, but it worked for them for now. Unofficial but exclusive. In love but avoiding the finality of commitment. As I watched them dance with a smile, I was struck with a sliver of jealousy.

I longed for a taste of what they had.

I brought the beer to my lips, and the condensation left a ring of moisture on the wooden table. The carbonation hit my throat, a soothing relief after a week of presentations and meetings.

One of my favorite things to do when Gabby dragged me along with her was to people-watch. I learned a lot about body language when learning to interpret people's reactions to my presentations, and I liked to apply what I knew in real life. It made for an entertaining dialogue inside my head.

A group of girls in very shiny outfits who seemed barely old enough to be in here believed a frat guy's story about bull riding and being able to last more than a minute. He was clearly lying, given that professionals didn't even go that long most of the time. Maybe he was talking about one of those mechanical bulls you find at state fairs.

A love-struck woman was being dipped on the dance floor. She stared at her partner, and he stared back at her. He whispered something in her ear that made her laugh.

Another couple was arguing in the corner by the DJ booth. The woman looked like steam might come out of her ears any minute. The guy stood with his arms crossed in front of her. I wasn't sure he understood why she was angry at him.

After a few minutes, I pulled out my phone and checked the time. Ten minutes had passed since our agreed time, and there was no sign of Parker. I shouldn't feel disappointed that he didn't show, after all, I don't know the man. I should have been relieved and picked a stranger from the crowd, but a small part of me had hoped to see him again.

I looked to the ground and sighed. There were many options, but none of the men standing near me seemed like they would keep their hands off my butt.

"Sorry I'm late," a smooth voice with cowboy boots stepped into my sightline. I saw Parker smiling at me, a white t-shirt tucked into a pair of jeans with a black trucker cap. "The Uber took forever to get here. I think the guy was lost and didn't want to tell me."

"I was starting to think you wouldn't show," I chuckled, hoping the excitement in my voice was well-masked.

"I'm a man of my word, Blake," he frowned. "I only arrived in the city yesterday. My car won't be here until Monday, so I'm at the mercy of whoever can drive me."

He motioned for the bartender to bring two more of what I was having. I asked the bartender to put my beer on Nathaniel's tab since he offered to pay to celebrate a job well done. Parker protested that he was meant to be buying my drinks, but I insisted.

We silently sipped our beers as the slow song continued but started to wind down.

"So, do you and Gabby come out here often?" he asked. He stepped closer, and I caught a whiff of his intoxicating smokey smell.

"Gabby used to come a lot more, but it's mostly just her thing. I'm not a great dancer, and it's always deafening. I know it's weird, but the only thing I like to do here is people-watch."

A slow smile spread across his face as he excitedly looked around the room. I recognized that he was trying to find someone that was having an interesting interaction. He landed on the couple that had been arguing by the corner.

"Care to guess what they're arguing about?" he asked.

I guessed that he asked another girl to dance or that she wanted to dance, and he didn't. Parker thought she was yelling at him because he was already stumbling. I thought they were both plausible scenarios.

"Ready?" he turned to me when I set my empty beer bottle on the counter. He was asking me to dance. He put his bottle down and grabbed my hand, pulling me away from the comfort of the bar.

I was instantly nervous, something I always was when I danced with a stranger. I wasn't a horrendous dancer, but I also wasn't an expert. My feet sometimes tripped over themselves, and I lost count of the pace entirely too often. Usually, I depended on whomever my partner was to guide me.

If Parker didn't know what he was doing well enough and I couldn't follow his lead, this could be embarrassing for both of us. However, all my doubts evaporated when he pulled me close and set a confident hand on my waist – commanding yet respectful. His cologne hugged me, pulling me toward him.

His hands were firm on me as we glided around the floor. I didn't have to think about my next move. He had already decided for me.

"Do you do this often?" I asked through the music, prompting us to step closer to each other.

"Do what often? Take beautiful strangers from the gym two-stepping? No, I can't say that I do."

A warmth spread through my face and in my core. "I meant the dancing part."

"I did it a lot growing up. I grew up in Texas."

"Oh, a real cowboy then?"

"Not exactly," he chuckled. "I'm from the suburbs, but I always liked dancing."

"Well, you're really good!"

"Thank you. It's not every day I get such a gorgeous dance partner."

My cheeks felt even warmer as the upbeat song faded into a slower melody. Parker shifted his gaze at me, quietly asking if I wanted to stay or sit down. My brain advocated to pull away and sit, but my body didn't obey, not wanting to lose the feeling of his hands on me.

I gave him an encouraging smile, and he pulled me closer. Chest to chest. We danced as the floor thinned out. His hands now rested lower, closer to my hips than my waist, fitting the curve of my body perfectly. My arm hooked a little tighter around him for the last few seconds of the song.

At the end of the song, Parker kept one of his hands on my back and led us back to where Gabby and Nathaniel sat. She sat on his lap; his arms were wrapped tightly around her. She was telling him a story, talking a million miles an hour with arms flailing around. His gaze was fixed on her. To him, she was the only person in the room.

Almost a year ago, Nathaniel and I had a few too many drinks while celebrating the close of a project after a customer visit in Boston. The exhaustion of the trip, the high of the success of the project, and the ample availability of alcohol were a precarious combination. It led Nathaniel to bare his soul to me while sitting on a bench at the last bar we visited.

He admitted what I already knew. He was in love with Gabby. I had introduced them almost six months before that, and she had been interested in joining the softball league he was a part of. One day, while watching Gabby work on her swing, he realized that he could see that the bats were light brown. At that moment, he was even more convinced that she was the perfect girl for him.

When we came home, he told her how he felt, and she shared the same feelings. But Gabby wasn't ready to commit to more. During our senior year of college, her heart had been shattered by someone she thought she loved. She was scared of that feeling again.

Nathaniel didn't mind at first. Every few months, I asked him why he didn't ask for more of Gabby. He wanted a real commitment, but Gabby's theory of love being a choice prevented him. He knew she wasn't ready to choose him yet, and he wanted her to decide on her own. They were essentially together, and he would wait as long as it took to make Gabby officially his.

"Ah, you must be the handsome gym stranger I've heard so much about," he reached around and shook Parker's hand, giving me a wink. "Great to meet you."

"Handsome gym stranger, huh?" Parker smirked, and his fingers poked at my side slightly. The butterflies in my stomach intensified. I glared at Nathaniel.

We rested with them for a few minutes from the songs that already had us sweating despite it feeling like Antarctica in here. Nathaniel and Parker instantly hit it off. I tried not to stare at the handsome stranger as they debated the stats of a baseball pitcher. He confidently sat back, slinging an arm around the back of my chair. Gabby smirked at me, and I averted my gaze to the floor, avoiding any of her suggestive looks.

A few songs later, Parker pulled me back to the floor, wrapping his arm around my waist and pulling me closer and more confidently than before. I found a strange level of comfort in his arms. I chalked it up to the fact that it had been a long time since I had allowed myself to relax. Gabby was right. This was precisely what I needed.

Nathaniel watched the dance floor. Gabby had fallen asleep on his lap. It had very quickly become midnight.

"Ready to go?" I asked, leading Parker off the dance floor. Nathaniel nodded, his fingers tangled in Gabby's hair. "Do you want a ride, Parker? It'll be expensive to get an Uber back to the city from here."

"Sure, I'm only a few blocks from the gym if that's not too much trouble."

Nathaniel lightly woke Gabby up and gingerly guided her to the car. They took the back and Parker the front.

"You can drop us off at mine," Nathaniel said. "I've barely seen her in almost two weeks, Blake. I've missed her."

Gabby spent most weekends that she didn't work at Nathaniel's, but he had traveled a lot over the last two weeks. He had barely been home between his mid-year customer visits and dealing with Amelia's contract.

"I know," I sighed, understanding the longing in his voice.

By the time we were in front of his building, Nathaniel had convinced Parker to join their softball team while he was in town. Parker was a former college baseball player, so he was more than eager to join.

"Goodnight, Blake. It was great to meet you, Parker. I'll shoot you all the info about practices in the morning." He shut the door behind him and sweetly walked a sleepy Gabby to the door.

After hours of dancing, I expected to be exhausted, but I was anything but. My brain was wide awake, and I was feeling a second wind. My body was ecstatic to be doing something other than running and sitting at my desk. I tapped my fingers on the wheel, thinking about what to do or say. Parker watched me with an expectant smile.

I felt a surge of boldness overtake me, and I knew I didn't want this night to end just yet.

"Do you like ice cream, Parker?" I asked. If he didn't, we couldn't be friends.

"I love it. Only psychos don't like ice cream. Are you suggesting we keep this night going?"

"If you're down?"

"I'm game," Parker smiled from the passenger seat beside me.

I pulled away from Nathaniel's building and introduced Parker to my favorite ice cream place, Scooped. The little shop was at the end of the bar district, so it was open until late, especially on weekends. The number of people who impulsively bought ice cream after a night of drinking was somewhat shocking, but it was convenient for a midnight ice cream run.

We dodged drunk bodies on the sidewalk and entered the shop. The sweetness in the air made my mouth instantly water. The shop was brightly lit and packed. A giant ice cream cone hung from the ceiling.

I ordered my usual pistachio and Nutella combination. Parker was skeptical of my claims that this was the best ice cream in the world, so he stuck to trusty chocolate. As I was about to pay, he stopped my hand from handing the exhausted cashier my card.

"My treat," he said. "My real thank you for rescuing my stuff."

"I guess I'll allow it," I laughed.

The floor was sticky around the only open table. I picked up and pulled the chair out, worried that it wouldn't slide through the stickiness of the floor.

I brought the ice cream to my warm lips, and it was sensational, as always. A small moan involuntarily escaped me as the cold sweetness fell on my tongue. Parker's eyes narrowed on the plastic spoon connected to my lips before his gaze flickered back to my face and then to his ice cream.

"So, tell me about yourself," I said between bites. "Who is Parker?"

"Hmm...loaded question there. Where do I even start?" he chuckled. "All right, so you already know that I'm from Texas. I was born and raised in southeast Texas and still live there. My parents are teachers; my dad teaches English, and my mom teaches Chemistry. I have two older sisters. I went to law school wanting to be something kick-ass, like a district attorney who fights crime and puts bad people away, but I ended up as an associate at a private firm for a few years. A few weeks ago, I left my firm to come on board as chief counsel for my best friend's business. My job has absolutely dictated my life. Many people who know me well call me a workaholic, especially my sisters. They're not wrong, and I am trying to do better. I'm only in town for a few months, so I'm determined to get to know the area while I'm here."

"That's thorough," I laughed. "Usually, people give me a handful of words about themselves, and I end up having to pry more out of them. I will say, though...you don't strike me as the type to be a ruthless lawyer. You seem too...nice."

"I get that a lot. How about you? Who is Blake? And I expect the same level of detail."

"Oof... where to start? Well...I'm from a small town on the West Coast in California. My dad is an accountant, and my mom is a hairdresser, so I've never had to pay for a haircut in my life. I'm an only child, so having siblings always seems foreign to me, but I think it would have been fun. I grew up next door to my best friend, so I think it didn't matter either way. I studied marketing in college and moved here about three years ago for my job, which is also my life, so I share the sentiment of being a workaholic. I live with Gabby, I love to run, and I love to try new things. Although the last one has suffered since I've been throwing myself into my work."

"Okay, I know this is a little crazy because we just met...but maybe.... just maybe...we could explore together?" he gave me a small smile. "I don't know anyone here, and it sounds like we could both use motivation to step away from our workaholic ways."

I knew the campaign would consume my life while he was here, so committing myself to spending time with a virtual stranger was a new experience. Yet there was something about him that made me want to say yes. He didn't beat around the bush, and I was having a great time so far. He was also easy on the eyes, which certainly didn't hurt.

Gabby's voice echoed in my head, reminding me I needed to enjoy life more. This night had turned out great thanks to Gabby's impulsive decision to invite him to dance, and I was thankful. Maybe it was time I started making impulsive decisions of my own.

I drew my answer to his proposition from the uncharacteristic brazenness I had felt today.

"You know what? Sure! Gabby is always telling me how I need to enjoy my life more, and she was right about today, so why not?"

"How about we meet for breakfast tomorrow, then? We can start strong by trying out a new place."

"Actually, I go to the farmer's market every Saturday morning. How about you come with me instead?"

"I'd love to."

We finished our ice cream and walked around the bar district. All the bars would be closing in an hour, but right now, they were at max capacity. A while later, I dropped Parker off in front of his building.

"I had a lot of fun, Blake. I'll see you tomorrow."

"See you tomorrow, Parker."

He shut the door and walked away.

I stared as he made his way around the car and tried to convince myself that it was to make sure he made it inside safely. Although, there was nothing I would be able to defend him against that he couldn't handle on his own.

He turned toward the car, and I was glad my window was up so he couldn't catch me staring. His lips tugged up into a smile before he disappeared inside.

Chapter Seven

Saturday morning.

Two days before.

The sun warmed my face and forced me awake earlier than I expected. My blinds were cracked open, and the sun rose right in front of my window, causing the light to land directly on my bed. The apartment itself was dead silent since Gabby had stayed at Nathaniel's. The only noise came from the commotion of the street below.

For a minute, as my eyes met the light, I doubted whether last night had been real. Had I really spent the most fun I had in a while with a total stranger? Had I really invited him to join me on one of my favorite Saturday activities? Whoever possessed my body last night was unaware of how I typically acted. Maybe I had passed out after running at the gym from the pressure of the campaign and imagined everything.

However, when I checked my phone, I had a text from Parker confirming the time and place for the farmer's market. The dancing, the ice cream, and the handsome gym stranger had all been real.

As I stared at Parker's name, a text from Richard pinged.

Richard: I'll be at your door at 7 PM. Wear something nice!

Me: Looking forward to it!

I shook off my doubt about last night and focused on Richard for a minute. Gabby might have some weird vendetta against him, but my time with him was enjoyable. He was not the most outgoing or creative person, but he was sweet, and the conversation flowed. Everything about us was simple and predictable.

Before I realized I had forgotten to wash off my makeup last night, I thought I had gotten into a fight. I had only had two beers, so I would remember that. Going to sleep with makeup still on was a bad habit I had to break. I got ready for the market. My jeans clung to my hips, imitating the feeling of Parker's hands on them last night. I sprayed myself with a few pumps of pineapple mist and walked outside.

There was not a cloud in the sky. The temperature was comfortable, but the sun was intense. It beamed up high, making me long to see its effect on the colors around the city or the way it contrasted with the sky.

I followed the path I took every Saturday to the white tents by The Boardwalk. It was still relatively early, so little maneuvering was necessary as I walked. Parker sat at the entrance on a metal bench beside Mr. Alder's coffee cart. I stepped in front of him, landing with a slight hop. He peeked at me through the top of his sunglasses. A slow smile spread across his face.

"Please don't think I'm weird," he said, stepping back from a quick hug hello and looking me up and down.

"That's a great way to start this," I laughed.

"You smell delicious. Is that pineapple?"

"Yeah!"

I sniffed the ends of my hair. He was right; I smelled delicious. By the way that the ends of my hair split from each other, I could tell that I was due for a haircut. My mom wouldn't be visiting until Thanksgiving, so my hair would have to wait.

"Did you rub pineapple on your hair or something?"

"Out of all the products in the world that you could name like shampoo, conditioner, body wash, or perfume...you go with rubbing a pineapple on my hair?"

He laughed at his comment after I pointed out the absurdity of it. His laugh was melodious and deep.

"Wouldn't that make my hair all wet and sticky?" I pointed out.

He put both hands on my head, covering almost all of it. "Well, it's not wet or sticky, so I guess you didn't rub a pineapple on your head."

"Of course not!" I laughed. "That would be ridiculous."

"No need to come at me like that, okay? It's early, I haven't had my coffee, and someone kept me out until late into the night. Just take the compliment that you smell good."

"Well, thank you," I chuckled. "I do think you're weird, by the way, but I think we can still be friends. Let's get some coffee."

"Yeah...maybe weirdly awesome..." he muttered as we walked to Mr. Alder. I tried to stifle a giggle as he side-eyed me.

For the three years I had been here, I had only missed the farmer's market a few times. I had become a creature of habit, and this was one of my favorite things to do. Many vendors had come and gone during the time I had been coming, but a lot of them were as predictable as I was.

"Good morning, Blake! Iced vanilla latte and blueberry muffin?" The edges of Mr. Alder's wrinkled eyes crinkled as he smiled at me.

Every Saturday morning, my first stop was Mr. Alder's coffee cart, and my order was the same. His muffins were delicious, almost as good as Gabby's, but they often crumbled. It was a pain to eat them, but I loved seeing how his aged eyes lit up every time I ordered mine. I could live with crumbs on my shirt to put that smile on his face.

"Yes, please!" I smiled back. "You know me so well."

"Who's the fella with you?" he eyed Parker while making my coffee.

"This is my new friend Parker. It's his first time here, and he needs coffee for his brain to function. I was thinking we give him the special...so I trust you know what to do."

"Absolutely!"

Parker also ordered a chocolate chip muffin. I would have to warn him to eat them carefully and with a napkin underneath for when they crumbled. I reached out to pay, but Parker snatched the card. He handed Mr. Alder his card and gave mine back. The action earned him a smile from the older man and a glare from me.

"You paid for ice cream yesterday. I can pay for the coffee!" I objected.

"Nope. My mom would smack me upside the head."

"That's ridiculous, Parker. I can take care of my stuff."

"It's how I was raised, Blake. If my mom caught wind of me letting you pay at any point, she would reprimand me six ways from Sunday. Now, what's in this? It doesn't look like coffee."

He turned the plastic cup in front of him, inspecting the drink.

"A world of deliciousness and probably enough sugar to bake a cake. But you'll love it, I promise."

He skeptically took a sip while locking his eyes on mine. His light eyes widened, and the moan that escaped him gave away that he loved it, like I knew he would. I shuddered at the sound.

"This is so good. It might give me diabetes, but it would be worth it."

"Told you. I always keep my promises, Parker."

He rolled his eyes at me and continued sipping. Before I could warn him, he took a bite of the quickly disintegrating muffin, and crumbs covered his shirt. I tried not to laugh. He pushed most of the crumbs off his shirt and laughed, being more careful with the muffin.

"Oh, you missed some," I stepped toward him. A little mound of crumbs sat on his chest. My hand brushed him clean as we stood only inches from each other. He looked down at me, an intrigued look in his light eyes. I lingered in his space longer than intended before forcing myself to step back.

"Okay!" I broke us out of the trance. "Are you ready to meet everyone?"

"How well do you know these people?"

"Let's get started."

I waved at him to follow me and walked around the familiar tents. As we walked, I gave him all the fun facts I knew about the people I shopped from each week.

I introduced him to a small, smiling woman surrounded by mounds of aluminum-wrapped tamales and little plastic cups of salsa. Ms. Mabel was finally back after a two-week visit to Oklahoma. One of her daughters had moved out there for her husband's job, and she visited her about once a year. I missed her Sunday lunch tamales, but the pictures of her newest grandson were incredibly adorable. Her character was lighter and happier than it had been in a while, so it seemed like her visit was a significant uplift for her mood. She had broken her leg a few months ago and wasn't sure if she would go, so I was glad she made it work.

Parker was hesitant to try the free sample she offered him since he swore the best tamales were sold from a random back of a truck in an alley, but Ms. Mabel convinced him. He bought a dozen. No one could resist Ms. Mabel's delicious food.

Three tents down from her, James and Adam were selling tubs of their mom's gumbo. For some reason, there was a wide berth of Southern food here. I wasn't an expert, but people usually praised the market. To my dismay, they were sold out when we walked up.

"I'm sorry, Blake," James scratched the back of his head. "We had more people than usual stop by a lot earlier. I guess people had somewhere to be this morning."

"James! I am a creature of habit. What am I supposed to have for dinner tomorrow and lunch on Monday now?"

"I'll save you one every morning from now on. We will not let it happen again, Blake," Adam chimed in, trying to charm me with his smile.

"Next time your mom visits, I'll make sure to tell her how you broke my heart and left me starving in the process."

James rolled his eyes and laughed. "Aw, the poor princess can't get what she wants today. Don't be dramatic."

"You're damn right. I'm a princess," I winked at Parker, who stifled a laugh. If he would call me that, I would own it.

"Next week, Blake. We'll have more."

"You better."

Before I bought my first container of gumbo from them, I had never tried it. It quickly became a staple of my weekly meal plan.

I usually chatted more with James and Adam, but the market was crowded today, so we moved along.

James and Adam were brothers. James was almost ten years older and worked as a construction manager a few buildings from me. Adam was finishing his degree in computer science at the University of Maine. He wasn't too far, but it wasn't close enough to be here every week during the year. Their mom, Callie, lived in Louisiana, but I had been fortunate enough to meet her the last time she visited.

"You know... I can make you some gumbo, princess," Parker dragged his speech on that last word, and we both chuckled. It was sweet of him to offer. "My grandma had a killer recipe for it, and I think I'm a pretty great cook."

"It's okay. I can pick up something else at the grocery store. They have a lot of those ready-made meals, and they're usually pretty good."

"Let me cook for you. It's been a while since I've had anyone to cook for. My best friend is a super picky eater, so she's no fun to make anything for."

My curiosity was peaked as to whether he was as good as he claimed. It had been a long time since someone other than Gabby cooked anything for me. Her encouraging voice crept into my thoughts again. Listening to Gabby's advice could be a slippery slope to bad decisions, but I found him fascinating.

Before agreeing, I finished showing him the rest of the market. We stopped by Mrs. Alder's tent for some vegetables and bought some cookies from Penny. Parker was shocked at my knowledge of the people we interacted with at each stop.

"How do you know everything about everyone?" he asked.

"I ask and listen," I shrugged. "I've been coming here every Saturday for three years. Many of them have been around for just as long. Some even longer. I've always liked to support small businesses and learn their stories. They're just like you and me, trying to make a living and take care of their families."

The sun shone on his face. He hid his curiosity behind his sunglasses and cocked his head slightly. I felt like a puzzle he was trying to decipher.

"For example," I continued. "The little boy Ms. Mabel showed us is her seventh grandchild, but he is only the second boy. Her daughters both live out of the state. One is in Oklahoma, and the other is in Washington, but she visits them at least once a year, and they visit her every Christmas. She brings them to the market, and the kids bring a breath of life to this place during the holidays. I feel good knowing my money goes to help her travel to see them."

"What else do you know?"

"James is going to propose to his girlfriend in Cancun next month. The ring is gorgeous. He planned to do it at the end of last year, but his dad got sick. He's better now, but it set them back slightly. Adam is intensely working to graduate and has a job offer in Seattle. He'll never admit it because he likes to seem manly, but James will miss him like crazy. Penny sells cookies every Saturday because she's saving for culinary school next year. Her parents don't support her, so she's been alone since graduating high school. Last Christmas, I bought a dozen cookies from her for everyone in the office. She's almost to her goal and wants to open her own bakery one day. The Alders come here to avoid the monotony of retirement. They were part of the original crew that established this market. I like to talk to people. You'd be surprised what you can learn from consistent five-minute conversations."

"You are incredible," he whispered in disbelief. "I don't think I've ever met someone like you." He pursed his lips, making me wonder what he was thinking. "Thank you for inviting me today. I'd like to join you again if you don't mind me tagging along. Maybe I can learn to listen more during five-minute conversations."

"You're welcome to join me any time. I enjoyed shopping with you."

We sat back on the metal bench for a few minutes. The warm feel of the metal came through my jeans. People came and went from the market, empty bags quickly filling with fresh produce, great cookies, and more. The sun was warming up the air around us, and I was acutely aware of Parker's leg sitting millimeters from mine.

"Will you come by for dinner tomorrow? I was serious about the gumbo."

"How about you come to me?" I suggested, feeling more comfortable knowing that Gabby would be around in the evening to find my dead body if Parker was a serial killer.

"Sure," he smiled. "Text me your address, and I'll be there at five."

"Okay," I stood up and faced him. "See you tomorrow, Parker."

"Later, princess."

Chapter Eight

SATURDAY NIGHT.

Still two days before.

A nice dent in the shape of my butt lingered on the couch where I had been sitting for the last couple of hours. My goal of not working during the weekend failed. I was bored waiting for my date with Richard, so I reviewed the presentation Nathaniel gave Amelia.

It had been over a week since the last time I looked at it, and my brain needed a refresher on all the promises we had made. Within a couple of hours, I became an expert on Truly You again. I scrolled through their social media and took notes on what they had done before. I wanted their work with us to be unique. My goal was to avoid repeating the same kinds of content that they had already put out.

Gabby was still out with Nathaniel, so I didn't endure her judgmental stare as I got ready for my date with Richard. For someone as sweet as she was, she made it obvious when she didn't like something or someone. My hair was straightened, and I slipped into a short-sleeved black dress.

"Hey," Richard's bright smile greeted me at the door. "You look good. Shall we go?"

His sport coat hid his bony shoulders, making him appear broader than he was. His build was of a long-distance runner, which was ironic because he hated running in any capacity. I tried to take him running with me once, but he instantly complained of the sweat, the pain, and even the stretching. I wished I could shovel food in my mouth like he did and still stay in shape without trying.

I looped my arm around him as we walked the handful of blocks to the restaurant. He held the door for me.

The atmosphere of the restaurant was intimate. My eyes had to adjust to the dim lighting. Each round table had a miniature modern chandelier hanging over it. The rings of light placed a direct spotlight on the food when it sat on the table. The walls were painted dark, with twinkling lights draping down every few feet and some abstract paintings.

The classical music heightened the cozy feel without interfering with the conversations. Hushed chatter and quiet laughter livened the dining room. The place was packed, but Richard had been smart enough to make a reservation, so we didn't have to wait.

We sat towards the back in a rounded booth. I scooted toward him, and he did the same on the other side. A gorgeous daisy in a clear vase sat in the middle of the table. I loved daisies.

Richard raved about the book Connor recommended to him. It was a development book about habits that he seemed utterly enthralled with. He seemed to be paying attention to the lessons and talked about them in great detail. I loved that he was an avid reader, but I noticed he rarely used the lessons he read about.

Usually, I was more attentive. I would ask him questions about what he was reading, and whenever I talked about a book, he would do the same. Tonight, my brain struggled to process what he was saying as my mind ran rampant with ideas about the campaign and worries about what Monday would look like.

"Blake?" Richard reached for my hand across the tablecloth. "Are you listening to me?"

"Sorry...I was, but I was also kind of thinking about the campaign. I'm sorry."

"What else is new?" he chuckled, annoyance peeking through his tone.

"I know, I'm sorry. I just...there's a lot on my mind. Sitting here with you makes me a little worried about working together. I don't know..."

"Okay, Blake. Lay it on me. What are you worried about? Everything is going to be fine."

"I think we need to set some ground rules if we're going to work together," I stated. "I want to ensure that our two different relationships stay separate."

"Okay? Shoot."

"Umm...okay. Rule one: No referencing any...dates or anything while working. I don't want anything we say or do to imply that we have more than a professional relationship," I waited for a reaction, but he stoically nodded along. "Rule two: don't be afraid to express your opinion if you disagree. I don't want you walking on eggshells around me just because you're scared of hurting my feelings. I'm a big girl, and I trust you to be good at your job, including calling out any issues you see. Rule three: Don't undermine my authority and expertise in front of anyone else because of our relationship."

"I can live with that."

His words agreed, but his body told me something different. Lips frowned. Arms crossed. Gaze dark.

I needed these rules in place so I could focus on my job. After what happened with Erik, dating within the office seemed like a bad idea, but things with Richard weren't serious. Regardless, I didn't want our business aired around. We were all friends, but we were also a small office, meaning gossip spread like wildfire.

After a delicious steak and potatoes dinner, we walked around The Boardwalk. The sun had left enough remaining heat for it to feel enjoyable amidst the chilly wind. I pulled my hair in a clip to prevent it from matting and blowing into my face.

My least favorite part about living here was that it was a few hours from the closest beach and an hour from a lake. I missed the water, but at least we had The Boardwalk.

The city built a massive pond where people could canoe, fish, and hang out to counteract a lack of water-related activities. Most of it was surrounded by a wooden boardwalk lined by restaurants. It was a crowd-pleaser, often packed with people and full of life.

As we walked, Richard told me about a trip he was planning to take with his brother. Somehow, he managed to keep telling jokes. I could skip core day soon since I would be sore from laughing. The animated story he told about the last time his brother took him on a trip was a refreshing change of pace from our usual conversations.

For the remainder of our date, we avoided the topic of work almost absolutely, which was also unusual for us. Our walk back toward my apartment took us through the bar district and past Scooped. Suddenly, I had a craving for my favorite treat.

"Do you want to grab some ice cream?" I stopped in front of the store.

"I'm okay. I'm not big into ice cream."

A small gasp inadvertently escaped me, and Richard let out a chuckle. I thought about what Parker had said about people who didn't like ice cream. I pushed thoughts about Parker out of my head. I needed to focus on the man in front of me.

We kept walking in silence. Richard walked me home and lingered as I unlocked the door. Before I opened it, he caged me against the wall and brought his cold lips to mine. The wind had chilled them. He had been clearly signaling what he wanted, but I knew I wasn't ready to move forward.

"Goodnight, Richard," I pulled away, sinking into the door but remaining between his arms. His gaze flickered from my lips to my lace-covered chest and back. "I had a great time."

"Oh, come on, Blake. When can I make it past this door?"

"When I'm ready," I rose to my toes and kissed his lips. "Let me know when you get home."

His frustrated groan echoed in the elevator as I heard the doors shut. I knew I disappointed him, but I needed to move at my own pace. He was eager to get inside, but I wanted to be sure about him before we went there.

I leaned over my sink as I wiped off my makeup, which was out of character for me. A momentary surge of pride coursed through me as I did what I told myself I would. I went to bed bare-faced and moisturized for the first time in a long time.

This weekend had already been out of character for me, and I still had one more day left. I spent so much time with my head buried in my computer, even on the weekends, that sometimes I forgot how to step away. The smell of Chinese food seeped into my memory as I thought about the weeks Nathaniel and I spent holed up in the conference room.

I liked the fresh air better. I decided to listen to Gabby more often.

Chapter Nine

Sunday afternoon.
The day before.

I paced around the living room in my socks, excitedly waiting for and nervously regretting inviting Parker over. In the three years I had lived here with Gabby, Nathaniel and Mason were the only men not related to us who had stepped into this apartment.

After leaving California, I needed a haven, and Gabby didn't love hosting, so our apartment was the perfect place to create that. There were expectations of me everywhere but here. This was the only place where I could kick back and do nothing. It was only an apartment, but it was my haven in my fast-paced and demanding life.

As such, it was the unspoken rule that we rarely brought people by. I had broken that rule today. I knew Gabby wouldn't be mad, but I was nervous.

My watch announced it was five, followed by Parker's punctual knock on my door. My heart raced, and I didn't understand why I was so worked up over him coming. He had a bottle of wine in one hand and a bag filled with ingredients slung over his shoulder.

"I know that wine doesn't go with gumbo, but I figured it was a safe choice drink outside of beer," he laughed.

"Why didn't you get some beer? That seems more fitting."

"Because I panicked? I don't know. It just felt like a wine kind of Sunday."

"Okay, I respect the logic."

I moved away from the door and let him inside. He looked around the living room and seemed to spend time familiarizing himself with and studying the space around him. He perused the pictures that hung on our back wall, lingering on one of Gabby and me at our college graduation.

His bag thumped on the island as he unloaded the ingredients. Immediately, he moved things around and looked for bowls to parse his ingredients into.

"Anything I can do to help?" I offered, needing to force myself to do something other than stare at the handsome man in my kitchen.

"Sure. Are you willing to get greasy, princess?"

"I know you're mocking me, but I'm still willing to help you."

He let out a hearty chuckle and handed me some chicken to shred. I slowly tore it apart while he busied himself with everything else. Our dish towel with little muffins hung over his shoulder, and his shirt clung to his back muscles. I had to remind myself that I was supposed to be shredding chicken, not staring at his perfect back, moving around the kitchen.

He threw the ingredients together in the pot with no measuring cup in sight. He didn't say a word for a bit and worked methodically. I would be genuinely impressed if this tasted like the gumbo I bought from James and Adam.

I was terrible at cooking. Every time I tried to make something new, I either burnt it, didn't cook it enough, or the food tasted weird. Instructions weren't hard to follow, but I still couldn't get recipes right unless it was only a few steps.

"I'm done!" I announced, proudly showing him the shredded chicken in the bowl like a child showing off their macaroni art.

"Great," he reached over my shoulder, his smokey scent drawing me in. "Shouldn't be much longer."

I wiped up the island to take care of some dirty spots where I had dropped pieces of the cooked chicken and hopped up. I sat facing him, dangling my legs over the edge, and watched as he placed a lid over the pot.

"While we wait.... where do you keep the wine glasses?"

"Oh, I'll get them."

I almost jumped down before he set his warm hand on my thigh and pressed it down. His firm palm against my thigh kept me in place.

"You look...comfortable. Point. I'll get them."

I pointed to the cabinet on the right of the fridge. The wine glasses lived on the top shelf since we rarely used them. Gabby and I were partial to using our regular water or plastic cups out of laziness.

"Can you even reach those?" he laughed, noticing that the shelf was too high for me to grab anything comfortably.

"Nope. I either have Gabby grab them or use the step stool in the space between the fridge and the cabinet."

Parker checked the space to confirm that there was a step stool there before setting the wine glasses on the island. He rummaged through the drawer to find the corkscrew and opened the bottle. The smooth, dark liquid poured into the glass, and he handed me one, encouraging me to keep it raised.

"To new friends and the new experiences that we'll have...all because I couldn't open a locker."

His hand rested next to my exposed thigh. Parker stood before me, locking me to my spot on the island with his body. His smile, straight out of a magazine, didn't disappear when he sipped on the wine. Suddenly, my excitement for honoring our agreement awoke.

"So, are you ready for work tomorrow?" he asked.

"No," I rolled my eyes and leaned back, using my arms to support me. His gaze flickered to my exposed collarbone, peeking out of my off-the-shoulder sweater before he returned his eyes to mine. I felt a sudden shiver spread through me and tried to ignore his eyes on me.

"A self-proclaimed workaholic like you isn't looking forward to work?" he asked as if it was the most unbelievable thing in the world.

I had an honesty moment with myself. I was petrified of seeing Erik tomorrow. He grew to represent everything I attempted to leave behind in California. I was chaotic and unpredictable then, but the image I crafted for myself here was the opposite of that. Here, I exuded competence, but with Erik around, my childish side threatened to come out. My reaction to him tomorrow could go either way.

My worries over Erik and the thought of having Amelia and her team in the office made my stomach churn. I didn't want to embarrass myself, Capital Media, or anyone on my team. This was the largest and most important project I had ever worked on. The opportunity was ginormous, and failure on my end would be catastrophic.

"It's a long story," I sputtered.

His eyes and stance softened. "We have time."

I swirled my wine and looked up at him through my eyelashes. Unloading all my fears and worries on him seemed like speaking to a void that would likely forget everything I told him or a terrible idea that would haunt me later. But I needed to talk to someone with no stake in the situation.

He listened intently to my rant about Erik. Once I started talking, I couldn't stop. I told Parker about our history, my thought process for leaving home for my career, and my nervousness about seeing the man. I sprinkled in the discomfort of juggling those feelings with my current situation with Richard.

Since the partnership with Truly You was not publicly announced yet, and I apparently couldn't control my word vomit, I said very little about the work aspect. I just focused on that there was a project, and I was going to be uncomfortable. I shared with him my deep-seated fear of failure, the looming workload on my lap, and my potential promotion that hung in the balance.

It felt like an hour had passed, and I had been talking at a million words a minute. I didn't even notice him turn off the stove. But when I was done, I felt a hundred pounds lighter.

"Well, you seem incredibly passionate about your job, so I'm sure everything will work out with whatever is coming up. It seems like you and your ex have been able to work well so far, so there's no reason why you wouldn't be able to continue doing that. Plus, that Richard guy you're seeing probably feels just as awkward."

"You're probably...right. I have a bad habit of worrying about nothing. You know, telling you all of this is strangely comforting."

"Thank you? I think..."

He offered me his hand to get off the island, but I jumped off without grabbing it in a fit of independence, forgetting I was only wearing socks. Given how quickly he reacted, he could have been either a psychic or a cat in a past life. Parker caught me when I lost my balance on the landing.

His arm wrapped around my waist, bringing me back to my feet. My hip was encased in his other hand, similar to when we were on the dance floor. I grasped his arm, feeling his veins protruding under my fingertips.

"Thanks," I breathed out. His light eyes entranced me, and I couldn't move a muscle.

"No problem."

I breathed heavily, partly from almost falling and partly from seeing how his eyes filled with lust. He slowly brought me upright again but kept his hands on me. His eyes were pinned to mine, except for the hesitant flicker at my lips. His fingertips pressed into my side, and his grip stiffened on my hip. Slowly, he moved closer and brought our bodies together, giving me plenty of time to refuse him.

In this split second, I should pull away. I should turn around, thank him for saving me from hitting my head, and eat dinner in the weird silence of what almost happened. But everything I should do went out the window the second his lips hovered over mine.

I was already on my toes when our lips connected. Warm. Soft. His kiss was hesitant, like testing the water before getting in. Then, he took the plunge and finished closing the distance between our bodies. My hands moved to his chest before traveling to his neck, pulling him down closer to me. His thick hair was soft under my hands.

My back hit the cabinet with Parker's hand as a cushion. The hand on my hip now gripped the side of my face with a mixture of desire and affection. I could have stayed in his arms for hours had it not been for the front door flying open, forcing us apart.

"Honey, I'm home!" Gabby called out. "There's no way you cooked. Something smells incredible!"

"Whatever it is, I hope you have enough for three," Nathaniel's deep voice followed.

Gabby rounded the corner. Her mouth dropped open at the sight of a flustered Parker and nervous me in the kitchen. I smoothed over my hair where Parker's hand had dug in as her face broke into a wide smirk. Her eyes turned suggestive.

Nathaniel bumped into her.

"Are we interrupting...something?" Gabby asked, knowing that she was.

"No!" I panicked. "Not at all."

"Y'all want gumbo?" Parker immediately asked, clearing his throat. "I made a whole pot."

Nathaniel jumped at the offer and set the table for four. Gabby mouthed an apology. I locked eyes with Parker, and we both stifled a laugh.

Dinner was served, and Nathaniel and Parker intensely discussed their favorite baseball teams. Apparently, there was a very good Texas team that Nathaniel hated, and I caught something about trashcans that I didn't understand. I didn't know trashcans were part of baseball.

I tuned out most of the conversation, trying to process what happened in the kitchen. Gabby's comment about Richard dating other people slipped into my mind. I wondered if I was holding back my chances of seeing in color by constantly making myself busy.

I loved my job, but I hoped to see Stephen's work one day, both the designs displayed on his arms and the graphics he created. I wanted to see the leaves change and why it was such a big deal. I yearned to know the color of the ocean. Growing up, seeing greyscale never bothered me because I always figured Erik would be there when I was an adult. But after I left, I had moments of sadness about what I was missing in the world. I tried not to think about it, but it was getting harder lately.

My logical side intervened to get my thoughts back on track. It reminded me that Parker was only here briefly, and any notion of permanence would be ill-advised. I looked between Nathaniel and Gabby as he saved her hair from dipping into the gumbo. Her advice had worked out this weekend, so I shifted my perspective closer to hers. I wouldn't worry about anything until I had to.

Just because it wasn't permanent didn't mean it couldn't be fun.

Nathaniel bowed out shortly after dinner, claiming he had to be well-rested for tomorrow. With that statement came many innuendoes about his lack of sleep over the weekend, which left Gabby blushing and me nauseous. She kissed him goodbye and hid herself in her room.

"You can keep the rest of the food," Parker said, helping me wash the dishes. "It should fill the same number of meals you would have with the other one. Sorry that they ran out before you could get it."

"I'm not complaining about missing out on that one," I said. "Yours may be a little bit better, but if you tell James or Adam, I will adamantly deny it."

There was his deep laugh again. "I'm happy you liked it. Grandma's recipe is always a crowd-pleaser."

"Well, Grandma knows her stuff."

"I should go. I have an early start tomorrow, and you have a big day to prepare for. I need to be at the airport to pick up some people first thing," he turned to me when we got to the front door. "I'm sorry, by the way."

"For what?"

"Kissing you. I'm not typically the kind to go around kissing women I just met...I guess I just got carried away in the moment."

"Do you regret it?"

Here was my streak of boldness for the weekend surging again. I wasn't sure where it had come from, but it would come to an embarrassing end if the answer was yes.

"What? No!" he shifted his weight and crossed his arms. A flash of fire stormed his eyes as he cocked his head. He snapped a rubber band on his wrist.

"Why are you doing that?" my eyes narrowed at the mark on his wrist.

"Sorry, it's something I do when I get worked up, but I do not regret kissing you. I'm just not trying to add one more thing to your already full plate or if that's even something you wanted. I've enjoyed spending time with you the last few days, so I don't want one stupid, bonehead move to –"

I balled up his t-shirt, feeling the cotton wrinkling under my fingers, and pulled him down to meet my gaze. It effectively stopped his rambling. I seized the last bit of boldness I had in me.

"Parker, be quiet."

I pressed his lips against mine, an involuntary smile spreading across my face. He relaxed his shoulders and straightened up, letting go of the empty bag. Parker pulled me into him until my chest pressed up against his.

"So, I guess that answers that," he chuckled into my lips. "Umm...what happens now?"

"It depends. Do you still want to hang out with me?"

He nodded.

"We're both adults," I stated. "I pitch that we explore the city in our attempt to be better at life outside of work like we planned and just go with whatever happens. No strings, no commitments, just temporary fun. It's like the start of a joke...two workaholics make a pact to work less and enjoy life more."

"Well, then, I'm excited to discover what a life outside of work is like. Would you like to meet me for a drink tomorrow? You might need it after spending the day with your ex."

"Absolutely. I'll text you a time and place."

"Yes, ma'am," he said, lightly brushing his lips across mine. "Goodnight, princess."

"See, now that felt like a compliment. Goodnight, Parker."

I took one last glance at him before shutting the door. My hand lingered on the knob as I processed what I had just done. Gabby's advice was batting a thousand right now.

My bedroom ceiling stared back at me as I lay in bed, not quite believing who I was this weekend. Erik, Richard, and Parker consumed my thoughts and feelings. Amelia plagued my worries. My fear of failure kept me awake longer than I intended to stay up.

Come the morning, I needed to pack everything I felt away. I would move everything aside and forget about the fantastic weekend I had. Every worry, every smile, every doubt. Feelings didn't matter. I had to focus on the most important thing in my life.

My job.

Chapter Ten

Monday morning.

Arrival day.

Eighty-two days left.

My side table lights gradually came on. My phone buzzed, and my alarm beeped. It was the expected sound and feel of a Monday morning.

The excitement and anxiety of the day had me checking my phone every twenty seconds while I got ready to ensure nothing had gone wrong. In my head, my brain generated an ever-growing list of things that could go wrong.

The Truly You team backs out at the last minute.

The California team missed their flights yesterday.

The office catches on fire and burns everything down.

Usually, I wore comfortable pants, a blouse, and a pair of flats with the occasional dress or blazer. But today, I felt the pressure to look perfect. My image had to reflect what I wanted Amelia to think of me. I tried to channel confidence and competence. I needed to show that I was perfectly capable of handling the task in front of me.

I slipped into a black pencil dress paired with a white blazer. I curled my hair and did my makeup, something I rarely did for work. The mirror looked back at me, unsure of what it was looking at.

Today felt paramount. The pressure of making a good impression weighed heavily on my shoulders. I had something to prove.

The living room lights were on when I grabbed my lunch bag from the fridge. Gabby's empty coffee mug was sitting in the sink, meaning she was already gone. I had forgotten to ask her for the muffins and coffee I wanted to bring in today, so I stopped by the café on my way to work.

She had opened about thirty minutes before I walked in, but people had not started flowing yet. It was still too early. A sharply dressed woman waited for Gabby to finish ringing her up. Jeremy, one of her employees, served coffee to a pair of businessmen who already seemed to be working. He smiled at me as I walked in.

"Hey, Gabs! Hey, Jer!" I called in.

"Hey, Blake," Jeremy went behind the bar to return the coffee pot. "Early morning, huh? It's barely six-thirty."

"Big day today."

"Gotcha. Good luck!" he disappeared into the kitchen.

Gabby's face lit up when she saw me once she was done handing the woman her change. Her hair was in a bun, and her checkered apron was covered in flour.

"You look incredible!"

"Thanks, Gabs," I twirled to show her my outfit. I was starting to feel confident about it.

"Trying to show Erik what he let walk away?"

"Amongst other things," I laughed. "I mainly want to make a good impression on Amelia and her team. I know it's a little late notice, but could you drop off enough coffee and muffins for the team around eight-forty-five?"

"Sure, I'll even bring them in myself."

"You just want to see Nathaniel all dressed up," I teased.

"The very thing I live for."

I hugged her across the counter.

The rest of my walk to work let me relax, and empowerment flowed through me as I walked into the lobby. My heels clicked on the tile floor. The security guard conversed with someone on the phone. My heart started pounding. My future depended on proving to Connor that I could be the manager he needed.

The elevator door squeaked open to reveal the desolate floor. Almost no one would be here for another hour. The only faint indication of life came from Nathaniel's office down the hall, on the other side of the conference room from mine. His door was wide open, and the lights were on.

"You're here early," I poked my head in.

He stood at his desk, staring at the computer screen. He was also sharply dressed. A perfectly tailored jacket contoured his broad shoulders. His pants clung to his toned legs, ending at spotless white shoes. The shades of gray of the coat and pants differed, telling me it wasn't a matching set. His hair was styled slicked back in his typical fashion. His usual cocky grin was replaced by a troubled look as he tapped his fingers on the wood.

"You look nice today," I complimented him, trying to ease his mood. "Are you okay?"

"Thanks, kid. I'm fine, just a little anxious."

"Is that why you're here so early?"

"Yeah, I've been up since four. I couldn't sleep. This is my biggest deal ever, and with the promotion almost at my fingertips, I'm feeling the pressure."

"Wow, it's almost like you're a normal person, not a sales machine."

"Hey, I have feelings. Not many, but they're there."

"Relax. You did your part. Let me worry about mine. I will not let you down, I promise. After this, we'll truly be a force to be reckoned with."

"You're going to do an incredible job, kiddo. I know you are, even if I sounded unsure the other day. You know... I mess with you often, but I'm glad we're friends, Blake. I'm not sure I'd be half as successful without you."

"Aw! That's so sweet," I smiled. "Look at you, showing your feelings again! The sentiment is mutual for sure."

"If you tell anyone I'm nice to you, I'll deny it."

"Don't worry, your secret is safe with me. Oh, the love of your life is coming by to drop off muffins in a couple of hours."

His eyes lit up with excitement. He fiddled with the edges of his jacket. It was always heartwarming to see him flustered around Gabby and see how much he felt for her.

"You also look great today, by the way. Erik will take one look at you and regret letting you walk away."

"That's what Gabby said. Honesty moment? I think I'm trying to impress everyone. I want people to feel confident in me; I've never had that feeling before. On the inside, I want to crawl into bed and hide. On the outside...I'm cool as a cucumber."

He stifled a laugh. "You're going to blow everyone away, kid. Today is going to be great."

"Ah, the day is young. A lot can still go wrong."

"Don't be so negative. Do you have plans tonight? Maybe the three of us can get a drink and either celebrate a great kick-off or drown our sorrows in discounted margaritas."

"Actually...as much as I appreciate the offer...I'm having drinks with Parker after work."

Nathaniel's smirk matched the one Gabby gave me during dinner last night.

"Seems like the handsome gym stranger has you captivated."

"I've had a lot of fun with him, and it's temporary, so there's no chance of it interfering with my long-term goal of ruling the marketing world. I'm finally listening to Gabby."

"You're taking life advice from her? I love the woman more than life itself, and you know that, but I'd tread carefully around her advice."

Nathaniel knew how much of a wildcard Gabby could be better than anyone.

"She just said I need to start living my life more, so I've decided to do that. I'm letting Parker show me a fun time while he's here."

"As long as you're happy, I'm in your corner. I like him. He was cool to hang out with."

"Thanks. I'm going to get settled in for the day and pray to every single deity I can think of that today goes well."

As I walked out of his office, a similar list to earlier flashed in my mind, reminding me that my brain was still generating worst-case scenarios. These were tailored to seeing the California team.

I could break down and cry at the mere sight of Erik. That would be deeply concerning and embarrassing.

I slap Erik flat across the face for the way he let me drive away without saying goodbye. That would be equally as bad.

Wild animals eat them before even making it into the building. I would just be sad and scared of going outside if that happened.

My brain had to stop coming up with these. It was derailing my attempts at pretending that I wasn't shaking.

Tens of emails flowed in as soon as I turned on my computer. A constant stream of dings had me muting the sound. Questions about ongoing projects, requests from the sales team, and a companywide communication announcing Project Porcelain. Most of these emails could be addressed right now, so I took care of them while waiting for the true workday to start. Others would have to wait until I could debrief Lainee about them since she would be running point on most of our other projects.

My phone chirped next to me, scaring me since I always had it on silent in the office. Parker's name flashed across my screen.

Parker: Wishing you the best of luck today. You'll do great!

Me: Thanks! I'm getting more and more nervous as the minutes march on.

Parker: Think about it this way – as each minute passes, you're one minute closer to hanging out with me ;)

Me: Feeling a little cocky this morning, are we?

Me: But I am looking forward to it. The Boathouse. 5:30 :)

Parker: Can't wait :)

A soft knock made me jump and throw my phone. I slammed it down onto my desk, trying to catch it. I dejectedly sighed and saw Lainee sheepishly standing by the door. She held a laugh back from seeing my phone's journey from my hands to the desk. I had to get my jumpiness under control.

"Sorry, Blake. I didn't mean to scare you. I wanted to run the itinerary for the day with you."

Lainee took a seat across from me and reviewed the schedule for today.

The California team would be arriving here within the hour. She had already requested IT, meaning Gordon, since he was the only one who could do it, to set up their computers. He had committed to doing it by the end of the day. She had also booked the conference room for our kickoff meeting.

After lunch, Amelia and her team were due to arrive. Gloria, the receptionist downstairs, would notify Lainee when they were here, and she would greet them. The temporary badges that allowed them to access our office had already been requested. All she needed was their picture. She had also ensured that the small team room was set up like a coworking space for the days they would be here.

Lainee was incredible. She never gave herself enough credit for how much easier she made my life. I made a mental note to talk to Connor about promoting her or giving her a hell of a raise. She walked out of my office, satisfied at my signing off on everything she said.

Every minute that went by was a minute closer to seeing a part of my past I would have preferred to leave behind. It was a minute closer to meeting the team that would help determine if I got to take the next step in my career. But it was also a minute closer to seeing swoony light eyes that made me smile and forget about everything else this weekend.

Another knock startled me. I was entirely too jumpy today for my office door to be revolving. I looked up to see Connor. He wore a black suit, which was typical of him. Today, his tie had little lipsticks printed on it. I had to give it to him; he was committed to being on theme. He owned a tie for every kind of client we had.

"Big day today, Blake," he sat across from me. "How are you feeling?"

"Do you want honesty or a canned response?" I asked.

"I don't pay you to lie," he laughed.

"I'm terrified. Nervous. But weirdly excited."

"I'd be worried if you weren't all three. This isn't going to be easy. It'll probably be the hardest project you've ever managed."

"Is this supposed to be a pep talk? Because if it is, you might need to understand the concept of one better."

"No," he chuckled. "You don't need one. I was going to wish you luck and let you know that I'll be here for the first bit of kick-off, and then I have lots of meetings. But I'll be back, briefly, after lunch to meet Amelia and her team. My daughter has a school awards thing that I'd like to attend."

"Family first. I'll ensure everything is under control. Gabby will be here with muffins and coffee soon, so I hope you're hungry."

"For Gabby's muffins, there's always room."

Connor's confidence in me was both comforting and unnerving. I was glad he felt like I had a handle on everything, and he didn't look over my shoulder, but part of me wanted him to. Part of me wanted him to be an overbearing and micromanaging boss so I didn't have to be the responsible adult in the room. But that wasn't his style.

He was throwing me into the deep end; it was sink or swim.

Nathaniel crossed paths with Connor at my door and peeked his head in. Before he could say anything, Gabby's infectious laugh traveled down the hall and pulled him away. Lainee instructed her to take the items to the conference room, and the scent of coffee and muffins awakened everyone.

"I don't know how you concentrate with him around," Gabby stood beside me by the door. I didn't need to look to see who she was looking at.

"Easy. I'm not in love with him."

"Shut it," she whispered through gritted teeth as if Nathaniel and the rest of the world didn't already know. She gave me a slight push as I laughed. "Well, my sweet Blake, I shall leave. I baked, I delivered, and I saw Nathaniel's fine body all dressed up. You'll do great today. Don't let dumb Erik being here throw you off your game."

She blew a kiss at Nathaniel, who was stuck in conversation with Connor and couldn't break away. It seemed to physically pain him not to kiss her goodbye. I grabbed a blueberry muffin and sunk my teeth into it. The flavors brought me the comfort I craved as I waited to face my past and future.

"Are you ready for today?" Richard came up behind me, a little too close for comfort. He seemed relaxed. One hand was in his pocket, and the other held a steaming coffee.

"As ready as I'll ever be."

"You're holding it together well. I'd be a nervous wreck."

"Thanks, Richard. That's helpful..."

"Sorry, comforting people isn't my strong suit. That was supposed to be a compliment."

"Hey, Blake," Lainee called from the door as I was about to respond. "The California team is coming up."

My legs almost buckled, and I felt my heart rate increase. My palms were sweaty. My breath was forced, and not enough air was getting to my lungs. Nathaniel warily walked over to me, recognizing the signs of what I was on the verge of.

"Can I talk to you for a second, Blake?" he pulled me away from Richard and the door.

"Breathe, kid," he said, trying to hide his worry. If anyone in this room could walk me through calming down, it was him, and I had to trust that. He led me through some deep breathing, and I brought myself back from the brink of a panic attack. I hadn't had one of those in almost three years.

"Look at me. You are just fine. Breathe. He's just another coworker."

"He's just another coworker," I whispered back at him. "I can do this."

"Exactly. You're superstar Blake right now. Everything will be just fine."

When we started traveling together, Nathaniel had become an expert at talking me off the ledge of a panic attack. I was scared of flying and having to present in front of strangers sent me into a panic, so there were plenty of opportunities for him to hone his skills. Over time, we learned to recognize the pattern of how they started: increased heart rate, clammy hands, and a lack of air. If I managed to calm down by the time I couldn't breathe, it wouldn't progress to shaking and crying.

He kept breathing with me, knowing we were running out of time as the voices got closer. I couldn't let this happen now. I had come too far in my healing to fall apart right now.

The voices got louder, and I sensed the presence of the other team in the room. It was now or never. I needed to step away from Nathaniel and take charge of my emotions for this meeting.

I turned away from the safety of Nathaniel's comforting gaze and looked up to meet the dark eyes I had once been so familiar with. Laughter. Sadness. Friendship. Pain. Years of memories and emotions flooded back, threatening to undo all the walls I had built over the last three years. The pit in my stomach grew.

All the other voices in the room faded into a muffled mumble as people greeted each other. Heat spread throughout my body, reaching everywhere but my hands, which were clammy and cold. My fight-or-flight response was confused. It wanted to run away and hide but knew that would be the wrong reaction. My feet felt bolted to the ground until Nathaniel pushed me slightly forward to the head of the conference room.

"Everything is okay, kid," Nathaniel whispered.

He walked around me and greeted the team. I took a deep breath and reminded myself that I was a different person, and so was he. It had been years, and I had changed. Running and crying wasn't what this Blake did, although the want to do that tried to claw its way out of the carefully crafted cage it was trapped in. I allowed myself to breathe and be the Blake I trained myself to be.

Connor's concerned eyes carefully watched me. For the first time in five years, I felt his doubt grow. I shoved my feelings in a box and took a deep breath again. I arranged myself at the front of the room, looking at Connor for a nod of approval to start.

"Good morning, everyone!" I called out to the filled room, avoiding further eye contact with Erik.

Everyone muttered a greeting and took their seats around the wooden table. Muffins and coffee sat on the table like another regular Monday morning. I tried to find comfort in what I knew was the same today. Lainee picked at her chocolate chip muffin; she always took the chips out and ate them separately. Stephen scowled at his black coffee; he rejected the notion that muffins were breakfast. Jamie added three packets of sugar and cream to her coffee. All these things remained the same.

"Thank you all for your attention this morning. As you all know, or at least I hope you do, today is officially day one of Project Porcelain!"

There was a round of proud applause around the room with a burst of quiet snickers.

"For the first time in our five-year history, Capital Media has been awarded a contract to develop and implement a nationwide campaign. I want to thank every single person in this room for their intense dedication and hard work over the last couple of weeks that made this happen. It wasn't easy, but our hard work has paid off thus far."

I took my millionth deep breath of the last ten minutes. "I want to extend a warm welcome to our colleagues from the California office who have gracefully committed to camping out here for the next twelve weeks. Sorry we stole you from your families for a bit, but thank you so much for being here. We are pleased to welcome you to New Windsor, and I know we're all going to have a great time working together."

"Thank you, Blake," Erik's booming voice echoed through the room, accepting my welcome from his seat.

In a different life, his voice was the voice of comfort. A voice that made everything okay and helped me through some of the hardest times growing up. Today, it made me feel nothing but nervous. "On behalf of the California team, we are incredibly excited about the opportunity to work closely with your team on this."

"Thank you, Erik."

His name caught in my throat. I turned to Nathaniel. He gave me a reassuring look and a slight nod.

"Per the stipulations of our contract with them, Amelia and a few members of her team will be in this office approximately three times per week for the next twelve weeks," I ensured we were all on the same page. "Assuming everything goes well, which is almost guaranteed with this team, they will love our work and give us full reins after phase one, as agreed. Her team will arrive after lunch today, and I expect everyone to welcome them warmly. However, I'm confident that won't be an issue for this team. Connor, would you like to say a few words?"

"Thank you, Blake," Connor joined me at the front of the room. He had relaxed. His faith in me was slowly coming back. "I want to sincerely thank each and every one of you for your hard work over the last few weeks and the work you'll put in over the coming months. We have an incredible amount of talent and dedication in this room, so I am sure that you will blow them away. We could not do what we do without this incredible team. I look forward to seeing what you all come up with and embark on taking this company to the next level."

"Thank you, Connor," I watched him return to his seat. "Now, we have about ten minutes before the official meeting starts. Lainee, please help the California team get settled in. Please eat a muffin from Gabby's and enjoy a cup of coffee. We'll need our energy today as we prepare to hit the ground running."

Everyone continued their conversations from when the team first walked in. I quickly excused myself, escaping to my office.

Before I could face Erik for one more second in any capacity, I had to compose myself. Seeing him elicited more conflicting feelings than I expected. I closed the door and collapsed on my chair, feeling the air leave my lungs. The day had barely started, and I was already overwhelmed. If this pattern held, I was in for a chaotic three months.

"Do I not even deserve a hello?" Erik stormed into my office seconds later. "What am I? Chopped liver?"

Obviously, this was off to a great start.

"Not right now, Erik," I pleaded, facing the window behind me. I focused on the people walking below, trying to find an ounce of calm to hook onto. "I can't do this right now."

"Blake, please look at me," he stepped closer, but I kept my gaze locked on the people walking down below. "Blake Elena, look at me. Do you really hate me so much that you can't look me in the eye?"

He was wrong. I didn't hate him. Everything would be so much easier if what I felt for him was pure hate.

I swiveled my chair toward him but kept my eyes on the ground.

"I'm not going to berate you, but after three years of barely talking to you and the first time seeing you since you left, I didn't even get so much as a hello?"

"I welcomed you and your team. I don't know what you mean."

My breath trembled as I wiped the tear tittering on the edge of my eye. Thankfully, I opted for waterproof mascara so it would last longer, not knowing it would also prevent the black streaks I feared would appear on my cheeks. I had never cried at work before.

"I don't care about the team. I want you to look at me and acknowledge me, acknowledge the fact that I still exist. I want to see your eyes," his voice was as broken as I felt. He always said my eyes were his favorite part of me, yet he had never seen their color. "Please, Button, let me see your eyes."

Button.

Erik was the one person in the world that called me anything but my name. He gave me that nickname when we were eight years old. I dared him to swallow a bug, which he did. He dared me to swallow a button, and I wouldn't be outdone. My parents were not happy with the doctor's visit that ensued, but it stuck.

The nickname hung in the air, forcing me to look at him. Tormented eyes. Sad smile. Twenty years of memories rushed into my mind. The heartbreak of the day I left felt as fresh as it was three years ago.

He hesitantly walked behind my desk and grabbed my hand, slowly prompting me to stand from the comfort of my chair. He studied me as if three years had made me unrecognizable before pulling me into his chest. I crashed against him and wrapped my arms around his waist. The smell of clean linens and detergent crowded my nose.

"I'm sorry I stormed in, but can you talk to me? Please?"

"Not here. Not at work."

"Okay," he whispered, almost inaudible. "I've missed you."

"I've missed you too," I matched his tone. I didn't realize I meant those words until they escaped my mouth. I could hear his heart from where my head landed on his chest. He squeezed me tighter before pulling away, and I took a few steps back. It was my turn to look at him.

He had always taken care of himself, so it didn't surprise me that he was still in perfect shape. Thin yet toned. His dark hair was longer, reaching almost past his ears. I hadn't seen it like that since high school, but it was always my favorite look of his. It made him seem relaxed and boyish. The button-down with rolled-up sleeves tucked perfectly into his black slacks was his signature look.

He looked good, and I wanted to hate him for it.

My calm breathing faltered when my eyes landed on the bracelet tied around his wrist. I wouldn't have expected him to keep it, much less still wear it.

"How about tonight? Over some food?" he asked. "We can get Pad Thai."

My thoughts flashed to Parker's smiling face, whether he would understand. I decided against canceling drinks with Parker. I had enough turmoil for one day and had been looking forward to seeing him again. He had been right last night; I was going to need that drink.

"I have plans tonight. Maybe another night."

I also wasn't ready to talk to him. Not yet. He eyed me skeptically; it wasn't like me to have plans during the work week.

"Okay."

Nathaniel knocked on my door, slowly pushing it open since my blinds were drawn.

"Hey, Erik," Nathaniel walked in. "Can I get a minute with Blake, please?"

Erik nodded and left without question or argument. His body tensed as he walked past Nathaniel. Nathaniel grabbed my shoulders and looked down at me. We were less than an hour into the day, and I was unraveling.

"Are you okay?" he asked.

I shook my head, and he pulled me into a brotherly hug. I had never let my emotions get the better of me at work, so this was uncharted ground for me. I had to figure it out since I promised Connor I could work with Erik.

My confidence was shaken, but I reminded myself that it would all be okay once the initial shock subsided.

"I'm sorry," I wiped my cheeks. "I don't know what's happening to me."

"No need to apologize, kid," he handed me a tissue. "We knew this was going to be hard on you."

"I overestimated how much I would be able to compartmentalize once I saw him. He wants to talk, but I don't know if I really have anything to say to him."

"Blake, after the way things ended between you guys, I agree. I think you need to talk to him. Trust me, you have things to say, and it will be the only way you can truly move forward."

I sighed. He looked at me. Concern lit up all over his face.

"Look," he pushed aside big-brother-comforting Nathaniel and became matter-of-fact Nathaniel. "Crying isn't going to solve anything at the moment, and I won't allow you to think about this right now. We need superstar Blake to see Erik as nothing more than a coworker. Then, after work, you will have drinks with Parker and let your mind relax for a minute. After that, and only then, you'll think about Erik. But right now, I need you to do what you do best and be my superstar. Understood?"

I nodded, and he led me through some more deep breathing. Having to do this without him would have been impossible. His words landed harshly, but it was the only way to stop the spiral. He was right. I needed to focus on what I did best.

He walked out of my office, and I took a couple of minutes to breathe on my own. I texted Parker.

Me: I have to give it to you and your premonition powers. I'm going to need ten drinks this afternoon. Get ready for Hurricane Blake coming to you.

Almost immediately, he replied.

Parker: That bad?

Me: Worse than expected. Definitely shaken. Had never cried at work until today.

Parker: Please don't cry. I really hate the idea of you crying. Anything I can do?

Me: Get me lots of tequila?

Parker: That can certainly be arranged. I'll also make sure to bring enough tissues.

The little chuckle that escaped me helped me feel a little better.

I started out the kick-off meeting by making sure everyone on the team knew their roles and responsibilities. I would be managing the project as a whole and be the main point of contact for Truly You. Erik would report to me but was still responsible for his portion of the team.

We had twelve weeks to develop and launch the first phase of an incredible campaign for their new line. Later today, Amelia's team would provide us with their goals and target metrics, which will help us tailor our approach.

Nathaniel presented the promises he made Amelia, all of which I had previously approved. We reviewed the contract's requirements, and I ended the meeting fifteen minutes late.

Chapter Eleven

Monday afternoon.

Arrival day.

Eighty-two days left.

Nathaniel and I sat across from each other while I hid in my office. He had ordered food from Gabby's, which Jeremy had delivered, much to his disappointment. I picked at the gumbo I packed.

"Is that Parker's gumbo?" he asked.

"Yes..."

"You like him," he said in a singsong and mocking tone.

"Will you keep your voice down? The door is wide open."

"Why? Afraid Richie might hear?" he exaggeratedly whispered.

Nathaniel and Richard also didn't get along. I had asked all three of them, at separate times, why they disliked each other, but no one ever gave me a reason.

"No, I don't. I barely know the guy. It's just for...fun. Just to try and enjoy my weekends a bit more, like your future wife told me to."

"Oh, I'd say you enjoyed your weekend," he smirked. "Making out in the kitchen, Blake? How cliché of you."

I gasped. "How did you know?!"

"My future wife doesn't keep secrets from me."

I rolled my eyes and finished my food.

Panic started to set in when I noticed it was almost time for Amelia's team to arrive. Eating lunch seemed like a terrible idea now as I had to try to keep it in my stomach. Nathaniel scrolled on his phone, tapping his fingers on his knees, while I paced around the office.

A ding from the elevator prompted me to walk out and see if they had arrived. The doors opened, and it was just Gordon and Barry coming back from lunch.

"Are they here?" Nathaniel asked, stopping to fix the name tag on my door since it was slipping out of the plastic holder again. I needed to tape it shut.

Lainee wasn't at her desk, so I felt confident that the next people to come out of that elevator would be the team from Truly You. I forced a smile through the fear and waited for the elevator doors to open.

Seconds later, the door squeaked, and the bell dinged. A woman, not much older than me, stepped off. I recognized her as Amelia from all the social media pictures. She was talking to Lainee and was followed by a woman and two men.

"This cannot be happening," I groaned through my smile, barely loud enough for Nathaniel to hear. Heart rate increased. "It's like I'm stuck in a bad sitcom."

"Oh, crap," Nathaniel muttered when he saw the same thing I did. He was also careful to keep a confident smile on his face. His hand landed on my shoulder, and I could tell what he was thinking. My hands went clammy. "Shake it off, Blake. You look like you saw a ghost."

"A ghost would be better than this."

I struggled to breathe normally.

"Nathaniel!" Amelia exclaimed, enthusiastically shaking Nathaniel's hand.

She was taller than I expected. Her perfectly styled hair was long and wavy, almost reaching her butt. A black jumpsuit hugged her figure, adorned with a metallic belt that reflected the light.

"Wonderful to see you again, Amelia. Welcome to Capital Media, and welcome to New Windsor!"

"Happy to be here!" her voice had a slight twang.

"Let me introduce you to the promised superstar, Blake Johnson," he continued. "Our best and brightest. She will be your main point of contact while you're here and the one overseeing your campaign."

"Lovely to meet you, Blake!"

"It's a pleasure to meet you, Amelia," I shook her warm hand, praying she couldn't feel how mine shook. "I've been following your rise; you are truly an inspiration. Thank you for trusting us for this. You will not be disappointed."

"I'm confident y'all will do a great job. Let me introduce you to my team."

The two men and the woman stood behind her. All of them wore a bright smile, except one was forced.

"This is Amanda Wood, our national sales manager."

Amanda was barely taller than me, with a pixie cut that perfectly matched her angular face. She wore a white pencil dress and flats. She stood tall and proud to be at Amelia's side.

"Next to her is Nick Wolf, our product development manager."

The first man was Amelia's height, with a shaved head and a long beard. He looked like he could be the lead singer of a rock band or the leader of a biker group. Not what I had expected.

The last man and I locked eyes. He wore a perfectly tailored pair of black slacks, freshly shined shoes, and a tucked-in button-down that concealed his tattoos. He fiddled with the rubber band around his wrist, his gaze revealing an equal amount of shock.

"And last, but certainly not least, this is Parker Robinson. Our chief counsel and my right-hand man."

I shook Parker's hand hesitantly. The hand that fits perfectly on the small of my back. An involuntary smile spread across his lips. The lips that had sent feelings through me in my kitchen.

"It's a pleasure to meet all of you," I smiled, or at least did my best to.

"It's a pleasure to meet y'all as well," Parker shook Nathaniel's hand, pretending to be total strangers.

Lainee stepped in and led them away from us to get them set up in the conference room before our meeting. Before walking into the room, Parker turned toward Nathaniel and me as if he was ensuring this wasn't his imagination. I shoved Nathaniel into my office and shut the door.

"How did you not know?" I whisper-yelled. "He's chief counsel. You do contracts. How did you not know?!"

"I never met him! I didn't even know they had a chief counsel. I dealt mostly with Amelia and occasionally with Amanda!"

"Were there no pictures or anything? No pictures of their team when you visited their office?"

"I was preoccupied while I was there. You're the one that did all the research on them. How did you not know?"

"There were only pictures of Amelia!" I groaned, pacing around my office.

"Well...you know how I told you today would be fine? I think I lied..."

"You think?!" I panicked.

"Okay. Breathe, kid. In and out. You only have to get through the next few hours pretending you weren't making out with him twenty-four hours ago."

Nathaniel's face went from panicked to entertained when the absurdity of the situation dawned on him.

"This isn't funny!" I smacked his chest.

"Honesty moment? I have no earthly idea of what to do or tell you now, but it is kind of funny."

"This is literally the worst day ever."

"Let's not be dramatic. Just try and get through the next few hours and then hash it out with him over that drink."

"I can't do that! He works for Amelia."

"Be an adult, Blake. You at least have to talk to him about it."

"Easy for you to say!"

I groaned and buried my face in my hands. Out of all the lists my brain had devised of how this day could go terribly and horribly wrong, this was not on it. He sighed and walked out of my office, leaving the door cracked.

I turned to the window, wishing I was one of the people enjoying the sunshine in the park across the street. A woman was doing yoga, and a man was working on his laptop in the sun. My forehead felt the warm window against it, and I closed my eyes. I was breathing and trying to settle my heart rate.

I jumped at the knock on my door, bumping my forehead into the window. The revolving door of people continued.

"So," Parker walked in, whispering. He lightly shut the door behind him. "This is...umm...unexpected."

I turned to face my handsome stranger from the gym and felt compelled to walk over to him. "That is the understatement of the century."

"Are you okay?" his voice was soft. "I know seeing me wasn't what you needed after the morning you had."

"No, I'm not okay, and you being this sweet to me isn't making it any easier. Look, I don't know what this means for our plans, but we should get out of here before anyone comes looking for us."

"Blake," he stopped my attempt to get to the door, strong fingers wrapped around my wrist kindly. "Let's still have that drink tonight. We can talk about this then."

His eyes begged for me to say yes. His grip on my arm was uncertain. He pulled me and turned me to face him. Instead of looking at the floor, I was now staring at the transparent button of his shirt. He brushed his fingertips across my temple and tucked my hair behind my ear, forcing me to look up at him with his knuckle under my chin.

"Please."

"Okay," I sighed.

"Promise me. Promise me you'll have that drink with me."

"I promise," I said, keeping my eyes on his. He smiled and turned, walking out of my office.

Another piece of my carefully curated self quickly unraveled, revealing the chaotic emotional interior I tried so hard to subdue.

Thankfully, Connor took charge of the beginning of the meeting, giving me time to adjust to being in the same room as the three people who chipped away at my composure. He warmly welcomed everyone and apologized for needing to leave early. He assured Amelia that they were in good hands – my hands – and Amelia seemed receptive.

Then, it was my turn.

I stood at the front of the conference room. It took all my energy to stop me from collapsing from the stress of the watchful eyes on me. Erik's familiar dark eyes tracked my every move. Richard's focused look studied my words. Parker's concerned gaze threatened to undo me.

I searched for comfort, holding to what I knew to be true. I had gumbo for lunch, like every Monday. Gordon brought leftovers back from lunch because he never finished his food. Lainee used her thick pen for her notes because the thin ones were hard to read. I landed on Nathaniel's encouraging grin. He gave me a soft nod.

My speech was similar to the one from this morning, and everyone seemed comfortable. After the first hour, we took a short break, and some of Gabby's muffins from earlier were making their rounds again.

"You're doing great, kid," Nathaniel assured me.

"I feel like I'm going to pass out."

"Are you okay?" Erik's concerned voice came up behind me as I nodded. He stood next to Nathaniel, taking a closer look at me. "You look pale, Blake. Are you sure you're fine? Have you eaten?"

"She had gumbo for lunch. I saw her," Nathaniel said a little too loudly. Parker turned to us but averted his gaze to the floor with a smile.

Suddenly, we were back in the California office four years ago. Nathaniel and Erik had been concerned about me during an event because I had been so busy that I forgot to eat all day. I almost passed out on the way home. That happened a few times during that month as my deadline approached, and it was only one of the many times I met Erik's disappointed eyes. From that moment, one of them ate lunch with me every day.

"Yeah, I ate," I forced a smile while pinching the bridge of my nose. "I just didn't get enough sleep last night."

He was unconvinced but didn't argue. Nathaniel was called over by Amelia, leaving me alone with one of the people that made me want to collapse.

"Hey," Erik took a step closer, putting his hand on the side of my arm. From the table, Richard looked up, eyes burning a hole through Erik. "You're doing great. Amelia seems impressed with you so far."

"Thanks," I stepped back, letting his hand fall from my shoulder.

He walked away, and I collapsed on the chair closest to my computer. Across the room, Parker snuck a glimpse of me. I pretended not to notice. I needed him to disappear into thin air for a bit.

"These are incredible!" Amelia exclaimed, biting into Gabby's signature chocolate chip muffins. "Where are they from?"

"Gabby's café," Nathaniel answered proudly. "Highly recommended. It's only a few blocks from here."

Parker and I quickly glanced at each other, exchanging a knowing look. I had to stifle some laughter at his knowing smirk. My reaction earned me a puzzled look from Richard.

Amelia finished her muffin and took her place at the front of the room. Parker plugged into the projector, and they started their presentation. They were confident, and both looked in their element presenting. I didn't know what Amelia did before this, but I assumed Parker had plenty of practice talking in front of people.

They gave us a thorough history of their company and how it evolved from a drunken idea after Amelia had a bad reaction to a lotion she bought. The mission of their products was to provide quality skincare and makeup at a price that even college students could afford. I respected their mission. Sometimes, I was appalled at the cost of a tube of lip gloss.

I filled page after page with ideas and questions to cover with them. I peeked at the clock; it was almost five. Parker sat several seats down from me, checking his watch every five minutes. If I got up again like I had planned, as Amelia finished, the meeting would go past five o'clock.

"Okay," I shut my laptop, earning confused stares from my team since they knew the agenda and we weren't done yet. "There's still a lot that we need to cover, but that will take us way beyond the time, so I think we'll call it a day and pick this back up on Wednesday."

"Really?" Stephen didn't hide his surprise. "You're going to end a meeting without everything being covered? Who are you, and what have you done with Blake Johnson?"

Everyone laughed. My face got warm. I had to do a better job as a manager.

"I'm turning over a new leaf," I said. "You are more than welcome to stay working, but for the first time ever, I have plans that I would like to keep this evening. So, take it or leave it."

"No, I'm out of here," Stephen stood and rushed out of the room.

Richard's eyes questioned me, but I wasn't going to stick around to answer any questions. Amelia's team retreated to their conference room, and I dashed to my office. I shoveled my stuff into my purse and locked the door. Lainee stopped me to sign off some slides for her presentation tomorrow before I could run away.

"You run long meetings well," Amelia commented as she and her team caught up to me in the elevator. "I'm known for keeping my team later than I should."

Amanda snickered behind her and adamantly nodded. I was glad I wasn't the only one with an honest team. We chatted about our respective teams, even though hers was right there.

I wanted to be a better manager for them. They had been working hard, and I had been pushing them a bit much over the last few months. I had to be better about balance, both for them and me. Easier said than done.

"Well, your team seems to like you, and Nathaniel spoke very highly of you, so I'm excited to see what we can all do together. Where do you recommend we go for a drink after a long day? Preferably somewhere with sweet drinks, I'm kind of picky."

Parker gave me a panicked look as if I would recommend where we were going. My mind might have been racing a million miles a minute, and my thoughts were muddled, but I wasn't stupid.

"There's a cute little bar a few blocks north," I explained and pointed as we walked out of the building. "It's about three blocks that way and then on the right. It's called Shuffle. They have a great happy hour and yummy cocktails."

"Sounds great. Would you guys like to go?" she looked at Amanda and Nick, who were nodding. "Parker?"

"Umm...I had a... long... weekend, so I think I'll go to the gym and take it easy this afternoon," Parker shrugged. He avoided eye contact with Amelia. He was a terrible liar. A fact that brought me comfort.

"I've never known you to turn down a drink after work... are you feeling sick?" Amelia skeptically looked at him.

"Yeah, I'm fine, Ame. Just tired."

"Okay then? I'd love it if you could join us, Blake, but I believe you mentioned you have plans?"

"Yeah," I smiled at the ground. Lying wasn't my strong suit, either. "I'm getting dinner with a...friend."

"Hm. If my friends made me smile like that, I certainly would make sure I make that dinner," Amanda's squeaky voice chimed in.

I chuckled to hide my embarrassment. Parker shifted in his stance.

"Forgive her," Amelia rolled her eyes. "Amanda doesn't have a filter, even when she should."

"You heard Stephen earlier. I encourage honesty in all its forms," I laughed. "Maybe next time."

We said goodbye and walked in opposite directions.

Today's events replayed in my head like a bad movie. Seeing Erik was much tougher than I expected, and Richard watching my every move made me uncomfortable. Parker walking out of those elevators was the last thing I needed. His kindness and concern for me also didn't help.

I needed to keep myself together and be the person I forced myself to be here. Someone who puts their career above all else. Someone who kept their feelings at work in a box. Sure, it would catch up to me now and then, and I'd spend a day eating ice cream, crying, and watching TV. But it had afforded me success.

The pang in my heart confused me. I didn't want to, but I needed to tell Parker that we had to stop our plans and that our quasi-friendship was now a bad idea.

My thoughts flashed to Richard and Erik. There was nothing wrong with my relationship with Richard. It was uncomplicated. Albeit a bit boring from time to time. But sometimes, boring was good. Stability was good.

On the other hand, everything was wrong with my relationship with Erik. It had broken me completely to lose him once, and it took me years to rebuild myself. I couldn't get close to that heartache again.

I found a spot at The Boathouse that was furthest from the door. An empty booth in the back corner. I ordered some mozzarella sticks and a margarita while I waited. My phone lit up on the table.

Parker: I don't see you anywhere. Please tell me you came.

Me: Back right. Like alllll the way in the back.

"Are you trying to hide from me?" Parker slid in on the opposite side of the worn-down booth.

"I want to hide from the world," I rested my forehead on the table.

"That bad, huh?"

The waitress dropped off what I ordered and took Parker's order. I hovered my head above the table and gave him an annoyed look. He reached across and set his hand on my forearm, caressing me with his thumb. The tension in my body argued whether it was making me feel better or worse to feel his hand on me.

"Blake, look at me."

"I don't want to," I said. "If I look at you, it means that this is happening, and we have a big problem. It means that you're here for the same project I am on and that we can't do whatever this is."

I was rambling. Finally, the waterfall of tears that had been restrained all day fell. There was a cathartic feeling of relief in letting go and the tears soaking my cheeks. Even if it was in front of Parker.

"Yeah, I was worried you'd say that."

"It means that my day has been a total disaster. It means that I cried at work for the first time in my life. I felt like a total wreck."

He continued rubbing my arm with his thumb. I raised my head again to meet his eyes. Pain flashed across them as he noted the embarrassing number of streaks being carved on my foundation.

"Please don't cry, princess. Please. It's breaking my heart to see you like this."

It was inappropriate to cry in front of him. To let him call me princess, even if it had started as a way of mocking me at the market. All of this was wrong.

"I don't know what's happening to me," I let out a quiet sob and an embarrassed chuckle. "I don't cry. I never cry!"

Parker rushed to my side and pulled me into his chest. I didn't fight him and quietly sobbed against his shirt, scrunching it under my fingertips as I held onto him. He ran his fingers down my hair in silence for a few minutes.

"Parker, we cannot do this."

"Yes, we can," he spoke softly into my ear. "The last three days with you have been the most fun I've had in a long time, Blake. I can't just let that go."

"We have to. Parker, my job is my life. I can't risk that."

"And I'd never ask you to. Look, there's no reason why we can't hang out. It's not against the rules. It's not in the contract. I would know; I read all of it. No one has to know that we're friends if that makes you more comfortable. I'd go on a limb and say that Nathaniel won't tell."

I pulled back from him and stared. I wasn't sure I could do this.

"We first met while at the gym. I'd venture to say that we became...friends...before 'meeting' today. There's no reason why friends can't hang out outside of work."

"I don't –"

"I promise this won't jeopardize your job. Remember, we're trying to enjoy life more, and I know you had fun this weekend. What we do in our personal time shouldn't matter."

"Friends don't kiss in the kitchen while making gumbo. Friends don't tuck hair strands behind ears while staring into my eyes."

"I don't know what came over me this afternoon, but I won't let it happen again. I promise I'll keep my hands to myself."

I couldn't deny that this weekend was the most fun and most relaxed I had been in a long time. Work had barely crept into my mind while I was with him. It was a strange feeling – to forget about work for a bit. I had forgotten what that felt like. My brain screamed that this was a bad idea, but the shiver up my spine as Parker caressed my hair made it hard to concentrate on the advice my brain was giving me.

"I promise I will not do or say anything in the office. I will not touch you again within those walls."

"What about outside of those walls?" I almost whispered.

"That depends. Is that what you want?"

"I don't know what I want! I've had many feelings batter me today, making me question everything. But I was looking forward to exploring the city with you."

Parker touched my cheek, and I immediately knew I couldn't let this go. This was a bad idea. I knew it, and on some level, he knew it too. But it was only twelve weeks. What's the worst that could happen? He would eventually go home, and I would stay here and earn my promotion.

"So, we're doing this?" He held my face until I nodded.

The smile across his face helped ease my anxiety about the arrangement but didn't stop my mind from scolding me.

"We need to set rules if we're going to do this," I scooted back from him. He waited for me to explain. "One, don't hold back from expressing your opinion at work because of this. I promise I won't hold it against you unless you're a total dick to me about it. Two, don't use our relationship to influence me at work. Three, don't let this affect how you treat me at work. During work hours, we are nothing more than coworkers, and I will treat you as such. Four, we will not tell anyone the extent of our friendship. I don't want anyone to get the wrong ideas about us winning the contract."

"Sounds reasonable," he smiled. "I promise you will not regret this. You're going to have the best twelve weeks of your life."

"Don't make promises you don't know if you can keep, Parker."

His lips hovered over mine. "I promise, princess. These are promises I intend to keep."

We could keep our personas separate. We did it today; we could do it for twelve weeks.

Chapter Twelve

Friday night.

Seventy-one days left.

Our two teams worked together cohesively, and the easiness of working together made time fly. Amelia, Parker, and the team had been in our office three days the first week and just two the week after. The less they were in the office, the easier it was for Parker and me to keep our lives separate.

Lainee and Amanda had become best friends in a couple of weeks. Stephen had not ripped off Desha's head yet, even though they squabbled at least once per day. Nick and Amelia had flown back to Texas yesterday for the next week to deal with a production issue.

Erik continually tried to have that conversation with me, but I did my best to make it clear that I wanted to keep our relationship within the office walls. Talking to him was not a Pandora's box I wanted to open. My almost panic attacks had mostly subsided, and I wanted to keep it that way. He refused to let it go and was getting impatient at my avoidance of the subject. All the memories replayed in my mind every time I saw him, but I had succeeded in compartmentalizing them away during the workday.

Richard was not heavily involved with the project yet, which was nice. We continued with our routines, and I tried to push him out of his comfort zone. He had finally let me choose the restaurant we went to on Wednesday night, and I took him for sushi. Much to his surprise, he loved it. I was hopeful I could get him to expand into something other than having dinner at restaurants soon.

My goal of letting my team go at a reasonable time every single day had been successful for the entire duration of the project and set a new record for me. The results in morale were incredible, and everyone was in a better mood. I made a mental note to continue this even after the project was over. I had stolen too many of their afternoons.

My internal argument had settled, and I felt more at ease with everything that was happening. I still worked many hours but made it a point to be more intentional with self-care. I was running more often and had been Parker's inspiration to run, so he had joined me most afternoons after work. We kept our personal lives miles away from our professional world, and it worked just fine.

On Friday, I finally carved out some time alone.

Gabby and Nathaniel were out to the movies and would be gone all weekend. Parker had plans with Amanda since Amelia and Nick were gone. Amanda wanted to try a new Indian restaurant that had just opened. Parker invited me along, but that seemed like playing with fire, and I would rather not get burned. Some of Richard's frat brothers were in town, so they were out barhopping.

I decided to watch movies and eat popcorn for the rest of the night.

The initial soft knock at the door was almost drowned out by the popping coming from the microwave. The smell of butter permeated the apartment as I threw a sweater on to open the door. Erik stood on the other side, holding a brown bag in his arms.

"We need to have a conversation, Button. I'm done letting you avoid it."

The way he uttered my nickname turned my stomach upside down. It had that feeling of being in trouble coupled with a smidge of animosity. He set the bag on the kitchen island and unloaded it before I had even closed the door. I was surprised he still had Gabby's address from when we visited her years ago.

"Please, come in," I said sarcastically.

So much for time alone.

"I got chicken Pad Thai, no spicy, extra sauce, no green onions. I also got beef fried rice with extra eggs and crab puffs."

He motioned to the kitchen table chair while I stared at him. I took my seat and crossed my arms. I hated how well he still knew me. This had been our Friday night order from the moment we could drive.

"Okay then...talk," I waited for him to start.

I took a bite of one of the puffs. The cheese warmed my mouth, and the crunching was loud in my ears. Erik took a deep breath. His thumb and middle finger tapped repeatedly. He was nervous.

"Why are you avoiding me?"

"I'm not."

"Oh, please, Blake. Whenever I look in your direction, you make it a point to look away. Every time I walk toward you, you walk away. Unless it is imperative, you don't even breathe in my direction. I'll ask again...why?"

"No reason. I'm just trying to do my job and stay focused."

"Blake Elena, I know you so much better than that. I'm insulted that you think I can't recognize when you lie. I will sit here all night, and I'm not leaving until you're honest with me."

"Erik Michael, I'm not trying to avoid you," my voice grew quieter as he forced me to admit that I had been trying to keep him further than arm's length.

"Button, come on!"

"Stop calling me that."

I kept my gaze focused on the food. My heart rate increased. My hands were trembling.

"Why?"

He moved closer. A taunting smile.

"Stop."

His face was inches from mine, but I adverted my eyes to the tile floor. "Why are you avoiding me? Like right now, why won't you even look at me?!"

"Because it's hard, okay?!" I broke.

My hands slammed on the table so hard that all the food jumped slightly, some rice spilling off to the side of the container. I shoved the chair back. It tittered on its back legs for a millisecond before toppling to the ground. Erik backed up slightly, but nothing about my outburst surprised him.

This is who I was while Erik and I were together. Explosive. Unpredictable. We often fed off each other with loud results.

"These last few weeks have been hard when it comes to dealing with you! It hurts. It breaks my heart. It's painful. It hurts to have all the memories playing in my head every single time that I hear your voice. It's hard, Erik!"

My voice cracked and quivered. Tears rolled down my cheeks. I was fed up with all the crying.

"You left me.... remember?!"

"And you let me go! Do you think that was an easy decision?! It was the hardest decision I ever had to make. I left California, my home, my parents, and your parents. I left my entire life behind. You weren't just my boyfriend; you were my best friend!"

"Button, I —"

"Color or no color," I interrupted him, fearing that I wouldn't be able to continue if I stopped now. "I loved you. I lost so much more than our relationship. I lost the person who knew me best, the person whom I had confided in for over twenty years. I lost part of myself, which is really shitty to say. You said some awful things the night we argued, which deeply hurt me. It pained me so much more than you'll ever know. But driving away, knowing that you didn't care enough about me, either as your friend or your girlfriend, to come to say goodbye broke me completely! Did you barge in here to hear that?! Did you come here to make me re-live one of the most painful moments of my life?!"

I paced in the living room for a few seconds, trying to calm down. At least this time there wasn't any makeup on me to smear. Sadness and regret engulfed his face as he stood up. He pulled me into his arms, and I felt like I couldn't breathe.

"I am so sorry, Button. I said a lot of things I didn't mean. I was so angry and hurt that you weren't choosing me, and I shouldn't have taken it out the way I did."

The scent of my childhood came off his shirt. I was transported back to that night three years ago.

Erik and I had been arguing for nearly a week about whether or not I would accept Connor's offer. Finally, Connor got fed up with waiting for me to decide since he needed to move forward and gave me a deadline to have an answer ready the following day. Erik wanted me to stay, claiming that California was the only place to build the life we had always talked about.

I worried that the career I had come to love would be stifled if I stayed. I wanted us to move, together, and create a new life in Virginia. It would be a fresh start for both of us.

I paced in our shared one-bedroom while he stared at me from the couch, anger steaming from him. My decision had been made earlier that day, and I told him I was leaving. Connor's offer was too good to pass up, but I wanted Erik to come with me.

Erik refused to bend and leave his role in California. We argued about the decision, and like most of our arguments, it got loud and ugly – fast. He claimed that I was abandoning him and forcing him to give up his career, which is what he would be asking me to do if I stayed. He screamed a string of expletives and called me selfish at the end of his rant.

Usually, I would stop the argument once he brought out the curse words, but this was the one time I couldn't calm myself down. I accused him of wanting to hold me back and not letting me grow because he was insecure about my career outpacing his. He was convinced I was giving up on us and claimed he deserved the promotion, not me. At that moment, I knew the argument had nothing to do with the future we had dreamed of but more about his bruised ego over my success.

The next day, I gave Connor my answer, and Erik didn't speak to me until I was in Virginia. Part of me thought he didn't believe I would walk away, and I almost didn't. But my resolve to be successful in something I loved prevailed. I packed up my stuff while he was at work one day and stayed with my mom. A few days later, I played Tetris with my life as I tried to fit it all into the trunk of my car and hugged both of our sets of parents and some friends goodbye.

He watched from the window of his parent's house. Twenty years of memories, friendship, and love had been reduced to a single argument.

"I was so angry," Erik admitted. "The week before the promotion was announced, I saw purple and couldn't figure out how to tell you because you hadn't seen colors yet. I never told you how much I loved you or how proud I was of you. I regret not getting in that car with you. For the last three years, I have wished that you were still with me. I am so sorry for what I said that night, Button."

"Erik, I'm—"

"Let me finish," he tightened his embrace. "I'm only here for like a couple more months, but if you let me, I will spend every minute that you give me showing you that I deserve another chance."

"Another chance?"

"I want to give things between us another shot. You know we had something special."

"Erik, I've missed you, but I don't think so. We've changed a lot. A lot has happened in three years."

"Then let me take you back to before I knew what your lips on mine felt like. Let's go back to when we raced on the track, sat on opposite ends on the couch watching terrible movies, and went for midnight ice cream runs."

"Can I think about it?"

Part of me wanted him back in my life, but the more reasonable part warned me that it was a bad idea. Sometimes, it truly was better to leave things in the past.

"If you think about it, you're going to say no. What does your gut say? If you were to flip a coin, with heads being yes and tails being no, which side would you hope it lands on?"

Heads.

But could I handle that? Could I spend time with Erik knowing how my hands used to tangle in his hair? Could I welcome him back into my life knowing that, at some point before this, he resented me for being successful? Could I ignore the past for ten weeks and remember what it was like to have him back as a friend?

"Okay," I almost whispered. "But just friends."

"Friends, Button. Just friends."

Chapter Thirteen

SATURDAY MORNING.
Seventy days left.

Parker waltzed into my bedroom like he owned the place at nine in the morning, exactly an hour before I was supposed to meet him at the farmer's market. I was brushing my teeth in my bathroom in only a sports bra and spandex shorts. My hair was still pulled into the braids I slept in. Gabby had let him in, and I had left my bedroom door open.

His eyes held excitement within them and grew wide when he saw me. I wasn't ashamed of my body, but when he took his bottom lip in his teeth as he looked at me, I was sure a blush covered my face. His hair was contained within a baseball cap, and he wore workout clothes, which was odd because we weren't going to the gym.

"Cute...braids," he grabbed the ends and messed with them before hopping onto my bed. "Cute room."

I looked around, suddenly feeling self-conscious. Saturdays were also my chore days, so a pile of dirty clothes sat by my door. My bed was unmade since I had to change the sheets, and I had a collection of water bottles on the nightstand.

"What are you doing here?"

"Would you hate me if I proposed a change in plans for the day?" he asked. "Before you answer, I already went to the market and picked up the tamales and the gumbo. I was scrolling on my phone last night and came across something I thought we would both enjoy."

"What is it?" I hopped on the bed next to him, bouncing him slightly.

"I want it to be a surprise, but it's about an hour away. All you need are comfortable clothes you're not afraid of getting wet and walking shoes. So, how much do you trust me, princess?"

"Apparently enough to go out to a wet and unknown location an hour away with you," I laughed. "Give me ten minutes, and I'll be ready."

He nodded and laid back on my bed, eyes fixed on his phone. I changed in the bathroom and pulled my hair into a high ponytail instead, the loose part wavy from the braids. His feet hung off the edge, and he dangled them with excitement. Whatever he had planned had him giddy. He looked adorable.

Parker disappeared to the restroom before we left, and I waited in the living room. Richard's face came up on my screen.

"Hey," I picked up. "What's up?"

"I was just calling to see if you wanted to grab some breakfast," he suggested. I applauded him for his spontaneity.

"Uhm...I can't," I tried to come up with an excuse. "I have plans with Gabby today, but I appreciate the offer."

"How about dinner?"

Parker came out of the bathroom and called my name, asking if I was ready. I held my finger on my lips for him to be quiet. I hoped Richard didn't recognize his voice in the background.

"How about dinner on Friday night?"

"That works for me. Flemings?"

"Isn't that place expensive?"

He ignored my question. His lack of answer indicated yes. "I'll pick you up at seven. Looking forward to it, Blake!"

"Me too. I'll talk to you later, Richard."

"Was that work Richard?" Parker asked, clutching his keys in his hand. "Is everything okay?"

"Yeah. He wanted to have breakfast, but I told him I had plans with Gabby."

"Everything okay with you guys?" Parker caught my hesitation.

"I'm still trying to figure it out. Sometimes, it seems like all he wants to do is go out to eat, which is fun, but I would like to do other stuff. Sometimes he's fun, and sometimes it's like I'm talking to a wall or listening to one of those self-help podcasts...I don't know. It feels weird talking to you about this, though..."

He was asking to be a friend, which was technically what we were. Yet that wasn't entirely true either. I didn't know where we sat. We were friends that kissed sometimes?

"You can talk to me about anything, princess. But I agree...maybe Richard is not the best subject to the start of a great day."

Parker pulled my shirt and me toward him and kissed me. I felt his shoulders relax, and a smile spread across his lips.

He led the way out the door. The speakers blasted his favorite country music as we drove out of the city. He sang along, and I caught a few songs I knew. We quickly realized that we were both terrible singers.

An hour later, he pulled into a run-down parking lot. In front of us, there was a trail heading into the mountain. Other cars were parked, but it was silent, almost like no one was around.

"Gabby has my location, and Nathaniel will murder you if anything happens to me," I joked.

He laughed as we hopped out of the car.

Parker led our conversation and was curious about Gabby, Nathaniel, and me. He asked me a million questions as to how we were all connected. We had been spending a lot of time together, so he had seen Nathaniel and Gabby and how they acted toward each other. He was confused about why they weren't technically together, and I couldn't blame him.

Gabby and I had met in college during a Pilates class. We bonded over our love for trash romance movies and quickly became friends. She was originally from Virginia and had kindly let me rent her spare room when I moved. I loved the sunshine she brought everywhere, and it always lifted my spirits to be around her. My transition to Virginia would have been exponentially more difficult without her. She was my best friend.

Nathaniel and I had met in California, working. He was a handful of years older than me, and Connor had poached him from a local roofing company after Nathaniel almost convinced him to buy a brand-new roof for a house that was only five years old. He and I traveled a lot together to win more business, which helped us get close. I considered him to be the brother I never had.

One day, I invited Nathaniel to the apartment while we worked on a project. We had been working in the conference room for six hours and desperately needed a change of scenery but needed to finish our presentation. When he met Gabby, I swear it was the closest I had ever come to seeing love at first sight.

After a few more hours of work, I fell asleep on the couch. Nathaniel and Gabby spent the rest of the night talking. From then on, there was no stopping them, except that Gabby was not ready to settle down. Nathaniel knew he had found the woman he wanted to marry, so he would wait as long as it took.

"So," I finished my story. "For the last two years, they've been sort of dating. They don't date other people but are not officially together."

"I mean, even I can tell he's head over heels for her."

"Oh yeah. He can see color because of her."

"Really? Can Gabby see color?"

"Yeah, but she was born that way. I sometimes hate that she knows what the trees look like or the color of the water, but I have to wait for my heart or brain to decide that I love some stupid boy. She believes that you see color by choosing to love someone. She thinks that what matters is committing to a person and, if you do that, then the colors will develop."

"What do you think?" he stared at the ground.

"I don't know. I almost chose to be with someone who gave me no color, so I think any scenario is possible. I've resigned to thinking it'll happen when the time is right. But also, the more time that goes on, the more I think that Gabby is right. I think there needs to be a conscious choice to love someone, to fight for them daily, and to put them above anything else. But I've never been in that position."

"Not even with Erik?"

"Nope. I chose my job. I would argue that I did choose him, even if temporarily, but Gabby thinks I settled. She thinks that subconsciously, I wasn't fully choosing him, but I don't know. He was my best friend in the world for twenty years, then we decided to give our relationship a shot and moved in together. We lived in the same six-hundred-square-foot apartment for two years but fought all the time."

"What did you fight about?"

"You name it, we fought over it. We both have tempers. Towards the end, it was mostly my career and hours that caused the issues. He wasn't happy with how much I worked or how often I traveled."

There was a short yet heavy silence. He slipped his hand into mine as we walked.

"It doesn't matter, honestly," I sighed. "It would be nice to see color. To see the beautiful sunrise or the contrast of the clouds. I'd like to see what my eyes look like one day. Erik always said that was his favorite part of me. But I don't know a different world. I just want to die believing that I had been happy regardless of color."

"Are you happy?" he asked.

"At this second, or overall?"

"Both."

"Yes."

"Promise?"

"Promise."

It was true. I was happy overall. I loved Virginia, and my career was on an upward trajectory. My boy situation was...interesting...but I was happy.

The contentment I felt at this moment was also unmatched. The gravel path crunched under my feet as beads of sweat ran down my forehead. The chirping birds added background music to our walk, and the sun snuck through the small spaces between the trees. This was peace.

"Okay, stop," Parker said. "Are you ready? I'm going to cover your eyes before we turn the corner."

He moved behind me and covered my eyes. "I don't know. I'll let you know if I'm ready when we get there."

He gingerly guided me the few yards to where the trees opened. I wasn't sure what I would be looking at, but the sunshine warmed my body. Laughter from people still somewhat in the distance reached my ears, and the humidity in the air increased. He moved his hands from my eyes, lingering and placing them on my waist.

The picturesque view in front of me was incredible. My breath hitched. Parker sighed triumphantly, looking at my face. I didn't know something like this existed so close to home.

The incredible waterfall in front of me basked in the glow of the sun and stirred the tranquil pond at the bottom. A dirt landing on one side had tens of people enjoying the view, taking in the sun, and rustling through bags while sitting on towels. It was reminiscent of the beach. The water was completely clear, revealing a rocky bottom.

Even in a colorless world, it was incredibly breathtaking. Parker pulled me to him, my back pressed against his chest, and wrapped his arms around me.

"I remember you telling me that you miss the water. This was the best I could find within a short drive."

"This is incredible..." I turned, threw my arms around his neck, and hugged him tightly. He wrapped his arm around my waist and planted a hard, longing kiss on my lips.

"Well, princess, would you like to join me for a swim?"

"I'd love to, counselor."

He intertwined his fingers with mine and led us to the dirt landing. He pulled out a waterproof blanket and set it down, piling our bags on top. He pulled off his shirt, and I couldn't tear my eyes away from him.

I had seen him in a cutoff shirt before and had already admired the artwork on his arm, but what I saw as he faced away from me was surprising. Across the top of his back was a collage of historical tattoos, almost like a retelling of American History. It was incredibly intricate and detailed.

The sleeve that adorned his left arm traveled up his shoulder and into his chest. I stared at him a little longer than I should have. My eyes traced along the coast of Texas. I admired the block-T logo of his university. It was his life displayed as a work of art on his skin.

"Hey, princess," his smooth voice got closer, reducing to a whisper as his body cast a shadow over me. "You're staring."

"Sorry," I muttered. I took off my shirt and decided to swim in my sports bra and shorts.

He deviously smirked at me, bringing his hand to cover my cheek, and his thumb caressed my bottom lip. His eyes locked into mine, full of desire. Full of life.

He stared.

"Hey, Parker," I whispered. "You're staring."

"I know."

After a few beats of slightly labored breathing, he grabbed my hand and pulled me away from the dirt, heading toward the rocks where people were jumping into the water.

"Wait! No, I can't jump off those rocks!"

"Why not?" he turned to me with an entertained smile.

"I'm scared of heights!"

"Come on, it's not that tall. It'll be fun. I promise you'll be okay."

"I don't think I can do this, Parker. I really don't think so."

"Come on, Blake. Face your fears. I'll even carry you up the rock if it makes you feel better."

"I'm not scared of walking up there. It's the coming down that terrifies me."

A mischievous smirk spread across his face, and I started backing away. Without much effort, he bent down and threw me over his shoulder.

"Parker!" I screamed, trying to kick against him. His arm was hooked around my back, and his other hand was wrapped around my ankles.

"Blake!" he mocked me, continuing the climb up the stair-stepped rocks.

He set me down at the top. I looked at the distance between us and the water and yelped. My heart rate sped up. My breathing became erratic. I clung to Parker's arm, trying to get us away from the edge.

"I can't do this! I can't do this!"

"Hey, open your eyes and look at me," he crouched down so we were eye to eye. "Remember how you were scared to see Erik, and you faced that fear? How you were afraid to continue this but did it anyway? It's about the new experiences, Blake. Face this fear with me."

"I don't know," my lip quivered. "I don't think I can do this."

"Don't think then," he pried me off his arm but offered me his hand. "You can do this. Jump in with me."

I looked up at him, and he gave me the reassuring smile that often finds me in the conference room. He squeezed my hand.

The ripples in the water below made my stomach flip. The distance doubled since I looked at it the first time. I looked up to him again. He was watching me make my decision. My hand felt his squeeze again.

I tried to channel the boldness I had felt the first weekend I met him –that same bravery.

"Ready?" he asked. "I'm going to count down from three, and we'll run and jump."

I nodded, lying. I would never be truly ready for this.

"Three."

The falling water encouraged me, egging me on.

"Two."

My heart pounded in my ears. My grasp on Parker's hand tightened.

"One."

I regretted every decision I made today that brought me here.

"Go!"

Parker gave me a slight pull before we ran and jumped.

For the few seconds I flew through the air, I felt invincible. The wind caught my ponytail and lifted it from my back, sending a tickle down my spine. The people below cheered us on. My body crashed into the water, the heat of the day disappearing and the cool water washing over me.

I swam to the surface to see Parker's wide smile waiting for me. The water pressed down his hair as he pulled me toward him. I wrapped my arms around his neck and my legs around his waist as we floated in the water.

"I did it! I'm never doing something like that again, but I did it!"

"You did! I'm so proud of you!"

He peppered kisses along my jawline, ending at my lips.

"How did you know I wouldn't chicken out and just stomp my way back down the rock?"

"I hoped," he laughed. I pulled him into a kiss, and he pressed me closer, his hand on the back of my neck.

Although it felt like my heart was about to stop and I would die by falling, I was glad he convinced me to jump. These were the kinds of experiences I had been missing out on by trapping myself in the conference room. A month ago, I never could have envisioned jumping off a rock and plunging into water below with anyone.

We swam around for a little bit, talking about fears.

Parker insisted that he wasn't afraid of much. His only fear was missing out on all the things life had to offer. I had gotten a glimpse of his work ethic over the last couple of weeks, and he was, on some level, even worse than me. Because of his relationship with Amelia, he felt personally bound and obligated to be perfect at his job. He was still fairly new to their team, so it resulted in long hours as he tried to learn everything about his new industry.

"Before I left, my sister sat me down and told me that she was worried I would miss out on life, so she made me promise to have some fun while I was gone," he laughed. "So here I am, having fun with you. I had some time to think about it on the plane and while I was getting settled in. As much as I hate to admit it, she's right. I don't want to be on my deathbed wondering why I didn't see more of the world or just shared more laughs with the people I cared about. What about you? What are you scared of besides heights?"

"Unlike you, I am scared of everything."

Apparently, my new habit was to spill everything in my brain to Parker. I had many fears. Some mundane, some not.

I was scared of heights, spiders, elevators, needles, tigers, and airplanes. For some reason, elephants terrified me, and I avoided motorcycles like the plague. But I shared his fear. Sometimes, I worried that I would look back on life with regret. I was scared to make all the wrong decisions and look back wondering why I hadn't been happier.

"Seems like this is a great start to both of us making sure that our fears don't come true," he said.

We laid on a pair of towels and dried off under the sun briefly before hiking back to the car. The hike back gave us ample time to dry off some more. I was mostly dry when we got to the car, but Parker came well-prepared with towels to set down on both front seats just in case.

In the last month, Parker and I had explored more of New Windsor than in the three years I had lived here.

We perused the multiple exhibits of the entire museum district and learned more about DaVinci's inventions than I ever cared to know. Parker impressed me with the random facts and figures he knew; his brain contained more information than I thought was possible.

There were more restaurants near us than I had realized. The city had a wider variety of gastronomic choices than expected. Most new restaurants had been a hit, except for the Italian place that gave us food poisoning. That night and subsequent morning had brought a lot of bonding over a trashcan and a bucket.

I had lived more in the last few weeks than in three years. I had Parker and Gabby to thank for that. After this was over and I came down from the high, I wasn't sure how I would feel. But I knew that I would never regret these twelve weeks. That much, I was sure of.

After we showered and changed, Parker made lunch. He slurped his noodles next to me. His now dry hair was fluffed up, looking like a cloud on his head. I stared at him and felt an unfamiliar fear. For the first time, I had to remind myself that this was all temporary.

He was leaving in ten weeks.

Chapter Fourteen

FRIDAY NIGHT.

Sixty-four days left.

The sizzling of the onions on the skillet and the delicious smell of the peppers made my stomach grumble. Gabby was cooking dinner for her and Nathaniel while he typed on his laptop, sneaking glances at her occasionally from the island.

I waited, fidgeting with the buckle of my purse.

"Are you coming to the game next Saturday?" Gabby asked.

"You know I don't miss your games."

"Excited to see Parker play? He's pretty good."

"Yeah," my stomach twisted. "Except someone invited everyone at the office to watch, so Richard and Erik will also be there."

I shot Nathaniel a glare, and he gave me a sheepish smile.

"Don't talk to me about them. I don't know why you're entertaining those two in your life. You obviously like Parker!"

"I concur," Nathaniel adjusted his glasses.

"It doesn't matter if I do or don't like him. He's only here temporarily."

"You've been so much happier over the last few weeks, Blake," Gabby said, waving her spatula at me.

"Look, I –" The knock on the door stopped me. "I have to go."

Gabby rolled her eyes at me and went back to stirring vegetables. I opened the door to see Richard wearing a mismatched jacket and pants. He smiled at me.

"You look wonderful, Blake."

"Thanks."

He took a peek over my shoulder and greeted Nathaniel, who just grunted and gave him a wave. "Can't say I didn't try," he shrugged.

I offered him a smile as he offered his arm, and we walked to Flemings. Nathaniel's animosity toward Richard, combined with Richard's feeble attempt to say hello, told me that he knew why they didn't like him. But they were all keeping it from me.

"I feel like I barely saw you this week," he said.

"I spent way too many hours in the conference room with Lainee the last few days," I laughed. "We were working on one of our other projects."

During the walk, Gabby's words replayed in my head like a broken record, pulling me away from Richard's conversation. I tried to silence them and focus on the man next to me. A man I liked. A man who would still be here in three months.

The aromatic rosemary scent perfumed the room as we stepped inside. My stomach started complaining again about the lack of food it had seen today. I had an omelet for breakfast this morning and a protein shake for lunch, but I wanted to be plenty hungry for Flemings. Apparently, their food was incredible.

Richard ordered a bottle of wine, knowledgeable of its details. Based on the amount of information he repeated about it, I knew he had spent some time researching it.

His chatting died down a little bit after we ordered the food. I asked him questions about the project he was working on with Connor to draw some conversation out of him. They were building a new financial tracking system for our internal use to guide our projects. He excitedly talked about it for a few minutes.

I knew Connor was testing him for the promotion, and he knew it too. Connor would see that he was good at his job and give him the position. Richard was hungry for success, and I admired his dedication to growing in his career.

Project Porcelain came up for a short bit, but not much more than that.

Tonight's conversation felt forced. It was almost unwanted on his end. Maybe he was mad that I rejected him last week and was not feeling the date today. He had agreed to go on this date, but he didn't seem to want to be on it. His eyes were distracted, roaming around.

We finished our delicious meal, and I tried to ignore my uneasiness. Silence enveloped us as he walked me home.

"Is everything okay?" I asked him as we walked up to the front door.

For the first time in the time that we had been together, I felt insecure. I prided myself in knowing where I stood with Richard, but today I was lost.

"Yeah, why?" he took my hand, his touch lingering on my palms.

"You just feel a little distant today. What's on your mind?"

"Oh, just a lot of work stuff. Connor wasn't too happy with a test run of the software, but nothing that can't be fixed. Nothing bad between us, I promise. I'm sorry I wasn't great company today."

"Maybe next time we can do something a little...different...a little more active?" I pitched, standing by my front door.

"Noted," he smiled, one of only a few today. "Goodnight, Blake."

"Goodnight, Richard."

He kissed me sweetly before he turned to walk away.

Hesitation stopped his steps away from me, and he turned around. He drove me into the wall and kissed me again as if he had missed something the first time. It had a passion to it as he tangled his hand in the back of my hair.

He didn't ask to come in as he often did, but his kiss eased my doubt.

Chapter Fifteen

SATURDAY MORNING.

Fifty-six days left.

Thump.

Thump.

Thump. Thump. Thump.

"Blake!" Gabby pounded on my door. "Wake up!"

She rattled the doorknob, but I must have locked the door last night, which was weird for me. I never locked the door.

My alarm hadn't gone off, and now I was going to make all of us late for the game. Through the door, I heard Parker and Nathaniel's mumbled complaints. I knew Nathaniel was giving us all a ride, but I hadn't expected him to arrive with Parker as well.

For the first time, we were hanging out with coworkers outside of work for more than a happy-hour drink. It was nice for Nathaniel to invite everyone to the game, but it just meant that I had to be careful around Parker.

I had stolen a few too many glances at him throughout the two days this week that they were in the office. But I ensured to keep our distance and stay almost comically far from him. He tried to be discreet, but his own lingering glances weren't helping. We were eyeing our way to our own destruction.

I was sure Amelia was starting to catch on that there was something going on. When I saw her slyly smirk at me while chatting with Parker, I worried. What if Connor caught on? I wasn't sure how significant the fallout would be if something went wrong.

"I'm up!" I yelled.

I scrambled to get my sheets off and got dressed. My leggings got stuck on my foot, and I almost made us late by needing a visit to the hospital.

Finally, I walked out of the room, and they ushered me out without breakfast.

"Good morning," Parker turned to me when we were in Nathaniel's car, planting a soft kiss on my forehead.

"Hi," I felt my cheeks get warm.

"Here," he handed me a protein bar. "Eat."

"All right, get all your goo-goo eyes making in now because, Parker, I need you a thousand percent focused on the game," Nathaniel instructed. "We are playing the most awful team in our entire league, and you are our secret weapon this year. We need to cream them."

Only a handful of teams had been around in the league for more than a couple of years. Most teams formed and quickly dissipated when people had better things to do. For the most part, everyone got along. Tournaments and games were usually fun, except when our team played the team led by Bradley. Bad blood ran deep between the two teams, and Nathaniel had declared them the enemy in his own dramatic fashion.

"Why are they the worst?" Parker asked.

Nathaniel tensed, and Gabby set a reassuring hand on his shoulder. She told the story, and I thought Nathaniel would crack his teeth at how hard he clenched.

About a year ago, during a particularly tight game, Bradley had started messing with Gabby while she was at first base. It had started as harmless joking and flirting on his end. Now, Gabby was adamant about being able to take care of herself and let him down. He didn't take it well, and his anger led to some very lewd comments towards her. Nathaniel walked up and knocked him out with a single punch.

The fight quickly escalated to almost a brawl, and the game was over. The other team refused to kick Bradley off their team, so they faced each other a few times per year. Since that day, our team has won every game. Nathaniel intended to keep it that way.

The car pulled into the parking lot, and they all shoved their phones and wallets into my purse. It was a team rule that they weren't allowed to have their phones on them. Parker and I walked toward the chain-link fence that surrounded the field, a few steps behind Gabby and Nathaniel.

"Good luck," I gave him a thumbs up, mindful of keeping a friendly distance between us.

"I'd ask for a good luck kiss, but I can see Lainee and Amanda staring at me."

It took all my control not to look back at them. We chatted in the office sometimes. Parker and Nathaniel had become friends. Our talking was nothing weird.

"You don't need luck. Gabby said you're really good."

"Well, you just being here is all the luck I need," he shrugged as if it was a fact.

He turned and walked onto the field. I made my way to the benches where everyone was sitting.

Stephen held an ice cream cone for his daughter that was starting to melt onto his hand. Lainee and Amanda were whispering to each other and laughing at something the other team was doing. It was incredible how fast they had become friends. Even Gordon was here, although I think he might have been cheering for the other team.

A few minutes before the game started, everyone else arrived. I sat between Amanda and Nick. Richard was behind me with Erik. Amelia rushed towards us, worried that she had missed the start.

Nick brought everyone a cooler with beer and water, even though it was barely eleven in the morning. It was getting hotter, but the shade made it more pleasant than it should have been. Everyone joked as we watched Gabby, Nathaniel, and Parker start batting.

Nathaniel was the first one up to bat. The umpire was clearly in the other team's pocket from the start. The strike zone was too wide. But Nathaniel made it to first base with one more strike before he was out. Everyone cheered.

Gabby struck out.

"It's okay, muffin!" Nathaniel called out to her from first base. Bradley snickered.

Parker was the next one up. With his stance, you would have thought they were playing a professional game, not a beer league, on Saturday morning.

Amelia filled everyone else in on Parker's history. He had played baseball in high school and college. His skill had been incredible until he tore a ligament in his shoulder and needed surgery. It effectively ended his career as a pitcher before it even started. I could imagine him in baseball pants. It was an image I was keen to get out of my head with Richard and Erik behind me.

Parker struck out.

"Dust off the cobwebs, Parker!" Amelia cheered.

Nathaniel ended up stranded on first base as Allison struck out. The strike-out pattern held for both teams until the fourth inning. Nathaniel hit a double, and Parker followed it up with a home run. In a blink, they were up two to nothing.

Halfway through the game, they took a water break. Parker came up to the fence that separated us from them.

"Hey, Ame!" Parker said. "Can you take some pictures with my phone? I want to send some to my family."

"Sure, where is it?"

"Blake's purse!"

He jogged away from us and toward the dugout, where Nathaniel called his name. Richard cleared his throat and shifted in his seat. Erik's fingers tapped together. I rummaged through my purse to pull out his phone.

"Here," I laughed nervously. "The three of them just shoved their stuff in there, so it's super crowded."

Richard relaxed his shoulders. Erik stopped tapping.

"His parents love to watch him play," Amelia explained. "So, I'm always the designated picture taker when they're not around."

"That's so sweet!" Lainee almost swooned. She shifted her gaze at him, eyes twinkling.

"Oh yeah. Parker is a big family guy, but he's also the baby of the family, so a little doted on. His parents are awesome, though; his sisters are also the sweetest."

A twinge of jealousy stabbed at me. I was jealous at how Lainee had momentarily thought about him. I didn't like it. I was jealous of the fact that Amelia knew his parents and that she was close to his sisters.

The realization that I would never get to meet them slapped me. The stories he had told me would always remain stories. Which was fine, I repeated to myself. This is just temporary.

The protein bar had not been enough, and my stomach was grumbling. Further down, toward the other team's dugout, was the concessions area. An older woman was manning it, and some players from both teams stood in line during the short break.

"I'm gonna get a snack," I announced. "Anyone want anything?"

"I'll take a Coke if they have one," Lainee said.

I took note of it and walked over. The line had shortened since, and I was almost at the window when I heard a familiar voice behind me.

"Hey, Blakey," Bradley walked up behind me. He was too close to me but the perfect distance to hit him.

"Bradley."

"Are you still mad at me?" he taunted.

"No. I just don't like you."

"Come on, was getting knocked out by Natty not enough?"

"You should've been kicked out of the league altogether. Now leave me alone."

The chain link gate behind us shut, and I heard steps. The people in front of me were taking their sweet time in deciding what to get.

"Come on, you don't have to like me to have some fun with me."

"You're disgusting. Don't you have a game to get back to losing?"

He took a step toward me, and I felt the warmth of his body inches from mine. In the time I contemplated which part of his body to injure first, he grabbed my wrist and turned me toward him.

"Don't touch me!" I shoved him away with all my strength and into a brooding Nathaniel. He must've seen Bradley come up to me. Gabby and Parker were running toward him. Everyone looked from the benches after I screamed.

"You should walk away, Bradley," Nathaniel warned, voice deep and commanding.

"This is none of your business, Natty," Bradley squared up to him. "This is between me and Blake."

"I won't tell you again. Walk. Away. Asshole."

"Bradley, just leave," I pleaded.

"You're either fucking one or the other, you can't have both. Unless..."

"What the hell did you just say?!" Nathaniel's anger snapped.

"No, no, no," I stepped between them. "Hey, it's okay. Gabby!"

She broke into a full sprint, and she was soon between Nathaniel and Bradley as well. Parker came right up behind her, followed by a couple of members of both teams. Everyone from the office watched.

Gabby pulled Nathaniel back, and Parker stepped between them with me. His arm set a firm barrier between me and Bradley as he turned to Nathaniel. "Dude, if you let him get to you and assault him, you could lose everything. I'd happily help defend you, but it's not worth it. Blake is fine." He turned to me, a flicker of concern. "You are fine, right?"

I nodded. Gabby had forced Nathaniel to walk away, but his eyes were still pinned on Bradley.

Parker then turned to Bradley. He held his hand up to him to keep him in place. "I suggest you walk away, too."

"Who the fuck are you?" Bradley frowned.

"Someone who is saving you from being knocked out cold again. So do me a favor, walk away, and never think about talking to Blake again."

"You don't get to tell me what to do," Bradley hit his hand down. In front of me, I saw Parker's back tense and his jaw clench. I moved between them as I heard the rubber band snapping behind me.

"Bradley, just go," I stared him down.

"I suggest listening to her," Parker said through clenched teeth.

Parker's gaze must have been intimidating enough for Bradley because he actually walked away. Gabby managed to calm Nathaniel down, and they went back toward the field. Parker stood with me.

"Thank you," I sighed.

"If we weren't in public, I would've let him get in at least one punch. Heck, I probably would have joined him. But you're okay, right?" his eyes were concerned, but he kept enough distance from me.

"I'm fine. I promise. All he did was grab my wrist."

"Will you go back to where everyone else is sitting? I don't want you alone until that guy leaves."

I nodded again. "I was just a little hungry."

"Can you wait until pizza? If not, there's another protein bar in Nathaniel's car."

"I can wait."

He nodded, and we walked away. I went back to be hounded by everyone about what happened. I told them all the backstory on Bradley, and soon enough, everyone understood Nathaniel's anger.

The game resumed, and Amelia ran to the restroom, entrusting me with taking the pictures, which forced me to focus on Parker. The anger had fueled the team, and they were hitting more home runs than I thought was possible. By the time the game had ended, it was twelve to two.

As was tradition, the team went out for pizza after the game. I watched Parker kid around with some of the other guys from the team. Erik chatted with Stephen and made his daughter laugh. I tried to focus on Richard's story about when baseball and avoided looking at Parker.

Parker's eyes did find me repeatedly. They seemed different somehow. I heard the rubber band snapping against his skin, even from under the table.

Chapter Sixteen

WEDNESDAY AFTERNOON.
Fifty-two days left.

The office was eerily quiet most of the morning as everyone focused on their tasks. Only hushed conversation and keyboards clicking could be heard on the floor.

Desha and Stephen whispered at his desk and worked on a color scheme they had been stumped on. I wished I could give my opinion, but I was just glad to see that they had not killed each other yet. They actually seemed to be enjoying their time together.

Nathaniel was on local customer visits all day, so he was out of the office. Jamie and Melanie were glued to the computer, working on a demographic analysis of Michigan. Parker, Amelia, Amanda, and Nick were huddled in their conference room, reviewing our latest submission for an article we planned to release. Lainee and I had been in my office reviewing the projects she was monitoring.

She was doing an incredible job ensuring that nothing was dropped. I made a note on my computer to talk to Connor about promoting her once this project was over.

Once we were done, it was time to pile into the conference room for Richard to review a spend analysis he had worked on. Amelia brought in muffins from Gabby's after lunch, which were her current obsession.

I sat down and instantly regretted not grabbing a muffin. I noticed Parker standing by them.

"Hey, Parker," I called to him. "Will you bring me a –"

"Blueberry?" he said, holding the muffin in the air.

I nodded, and he walked the pastry over to me. Richard watched Parker closely. Erik tracked him across the room with his eyes. Parker set the muffin in front of me with a smile, earning a glare from both of them. It was just a muffin, but my hands went clammy.

Without wasting another minute, Richard started reviewing the numbers on the screen. Nick and Amelia had a lot of good questions, which was expected. I had already reviewed and approved what Richard was explaining, so I took notes of what they asked to make sure that we left no stone unturned.

"So," Richard walked behind me, still facing the room. His hands grasped the back of my chair and pushed it down slightly. My body went stiff but couldn't resist the gravity shifting it with the chair. The back of my head pressed against Richard's stomach. His hands moved to my shoulders briefly before he set them back on the chair. "We think this will be the most effective way to allocate the funds."

When he finished his sentence, Richard squeezed my shoulders and slowly dragged his hands away.

I was acutely aware of the closeness of his body to mine. Erik's eyes narrowed on Richard. Richard stared him down, daring him to say anything. Richard's touch was meant to be a warning, not to me, but to Erik. He was asserting a claim over me. I didn't like it.

Parker cleared his throat and straightened, not breaking eye contact with Richard's hands. His fingers moved to his wrist as he snapped the rubber band. The intention to pummel Richard was in his eyes, but his restraint, thankfully, won. Amelia moved her eyes from the screen to him, but by the time she looked at me, Richard was already back at the front of the room.

Amelia asked some questions, diffusing the tension, and walked off with Richard to talk more. Parker huffed out of the room. Erik reluctantly joined Amelia and Richard since the question pertained to his territory.

I let go of my breath and picked at the muffin in front of me. Richard intended to make a point. He intentionally warned Erik but unintentionally impacted Parker. I didn't think our rules needed to cover him keeping his hands to himself. I figured that much was implied by the fact that we were at work. He had never so much as bumped me at work, so I hadn't thought it necessary.

I stormed off to my office and shut the door behind me. Richard was the only one in my life that I had any notion of permanence with, but now I was angry at him. Furious. He was playing with fire if this was how he was going to behave.

While I tried to calm down, Erik burst into my office.

"Are you dating someone?" he demanded to know. His arms crossed in front of him. Fingers tapping.

"What?"

"Do you have a boyfriend, Button?"

"No, I don't..."

"Good. Then go on a date with me."

"Huh?"

"You heard me, Button. Go on a date with me."

"Erik, we talked about this. Friends, remember?"

"I know, but I can't. What was that thing that you and Nathaniel used to do? Honesty moments? Well, here is one. After everything we've been through and feeling what I feel for you, I can never be just friends with you."

"No," I said. I couldn't go down this rabbit hole again. We had already read this story, and it had a devastating ending.

"Give me one night. One chance to prove to you that we belong together. One night where we pretend the arguments never happened, and you let me show you that I can make you happy. No one in this world knows you as well as I do."

"Erik, it's not a good idea."

It was possibly the worst idea I could think of.

"You said the same thing the night we started dating, remember? We were great together, Button, like we were always supposed to be."

"We weren't always great, Erik. We fought a lot."

"But we always moved past it. There is nothing to lose in you going on a date with me."

The memories in my heart tugged at my brain to say yes. I was actually considering it. We had already broken up. We had already lost our friendship. Technically, when it came to him and me, there was literally nothing else to lose.

"Okay," I sighed.

"You won't regret it. I promise."

"Don't make promises you don't know if you can keep," I reminded him. "Now, leave before I change my mind."

Erik scampered off so fast that I thought he would pull a muscle. As I walked home, he texted that we were having a night in for our date at the apartment he rented. Against my better judgment, I found myself looking forward to it.

At home, Nathaniel and Gabby were on the couch. Gabby was passed out on his lap, and he motioned for me to stay quiet as I walked in. I hadn't left the office too late, but it was definitely past dinner time.

"She's been having some long days," I whispered. "I've heard her leave at four in the morning sometimes."

"Yeah," he said, wiggling out of her grasp and gently laying her on a pillow. "She's hiring more help, especially for morning prep. Jeremy is great, but he's only one person. How's the campaign looking?"

He sat on the stools by the island. His eyes were tired but calm.

"Good. On time and on budget. Richard went over the fund distribution numbers with the team today. Amelia must've asked a million questions, but she seemed pleased."

"That's good. I haven't heard otherwise from her, and Parker says that Amelia is super impressed with you so far."

"You talk to Parker about me?" I panicked a little bit.

Second to Gabby, Nathaniel was the person who knew me the best. He had seen every side of me and understood me better than most. The idea of him talking to Parker about me made me nervous.

"Honesty moment? You are a recurrent topic of conversation when we go out for drinks. Amongst other things."

"What have you told him about me?"

"Nothing that you haven't told him yourself, kiddo. We talk, we don't gossip. Speaking of...how are you handling your love triangle? I guess it's more of a quadrangle of sorts. Maybe a square?"

I chuckled and let out an uncomfortable sigh. I walked him through what happened with the muffins earlier, then ran him through what Richard did. He shook his head.

"That's...awkward...even for Richie."

Last, I got to the part where Erik demanded I go on a date with him.

"Did you say yes?"

I went quiet for a minute while heating up my dinner. "After a little bit of back and forth, yeah."

"I didn't peg you for the kind of girl that likes to be bossed around, but I guess powerful women want someone who can tame them for the night."

"Disgusting!" I threw my dish towel at his head. "He just wants a night to prove that we deserve to give us another chance."

"Do you want to give him one?"

"I don't know what I want," I defeatedly sat beside him. "If you haven't noticed, I've been kind of flying by the seat of my pants the last few weeks. I have nothing to lose by going on one date, I think. At one point, I thought I wanted to marry him, so what's the harm of one night? He's leaving anyway."

My feelings were all over the place. It felt like my heart was on a never-ending rollercoaster of emotions.

Parker was a temporary surge of life. He had made me feel more alive in the last weeks than I had in a long time. My sense of adventure and exploration was awoken again, and my weekends had been filled with laughter. But it was temporary. Once he was gone, I would have to adjust to eliciting these feelings on my own.

Erik was comfortable and familiar. But aside from the heartwarming happy memories, he brought a history of pain. We had so much history that it was hard to ignore. Yet, I struggled to resist imagining a future where we could be together again like we always thought we would be.

Richard was here, and he was staying. He had a bright future ahead of him and was actively working towards a career he loved. His intelligence was impressive, and he was predictable. He kept me calm. It didn't matter that our dates needed to be injected with a bit of creativity. That is easily remedied.

"Honesty moment?" I asked Nathaniel for his thoughts. He was staring at me, unsure of what to say.

"You're getting a little...daring, kid. Be careful. I really don't want to see you get hurt again."

"I'll be okay. I can take care of myself."

"I can beat up one guy, but if three hurt you, it's a little much. And I like Parker. I don't want to have to punch him."

"No one is going to hurt me," I laughed. "But I appreciate it."

I genuinely believed that to be true. None of them would hurt me. But I also believed that if this shattered my heart, I had been the source of my pain.

"How are you guys doing?" I asked, looking at the sleeping Gabby on the couch, begging him to let me change the subject.

"I'm gonna ask her to move in with me," he said. I looked at the emotional mountain of a man next to me. "I love her so much, Blake. I don't want to wait any longer. I want her there when I come home, to our home. I want to marry her, and I need her to know that."

"She knows that. You know she loves you more than anything, right?"

"Yeah, I know...I'm going to take her to bed. I'll finish some work in bed, but I'm pretty tired. I'll walk with you to work in the morning. Night, kid."

"Night."

Nathaniel slipped his arms under Gabby, and she slightly stirred. Every time I saw how Nathaniel looked at Gabby, I felt a pang of jealousy and sadness.

That's what I wanted.

My heart longed for someone who accepted me despite my faults and issues but wanted to help me work through them. I wanted someone who understood me, who listened. Someone who would be willing to choose to love me.

Standing in the darkened kitchen, my greyscale world represented how I felt inside. Empty and alone. My strength and independence since I moved had been a source of pride for the last three years, but the walls I had built to make that happen were crumbling. I felt myself slipping into an emotional mess, and I knew Nathaniel was right. I was getting bold, but I finally felt something again.

Tears rolled down my cheeks as I looked around me. My entire life, I focused on accepting beauty in the world despite it being colorless. I convinced myself that I didn't need color to be happy.

I cherished the sound of the tree leaves rustling in the wind or the crunching of the dead ones in the fall. The smell of freshly baked muffins always made my mouth water. I believed ice cream always tasted better in the sweet air of Scooped at midnight. The taste of my weekly gumbo and tamales brought me a feeling of hominess, and I loved how the bitterness of coffee woke me up before I drowned it in creamer. The feel of my silk pillowcase against my hair or the warmth of the sun, when it snuck past my blinds to warm my face, was comforting. It was all beautiful.

None of that seemed to matter in this moment. For the first time in my life, I craved nothing more than to see the beauty of the colors that I knew surrounded me. Not for what they would have looked like but for what they represented.

Chapter Seventeen

FRIDAY NIGHT.
Fifty-days left.

My date with Erik snuck up on me, and before I knew it, I was walking up to his apartment door. The door was dark, with the peephole staring back at me as I stopped myself from knocking. A pang of guilt and regret, outweighed by curiosity, rushed through me.

He didn't specify how I should dress, but he lived in workout clothes, so I opted for comfort. Finally, I found some courage to knock, and the sound of the hollow wood rivaled my pounding heart.

"Hi, Button," he opened the door with a wide grin and moved to let me inside. His smile didn't fool me; his fingers tapped furiously at his side.

The apartment was tiny, barely bigger than a shoebox. The door directly opened to the living room and the glorified corner that could be called a kitchen. The furniture was generic, and there were no decorations.

Erik looked at me expectantly as I turned to see his creation. It was shockingly similar to how I found our living room after work one time after a big fight. Almost identical to what we had spent doing for weeks one summer. I turned to him, his face instantly morphing into a smile at seeing the light in my eyes.

Deja-vu.

I walked towards the couch and touched the blanket draped over the TV. The velvety feeling was oddly familiar and unsettling at the same time. The image in front of me had to be a mirage. I worried that it would dissipate as soon as I touched it. The fabric of the second blanket felt soft between my fingers as I ran my hand over the seam.

He had built a fort. Not only had he built one, but it also looked exactly like the one we had built in middle school. We had spent countless hours trying to make a fort that wouldn't fall immediately and perfected a foolproof design that lasted for hours. Those forts became a staple in the game room of my mom's house, often staying up for days. They became my haven. Where I went when things got hard. Erik was the only one who crawled in when I would burrow myself between the pillows.

After a particularly challenging and long trip in my first year of work, we argued when I came home. He was mad that I had been gone for over a week. It was the first time I didn't apologize for traveling because that trip cemented that I was doing what I loved. It had been five days of meeting with six different potential clients, which all ended in rejection. Yet, I came home increasingly determined to improve and master my job.

When I walked through the door, the apartment looked like a hurricane had battered it for weeks. Four days of beer cans littered the living room coffee table. Plastic and real plates covered the island, along with dirty pots and pans. Last week's laundry I had started for him before leaving sat on the bedroom floor. I wouldn't have been as mad had he not started the argument with, *"You were gone for a week. What did you expect to come home to? A palace?"*. I didn't expect a palace. I expected the apartment to look like adults were living in it.

I turned around immediately and walked out the door. I slept at my mom's house that night. The next day, when I came back to talk to him, the apartment was sparkling clean. The smell of lemon and disinfectant greeted me at the door. An immaculate fort sat in the living room as a peace offering. We spent all weekend in it.

"This is adorable," I said. His tapping slowed.

"I figured you'd like it," he walked over to the other side and held the makeshift door open for me.

I got on my hands and knees and scooted in. A little pile of snacks was in the middle, accompanied by two bottles of chocolate milk. He scooted in next to me. As we got older and taller, the fort grew with us.

"What movie are we watching?" I asked, reaching for the sour gummies.

Erik remained quiet and pressed play. The screen lit up, and Legally Blondestarted playing on the TV – my all-time favorite movie.

"You remember?" I turned to him.

He got closer to me and pressed his lips to my forehead before wrapping his arm around my shoulder and pulling me into him when the soundtrack started. Dark, thoughtful eyes stared into mine. Clean linen smell.

"I could never forget anything about you."

I looked away and relaxed in his arms, remembering what it felt like to be his. I would be lying if I didn't say that I missed this.

The comfort between us was still alive, but my feelings were conflicted. My heart was trying to determine where Erik sat. Nestled in his warm embrace, part of me wanted to give him another chance. I could forgive him for the things he said like I had many times before. We could learn not to be as explosive and escalate with each other. For a second, I believed we could make it work again.

He let out a long breath and leaned his cheek on my head. Years of forts, hugs, and kisses – both secret and not – flooded my memories. We had so much history. He had been my first everything. My first kiss, my prom date, my best friend.

He held me tightly like he was afraid I would vanish into thin air. It was like he could sense my hesitation about being here. The wrong scenarios played in my head, but I allowed my thoughts to be overshadowed by the feeling of being in his arms. His finger swirled around on my exposed thigh as Elle gave her graduation speech.

We crawled out of the fort once the movie ended, and I shook my thoughts off. Erik walked over to the freezer and pulled out my favorite comfort meal – nuggets and fries. He popped them into the oven as I stared at him.

"I figured reminding you of a time we were happy would be a good way to start," he explained. He mixed some ketchup and mayo to make my go-to condiment.

"It's definitely sweet."

He gave me his million-dollar smile that melted my heart. Once the food was done, we climbed back into the fort and watched another movie.He really was trying to take me back in time. I appreciated the weird sense of nostalgia that came with the evening.

After dinner, I decided it would be better to head home. Old, strong feelings were bubbling up, and I was liable to make bad decisions. Erik followed me to the door.

"Thank you," I hugged him. "I had fun traveling back in time."

"I'm glad," he kissed my head. "I want to show you that I want this again. I wanted to remind you of how good it used to be, Blake."

"I never forgot, Erik."

"Good. Will I get another date?"

"There's a lot I have to think about. There was a lot of bad between us too."

"It won't be perfect, I know. But we can work on it. We can be happy again."

"I'll think about it, but I'm not—"

He ran his fingers down the back of my hair, sending shivers down my spine, and pulled the bottom of it. It forced my face to tilt up toward him. He pressed his lips against mine without another word and pressed me up against the wall. Everything happened in a split second.

The kiss was familiar. Comfortable. Hungry. Begging for me to kiss back, so I did.

I felt the corrugated wall on the backs of my legs. One of his hands fell to the side of my thigh, fidgeting with the edge of my shorts. His other hand clutched at the stomach of my shirt. My breath hitched, and I broke our kiss.

"Sorry," he whispered, cupping my face before letting me go. "I wouldn't have forgiven myself if I let you walk out that door without kissing you one more time."

"Goodnight, Erik."

"Goodnight, Button."

I closed his door behind me and let myself breathe again. My fingers touched where his lips met mine just seconds before. My heart broke, remembering the kisses that helped shape me.

Throughout high school and college, I always knew Erik and I had something but always ignored it. It was terrifying to come to terms with my feelings for him. Feelings I wasn't supposed to be having for my best friend. Until he kissed me in his college living room, I had convinced myself they were one-sided. Then, we gave it a shot and lit up our relationship like a firework, only to have it explode at the end.

A year after we broke up, I still found myself feeling the other side of my empty bed for him, wishing he was next to me. Some Saturday mornings, I wished things were different. I wanted to find him making pancakes in the kitchen, shirtless with flannel pants hung low, and his hair wet from a shower after his run. It took me a long time to be okay with the choices I made.

As I walked into the apartment, I resigned myself to having my thoughts plagued by him tonight. Gabby was watching a movie on the couch by herself. I would have expected her to be at Nathaniel's by now.

"You're home?" I asked. "Everything okay?"

"Yeah," she said. "One of the guys from the team is having a guy's night, and he invited Nathaniel along. There's no point in being in his apartment by myself. He doesn't have any of the good snacks. Stupid, healthy eater."

"Seems reasonable."

"You had your date with Erik tonight, right?"

"Yeah."

"How did it go?"

I looked at her with uncertainty, not even having an answer for myself. She saw the hesitation in my eyes and headed to the kitchen. She grabbed a bottle of wine and set some fully filled plastic cups and the bottle on the coffee table. She patted the cushion across from her. I obliged.

The tears started flowing as soon as I sat in front of her. I buried my face in the couch pillow and sobbed. All the pent-up feelings spilling out of me.

"Wait, Blake, what happened?" She hugged me and let me cry before pushing me for more answers.

"I don't know!" I sobbed. "I don't know, Gabs. Nothing bad happened. Quite the opposite, actually."

"Explain, please."

"Gabby, it was really fun. Like really fun. He built a fort...and we watched my favorite movies...and ate chicken nuggets with my ketchup and mayo combo. He kissed me before I left. I don't know. It felt like we had been transported back to a really happy time, almost blissful."

She hugged me tighter. She smelled like freshly baked muffins. I think it was just part of her DNA at this point.

"I was comfortable with him. He cuddled me during the movies, and I didn't even shrivel at his touch. I welcomed it, and that scares me. I don't know, Gabby. Help me. My mind is all messed up."

She ran her fingers down my hair for a few minutes. She wasn't good at silence, but she was good at knowing what I needed to calm down.

"I don't even know what to think. I want to be with him but don't want to be with him. What do you think? What should I do?"

"Blake, I don't think you want my thoughts on Erik."

She was right and wrong. I needed someone to tell me what I knew my heart was trying to make me forget. I needed the truth, and that was what Gabby would give me.

"I need the truth," I sighed. "You'll tell me the truth. You always did."

She eyed me skeptically.

"Please."

Apparently, I wasn't above begging.

"I don't have warm feelings toward Erik, you know that. He was a great guy while we were in college and at the beginning of your relationship, but being with him broke you. The end of your relationship destroyed you. I remember the day you got here and the subsequent months. You wouldn't go anywhere. That heartbreak changed you. It's not a bad thing, just a fact."

"What do you mean?"

"You were always a workaholic, but you used to be excited about everything about life and saw the best in all of it. You loved to explore and enjoy life outside of work, no matter how overwhelmed you were with work. But when you got here, you stopped doing anything but working. You're still you...you know? Sweet, caring, and so kind. But that...spark...died. At least until recently."

I couldn't argue with her that I had changed a lot over the last few weeks. I felt like my old self. My mood was improving, and the balance in my life was too. I felt...truly happy...for the first time in a while.

"So, what should I do? What if I'm back to my old self...because he's back...there were so many things wrong with me back then, Gabs. I was erratic and unpredictable." My heart rate shot up. "What if he not only brings out the good part of me but also brings that side of me back?" My hands went clammy and started shaking. "The angry side. The disappointment. The yelling...oh gosh...the yelling. I mean, I don't –" The air wasn't reaching my lungs.

"Blake. Stop, you're spiraling," Gabby shook me a little bit. "I'm not letting you have a panic attack over this. Breathe."

"Gabby, I don't know what to do."

"That's okay. You don't have to decide today. Sleep on this."

I nodded. I ran out of words for the night. I gave Gabby a tight hug before I retreated to bed.

For years, my heart belonged to Erik, and his had been mine. Then I left and broke both of them in the process. Part of me would always belong to him; I knew it. I had given him a part of me with our relationship, many parts of me that I couldn't take back. Back then, choosing him seemed like a no-brainer.

Today, as I felt the cold silk of my pillowcase press against my neck, my feelings debated whether I could still choose him. Could I go back to the life I used to know?

Like a well-crafted predictive software, my mind computed a million scenarios where Erik and I somehow ended up together without one of us sacrificing a part of ourselves. Something went wrong in every single one. A happy ending with us together was unlikely.

There was no universe in which I could give him what he wanted. He wanted the picket fence. The stay-at-home PTA mom. The picture-perfect family. I commended women who wanted that; it was a hard job. But it just wasn't the job for me. We might have shared those dreams before, but it's not what I wanted anymore.

Yet, for the seconds that his lips were against mine, I believed it could have been possible.

Chapter Eighteen

SUNDAY MORNING.

Forty-eight days left.

The falling weights downstairs startled me, breaking me out of my staring contest with the track. There weren't many people at the gym, so everything echoed louder. Parker and I had agreed to run today, but I wasn't feeling it. My hamstrings were uncomfortable as I stretched them on the track. I was hoping having him with me would push me to finish the three miles for the first time this week.

I wanted to see Parker's reassuring grin, but my heart and brain were still reeling from Friday's rollercoaster. Nathaniel's warning was ringing louder in my ears. Richard's hands on my shoulders felt heavy. Erik's kiss was still lingering on my lips. Parker was walking up the stairs toward me.

"Hey, princess," he kissed the top of my head.

He sat down and joined me in stretching. I couldn't bring myself to say anything to him, fearing I would burst into tears. He didn't question my silence since my chatting before running was usually muted. We ran our usual three miles, and I was right. Having the stupidly attractive man running beside me was definitely encouraging. We sat back down on the edge of the track to stretch.

"How was your...thing...with Erik?" he prodded.

"It was fun. He built us a fort like when we were kids, and we watched my favorite movie."

"Legally Blonde," he nodded along.

"Yep," I was shocked he knew that. "He had all my favorite snacks and made chicken nuggets for dinner. It was sweet and nostalgic. It reminded me a lot of when we were kids."

"That's adorable," his tone was more annoyed than complimentary. "Did he convince you?"

"What do you mean?"

"Don't deflect, princess."

"Do I detect a twinge of jealousy in your tone, counselor?" I teased, trying to lighten his mood.

"I'm jealous of every man within five feet of you, Blake. Now, answer my question. Did. He. Convince. You?"

He had stopped stretching and turned to stare at me. I wasn't prepared to get attitude from him this morning. No strings. No commitments. That was our deal. Our relationship was time-limited, so I kept reminding myself that his jealousy was an illusion. Temporary.

"I'm not sure. He kissed me at the end, and it felt...familiar."

"He kissed you?!" he looked down at me. He paced, snapping the rubber band on his wrist.

"BUT!" I continued before he could say anything else. "It was like kissing a memory. A lot of old feelings were jumbled, but I think that's all they are. Just old feelings, but I don't know."

I extended my hand, and he helped me up. His pull was so rough that it lifted me entirely off the ground. I yelped slightly, and he grounded me with his hands on my hips.

I had told him about Richard kissing me before. We probably talked about Richard and Erik more than either of us wanted to. Never had he had this reaction. I looked at him, puzzled.

"I don't like that," he growled. "I don't like you thinking of old feelings. I don't like you having his lips on yours."

His hands stayed firm on my hips, and he was so close that I could smell the mix of his shampoo and sweat. Troubling thoughts were hidden behind his eyes. I tried to read them, but his own thoughts seemed to be confused.

His lips hovered right above mine for a few seconds before he came down to meet them. My sweaty hair was not a deterrent for him to slip his hand underneath my ponytail. I threw my arms around his neck. He pulled my hair slightly as I parted my mouth, allowing him to deepen our kiss. It was full of envy. Jealousy. He was trying to erase Erik's kiss from my lips.

"I think I like it when you're jealous," I took a breath from him.

I tried to step back, but he didn't let me go. His grip on me was possessive. Unyielding.

His smile returned as I stared at him. His face was only inches from mine. I had begun to memorize how his eyelashes curled at the end, how his left cheek got laugh lines with his smile, and how the small scar on the bridge of his nose creased when he read something complicated.

"Do you want to get some ice cream?" he asked.

"We just worked out," I laughed.

"Why do you think we work out?!" He grabbed my hand and pulled me in the direction of Scooped. "And after I walk you home, I'm going to spend all night thinking of what we're going to do on Saturday."

"It's not even Monday!"

"That just gives me more time to get creative! You're all mine on Saturday, princess."

Chapter Nineteen

THURSDAY NIGHT.

Forty-four days left.

The clicking of my keyboard and the music barely managed the monumental task of keeping me awake. It was really late, and my light was likely the only one on in the building. My eyelids were heavy, asking me to sleep. I debated taking a nap on the couch in the break area.

Today had been hard enough. I struggled to keep up with my workload and tried to step in to help Lainee, who was also struggling. Connor had spent two hours grilling me about discarded ideas on a different project and about how I thought Amelia's team liked our work. During lunch, I had to field a call from a concerned customer that a specific ad wasn't working yet. We released it two days ago. It wouldn't produce results in forty-eight hours, but I had to listen to them complain anyway.

In the whirlwind of the campaign and my emotional turmoil, I realized that the timeline draft for one of our smaller clients was due tomorrow. As of this morning, it had not been touched in weeks.

Most of the information was compiled and patiently sitting in a folder on our drive, but we had not gotten around to putting together the timeline or a minor draft of the ad we promised. The last nine hours of my day had been consumed by reviewing the materials and putting the documents together. I didn't want to alarm anyone, so I took care of it myself. The last thing I needed was for anyone to be worried.

Finding this slip-up was concerning, at best. Lainee had been tasked with reviewing all the upcoming deadlines within the next five weeks to ensure we had not missed anything else. Thankfully, this was the only item that fell through the cracks.

Parker, Nathaniel, and Gabby had been trying to call me since I was supposed to watch their practice and get some fresh air. I canceled at the last minute. With a quick text, I appeased them enough to get off my back and stop their worry that I had died.

"Blake?"

The faint creak of my door startled me. Erik peeked his head in.

"Hey," I rubbed my eyes.

"What are you still doing here?" he asked.

He was in running clothes. His hair was sweaty and messy, not slicked back, and perfectly styled. He looked like the Erik I grew up with. I figured he went for a run to tire himself out. He did that when he couldn't sleep.

"I'm just trying to finish something I let slip."

I put my chin in my hands and faced the computer, trying to make sense of the sentences I had written. The words were starting to slur together in my eyes. My brain had stopped cooperating with word processing.

"What is it?"

"A timeline for a different contract for a small customer in North Carolina. I've been working on it all day, so it's mostly done. I just need to finish the presentation."

"Button, it's almost midnight. Come on, why don't you let me walk you home?"

"Is it really?"

"Yeah," he whispered, walking around my desk.

He turned my chair to face him and crouched in front of me. His hands landed on my knees, and he cleared his throat. I watched his hands, fingers caressing my outer thighs.

"Hey, look at me, Button."

I shook my head. His disappointment at my lack of work-life balance was a familiar feeling for me. When we were together, I didn't tend to stay in the office until late since we commuted together, but my desk at home had seen many late nights. He would often come to get me from my desk around midnight and would dejectedly sigh to our bed. My insistence that he went to bed without me often made him angry.

"Button...please?"

I looked at him. His dark eyes were washed in concern. He looked at me with a sad expression. Not disappointment, worry.

"When was the last time you ate?" he raised his hand to my cheek.

"Not sure," I whispered, knowing how disappointed he would be. "What time did we finish our update meeting with Connor?"

"Around ten. Have you not eaten since then? All you had was like a banana."

"It was an apple."

"Blake."

"I'm sorry. I'm sorry. I uncovered that we missed this, and I've been hyper-focused. I'm sorry."

"Hey, hey, Button, it's okay. You're going to run yourself ragged. Let me take you to get some food, and then I'll walk you home."

"No, I can't. I need to finish this before the morning. I'm almost done."

"Blake, you're falling asleep sitting here, and you look like you'll pass out any minute. Let me help you. I'm going to run downstairs and get you some food. Then I'll help you finish this. It'll go quicker with both of our brains."

My stomach chose a terrible time to growl, and Erik chuckled slightly before he walked away. I was too tired and hungry to put up much of a fight.

As I waited for him, it dawned on me that this was a different Erik. In the two years that we worked and lived together, he had never offered to help me. Our discussions often resulted in arguments and with me apologizing after his berating.

Maybe he had changed.

Erik came back about fifteen minutes later. He had picked up a burger and fries from the nearby fast-food place. The smell of food sent my stomach into a frenzy. He took my computer to the conference room and plugged it in before setting the food in front of me. I felt reinvigorated with every bite.

My phone dinged, but it was on the other side of Erik. He reached for it and took a peek before handing it to me. There was a text from Parker on the screen. Erik gave me a strange look, but I just locked my screen and set my phone aside. Parker could wait.

I was still exhausted, but the food made a big difference in my energy levels. I could read the words on the screen again and focus on doing what I had to without my eyes closing on me.

Erik let me quickly walk him through everything I was looking at and what needed to be done. He provided valuable feedback on the mockup that Stephen had done. I wrote everything down. He helped establish an excellent timeline and raised some questions and discrepancies I hadn't considered before. By the time one in the morning rolled around, I felt confident that the draft was complete enough to send to the client in the morning.

Our big clients were important, but we couldn't disappoint the small ones that had given us the opportunities that led us here.

"I can't thank you enough," I turned to Erik as we left the building.

"It's nothing. Let me walk you home."

"It's okay. You've done more than enough, and my apartment is out of your way."

"It wasn't a request, Button. It's one in the morning. I'm not letting you walk home by yourself."

I didn't argue further or tell him I had done this walk at odd hours in the morning many times. He walked me to my front door.

The small talk during the walk gave me time to think about the many memories of us walking around our hometown before we were old enough to drive. To the dollar store for snacks. To the gas station for ice cream. They were the only place in town that always had good ice cream bars. It also brought back memories of driving home together after a hard day at work. This was familiar. Natural.

"Thank you, Erik. Let me know when you get home, okay?"

I hugged him. I tried to pull away, but he wasn't letting me go.

"I have to go to sleep. We need to be at work in like six hours."

"I know," he whispered. "I just... needed this."

"Goodnight, Erik. I'll see you tomorrow."

He kissed my cheek. "Goodnight, Button."

I closed the door behind me and stood staring at the dark apartment. I checked Parker's text from earlier.

Parker: You missed a really fun practice. Nathaniel took a hell of a tumble and rolled across the dirt. He's mostly okay but will have a gnarly bruise on his arm tomorrow.

Me: Wish I could've seen it. Had to finish some work. Just got home.

I didn't expect him to still be awake when I answered, but my phone buzzed as I brushed my teeth.

Parker: Just now? You should've called me to walk you home. It's really late.

Me: I managed. Thank you, though.

Parker: It's not safe for you to be walking by yourself this late, princess. Call me next time.

Based on his reaction to a date with Erik that he knew was coming, I didn't want to tell him I hadn't been alone.

Parker: Actually, there is no next time. Don't stay that late again, please.

Me: Okay.

Me: You're a great guy, you know? I don't think I've told you that enough.

Parker: Just wait until Saturday. I'm going to go from great to incredible.

Me: I'm excited about it. I just hope you can live up to the expectations you're setting.

I put my phone down and thought about tonight. Lainee would be able to send the draft to our client in the morning. As tired as I was, I couldn't shake the feeling of how great it was to collaborate with Erik again. To be a team.

My phone buzzed again, and I couldn't resist checking it.

Parker: Trust me, you're going to love me after. Night, princess. We've got work in the morning. Well...technically, later today.

Me: We'll see about that. Night, Parker.

I read his message a handful of times before falling asleep. An uneasy happiness sunk into my heart.

Chapter Twenty

SATURDAY MORNING.
Forty-two days left.

My Saturday plans were still a mystery when I opened my eyes in the morning. Gabby worked at the café one Saturday per month, and today was it, so she was also up early. I heard the blender crushing her fruit and ice together for her morning smoothie.

I walked out to the kitchen, greeted her, and scared her.

"What are you doing up so early?" she asked when she caught her breath. "It's the weekend."

"Parker has a surprise for us today, and he said to be ready by seven."

She smirked and hugged me on the way out the door.

Parker called last night and instructed me to pack a bag to be gone the entire day. I had no idea what we were doing or where we were going, and he refused to give me any hints. He told me to wear something similar to what I wore when we went to the waterfall but also to pack a jacket, a swimsuit, workout clothes, and a nice outfit. I knew he told me to pack all of that to throw me off the trail, so I had no way of knowing what items I would actually need.

I threw on my workout clothes and packed the rest. Right on time, he called to tell me he was downstairs. He was never late.

I hopped in the car, and he was giddy. Smile a mile long. Eyes lighter than usual. Two coffees sitting in the cup holders.

"A vanilla latte for my predictability princess."

"You know," I laughed. "That sounds like a compliment, but we both know it's not really one. It's like heart thing that southern people say."

"Bless your heart?"

"Yeah, that!"

"Oh, princess. Bless your heart."

He winked and reached for a kiss. He set his hand over mine and pulled away from the building. I was left feeling flustered.

"So, where are we going? And why did you have me pack so much stuff and wake up so early?"

"I'm not telling you. Just brace for a three-hour ride, which is why we're leaving so early."

"Three hours?!"

"It's not too bad. We've got one stop on the way there, which I hope will blow your mind. Although it's more for me than for you, just a heads up."

I briefly protested, but the wheels were already humming on the smooth highway. Plus, it's not like I would get out of the car and not go.

He curated the perfect playlist with some of our favorite artists for the ride. We sang off-key and off-beat to the music, and the first hour and a half passed in a blink.

Halfway there, Parker pulled over at a gas station where the convenience store looked plucked out of the middle of the woods. It looked like a Lincoln logs cabin. I had no idea how Parker found this place, but as soon as we walked in, I was glad he had.

The convenience store walls were lined with bags upon bags of beef jerky. There had to be thousands of pounds of jerky hanging from the small metal hooks along the walls. The only other things sold were beer and water in a small fridge by the restroom. This was carnivore heaven.

"I know that you think beef jerky is ridiculously overpriced and don't love it as much as I do," Parker fiddled with his hands. It was a rare sight to see him nervous or worried. "But I thought this would be a super cool stop!"

I looked at his brief, bright smile next to me. Full lips encased a perfect set of teeth. Perfectly trimmed beard. Eyes sparking with joy. He was, almost literally, a kid in a candy store.

He was right about the beef jerky. I would be willing to die on the hill that beef jerky was too expensive per package for a frustratingly small amount of meat. However, I would have paid an infinite amount of money and received nothing in return to see Parker smile like this.

"Are you kidding? This is awesome! I didn't know you could have this many flavors of beef jerky!"

He looked at me like I hung the moon and let go of his worry. His hand found mine, and he pulled me through every aisle in the store. He stopped to read almost all the bags and combinations of flavors. The packets were organized alphabetically. They sold normal flavors like barbecue, garlic, and just regular. But they also had some more adventurous ones. I saw amaretto, caramel, and pickle.

When we got to the cash register, his arms were loaded with as many flavors as he could carry. I grabbed a basil one. My threshold of desire to try adventurous flavors of beef jerky was low. He chatted with the cashier for a few minutes while he rang up all the bags.

When we got back to the car, I acknowledged my hunger and tried to open my beef jerky. Parker ripped it out of my hands, insisting it would taste better once we got to where we were going. He also promised that we would be able to eat in an hour and a half.

We kept driving, and I fell asleep. Frankly, I was surprised I hadn't fallen asleep before. I woke up to Parker running his fingers through my hair. The car had stopped moving, and he was crouched on the floor of the passenger side, waking me up. My seat was reclined mostly back, so I could only see him, the door, and the gravel at his feet.

"Don't sit up," his voice was low and husky. "You fell asleep at the perfect moment. I set everything up already. But I need you to cover your eyes."

He handed me a shirt. Parker definitely had a flair for the dramatic. Every time he wanted to surprise me, he made sure to cover my eyes. The first look always had to be perfect.

"Promise you won't look until I tell you?" he asked before helping me out of the car.

I nodded.

"No, princess. Promise."

"Ugh...I promise."

He reached over me and undid my seatbelt while I clipped together the edges of his shirt behind my head to make a makeshift blindfold. I pressed my lips to his cheek as he leaned forward. He grabbed my arms and carefully helped me get out of the car. My head bumped into his hand on the edge of the doorframe, ensuring it didn't hurt.

I didn't need to see where we were. As soon as I stepped out of the car, I knew exactly where he brought me.

The light breeze carried a bite of salt in the warm and humid air, pushing my hair around. There were no other voices. The birds flying around talked to each other. It was a sound I had not heard in almost three years.

"You did not!" I hopped up and down, keeping my eyes closed.

"I did," he whispered behind me, caressing my exposed arms. He unclipped the shirt and slowly removed it from my eyes.

The expansive coastline before me had foam-capped waves crashing onto the packed sand. They crashed rhythmically with the sounds of the birds. The sun shone off the water, giving the ocean a slight sparkle at the top. There were raised houses behind us, but no one was out on the sand other than an older couple walking their dog about a quarter of a mile down.

Parker had set everything up some yards in front of the car. There was a small tent set up over his waterproof blanket. Two beach chairs sat in the shade with a towel draped over each one. A cooler sat between the chairs, and a bag of beach toys was off to the side.

It had been almost three years since I had seen the beach, almost three years since I had felt sand beneath me. Growing up by the beach had been a large part of my life. My parents loved it, and it was only a short drive away, so we spent a lot of time there on the weekends. It was a six-hour round trip from New Windsor, and Gabby wasn't a big fan of sand. So, driving to the beach alone was usually not a thought for me.

I threw my arms around his neck, pulling him down. I kissed him with surprising force. He picked me up and leaned me against the car door, not tearing his body from mine. My fingers ran through his soft hair and pulled him more into me.

"You are incredible," I took a breath and ran my thumb along his laugh lines.

"Well, you deserve it," he peppered my neck with soft kisses. "You've been working really hard and doing an incredible job with our project. I am so proud of you, you know."

"Thank you, but let's not talk about work, okay?"

He nodded and put me down, but not before stealing another kiss. As he watched, I took off my shoes and shirt, setting them down in the car. It was easier not to get sand in my shoes this way. His eyes roamed my body, and heat rushed through it as he took off his shirt.

I had on a sports bra and shorts, but I also had a second set of clothes in my bag. These could get wet.

"I'll race you to the water!" I gave him a small push away from me and started running.

He stumbled back and watched me take off before reacting. "Wait, what?!"

My feet buckled slightly under the almost powdery sand. It wasn't too hot yet since the sun hadn't had time to make it burn. My toes reveled in the familiar feeling, but three years away had helped me lose my ability to run in it. The sand grew more stable and colder as I got closer to the water.

Parker quickly caught up to me with his long strides, even though I had a head start. As he passed me, he scooped me up, and we crashed into the cool water together. I held my breath as we went underwater. We giggled like children when we came back up for air. We swam around for half an hour before my stomach really started calling for food.

"I'm hungry and was promised food," I splashed him.

"I came prepared," he winked.

Parker unloaded the cooler to reveal a mountain of delicious food. Boiled eggs; rolled up turkey breast and roast beef; squares of Munster cheese and slices of Havarti; juicy watermelon and sweet cantaloupe. It was a whole spread along the blanket.

The beach started to fill up more as the sun heated the atmosphere and, to a lesser degree, the water. Kids were running around laughing, and parents watched them amongst the pages of their books. Watching all the families reminded me of the summers that my family and Erik's family would spend at the beach. I tried to push the image out of my head and focus on reality.

Parker ripped open the mesh that held the plastic building supplies together. It had been over a decade since I built a sandcastle, but he insisted it was a must when at the beach. I couldn't argue with that logic.

Together, we made the worst sandcastle I think I had ever seen. A career in construction would have been disastrous for either of us. When we tried to stack the cylinders of sand, one of them would inevitably crumble completely or on one side and take the others down somehow. The designs I tried to make all disappeared within seconds.

"Well, now we know why we're not architects," Parker laughed.

"We would kill so many people," I said. "All the buildings would come tumbling down."

We looked at our hideous creation. I started giggling. Parker looked at me and broke out in his own laughter.

"It looks like an earthquake hit it, or some catastrophic war broke out."

Parker inspected the half-crumbled sandcastle. A devilish smirk spread across his face.

"Are you ready?" Parker asked.

"For what?"

"Utter destruction!"

Parker threw his arm around my waist, pushing us into our sandy monstrosity. The few half-standing towers crumbled over us as Parker landed on me, holding up most of his weight. Sand tangled in my hair as I laughed, feeling Parker's chest on top of mine. He slowly lowered himself onto my lips, silencing our laughs, before rolling off me.

After laughing in the sand for a few minutes, we went back into the water. A group of kids kept splashing us while playing games until Parker started splashing them back. He then chatted with them for a few minutes and introduced himself to their dad, who was worried they were bothering us.

"You're good with kids," I said when Parker swam back to me after chatting with the dad for a few minutes. We floated within the waves.

"They're cute," he shrugged.

"Do you want kids? You know, in the future."

It was really none of my business whether he wanted kids or not, but I couldn't stop myself from imagining how great of a father he would be. Someone would be lucky to have him one day.

"Maybe. I've never given it much thought, but I enjoy hanging out with my nieces and nephews. I figure that kids will be something to figure out once marriage is on the table."

"You have nieces and nephews?

"Yeah. I have two nieces and one nephew."

"Cute."

"Do you want kids?" he asked, avoiding eye contact.

"Maybe one day. I'm not ready, but maybe one day I will be."

"Well, for what it's worth, I think you'll be a great mom one day."

"I think you'd be a great dad."

"Thanks, princess."

He looked at me kindly, almost with a hint of sadness.

Around six, we got out of the water and tried to dry off. We were damp, and the day had started to cool down.

We laid on the waterproof towel. I was sure I had thousands of grains of sand in my hair and other places that would require quite a shower to get out, but it was worth it. The sun was going down, and the sky changed. The clouds were darker and wispily spread across the sky. I snuggled up to him, and we watched the sun disappear behind the water.

"Do you think the sunset is as beautiful as people say it is?" I asked.

"I'm sure it is," he said, almost knowingly. "Otherwise, people wouldn't say it is one of the most beautiful things they've ever seen."

Today had been a perfect day. He pulled me closer as if he could feel my heart about to break at the realization that he would be gone in a little over a month. There would be no one to push me out of my comfort zone or give me secret sweet looks in the office. In a few weeks, he would be gone.

But today has been perfect, and I would rather have the memories than nothing at all.

Chapter Twenty-One

SUNDAY MORNING.
Thirty-four days left.

The commotion of the packed restaurant made it feel alive, even if it was a little too early in the morning.

"I'm so glad we got to do this!" Gabby squealed as the waitress took our order. I agreed. It has been a long time since we had time for just the two of us besides casual conversation.

Gabby had a tough week at the café but finally hired two new people to help in the mornings. She preferred being the only one there most of the morning, but word about her food had spread, so she couldn't handle it alone anymore. I was excited for her. She would be less tired and wouldn't have to wake up ridiculously early anymore to compensate for the lack of help.

"So, what did you and Nathaniel do last night?" I asked her. "He told me you guys were doing something special."

"He took me to dinner at Flemings," she blushed. "You were right after Richard took you. It was delicious! Then, we went for a nice long walk along The Boardwalk. We sat on one of the benches, watched the water, and just talked. It was really lovely."

"And...?"

There had to be more to the story. Otherwise, she wouldn't be stifling her smile as much.

"He told me he loves me."

"He tells you that all the time."

"But it was a little further this time."

I gave her a puzzled look.

"He told me he wants to make us official. Like for real. Like meet the parents and announce it on Facebook official. He asked me to move in with him and told me he wants to get married."

I almost spit out my water and chose to choke to avoid drenching Gabby. Nathaniel had told me all those things about Gabby a million times before, but I had doubts that he would actually tell her before she said those things to him.

"What did you tell him?"

She sighed. Oh, no.

"Gabby, what did you tell him!?"

Nathaniel was not an emotional guy with most people, but Gabby was different for him. Even then, I can't imagine that finally articulating his thoughts to her was easy.

"That I loved him. That I was sure about him, but that I needed a night to sleep on it."

"What?! Gabby!" I stared at her in utter disbelief. "Is that not what you want?"

"Of course!"

"Then why are you keeping him waiting?"

"I'm just scared, okay? I'm scared that if anything about us changes, things will start to fall apart, and I'll be left alone again. Totally and utterly heartbroken. I'm scared that things will change too much if we move in together and get married. I don't want things to change."

She sighed and took a large gulp of water.

"I've always been able to see color, Blake, so I can't be sure that I'm making the right decision, which makes it more difficult. My choices in the past have always been bad, and I've ended up devastated. I mean, you remember what happened with Jackson. I didn't get out of bed for weeks after we broke up. I couldn't trust my feelings to steer me in the right direction back then. What if I can't trust my feelings now?"

Finally, I understood why Gabby preached that she wasn't ready to settle down.

A handful of years ago, she had been very close to marrying her scum of an ex-boyfriend. Everything was perfect until they moved in together. Then, things started to fall apart. After they broke up, I did my best to comfort her from a distance and even visited her once, but she was completely heartbroken. Before Nathaniel came along, she had refused to entertain another relationship with anyone.

I assumed that some of her hesitancy came from the assumption that Jackson changed after they moved in together. She was scared that disturbing the status quo would ruin what she loved the most.

"Things will always be changing, Gabs. Whether you want them to or not, they will. I couldn't see color even when I thought I was deeply in love, so I can't speak much about color being able to steer you in the right direction. But what I can tell you is what I do see. I see that you love Nathaniel more than anything, and he loves you the same. I know he will wait forever for you to be ready, Gabby. If you're not ready, he won't push you. But I don't think it's fair to either of you to be in this limbo when you're perfect for each other."

"How can you be sure? I've had people tell me they love me before, and then they leave."

"I can't, but part of love is trust. You need to trust that Nathaniel will always be there for you. I know that can be hard, but it's the truth. Look at how much has changed over the last two years. You used to have a different date every night and maintained that you would never date anyone exclusively again. When we were still in California, Nathaniel was adamant that he would never marry or settle down with just one person. It was as if, independently, both of you had given up on committed relationships and were determined to never end up in this situation. Then, you met. You have had eyes for no one else. His eyes light up when you walk into a room. You sleep better with him. You accept each other for your faults. If what you and Nathaniel have isn't what love is supposed to be, then I'm confident love doesn't exist."

"I mean, I see your point..."

"I think you need to take your own advice and try something new. Moving in with him would be new. Completely committing to him officially would be new. You've never backed down from doing what scares you, so why start now?"

She nodded along with my words, and I could see the decisions being made in her head. Her lips formed a wide smile. I knew she wouldn't be here to see our food arrive.

"Go," I egged her on. "Don't leave him in suspense any longer than you already have."

"He was asleep when I left the apartment. He's probably still asleep."

"Gabby, go. Wake him up. Tell him how much you love him."

"I love you, Blake," she hastily grabbed her stuff and hugged me tightly. "Thank you."

I watched her run out of the restaurant as the confused waitress set down our plates. I asked for Gabby's food to be boxed up, and I would take it home. They deserved to be happy, and I was more than excited to see them do this.

It had been a long time coming.

Chapter Twenty-Two

Friday night.

Twenty-nine days left.

Richard knocked on my door on Friday night. I stepped out to the elevator landing. His appearance shocked me as I looked him up and down.

Usually, when Richard and I went out, he always donned a wrinkle-free button-down with a jacket and perfectly tailored pants. He wore the same thing to work. His hair was perpetually gelled back, and his glasses perfectly sat on the bridge of his nose. Typically, I matched his aesthetic with a nice dress for whatever restaurant we were headed to.

Today, he looked...different. He had a tight-fitting t-shirt that highlighted his slim frame. It sat over the waistband of a pair of jeans and some nice sneakers. For a while, I doubted that he even owned a pair of jeans. He told me to dress casually, so I opted for shorts and a crop top.

I adjusted my purse as Richard smiled at me.

"You look so different!" I exclaimed.

"Is different good?" he fidgeted with the bag he held.

"Yes! You look relaxed. It's a good look on you."

He gave me a shy smile and offered me his hand instead of his arm as we walked out of the building. He wasn't telling me where we were going, which was different from his usual carefully laid out schedule of events. But I recognized that we were walking toward The Boardwalk.

I told him about the movie Gabby and I had watched the other night and caught him up on what the last week at work had been like. There wasn't much to report since everything was normal. Nothing interesting happened, and there was nothing for him to catch up on as far as our project was concerned.

He had been on vacation with his brother, so he had lots of stories from their campout. The bridge of his nose was slightly sunburnt, and he looked tanner than usual. For the first time in a while, our conversation wasn't solely revolving around work, personal development, or books.

I was surprised that he had agreed to go camping. Richard's version of the outdoors was sitting on the terrace of his building or outdoors at a restaurant. His brother was a park ranger and loved it, so he appeased him for their vacation. He had fun but complained plenty about the bugs.

"I tried to get a little bit more creative," Richard started as we got closer. "But don't hate me if you don't like it."

"I'm sure it'll be fun!"

He led me to a small table on the patio of one of the closed coffee shops and started unloading the bag. He had picked up two sandwiches from the local deli down the street from the office. It was my favorite sub place. They had the best combinations.

"It's not like our usual meals, but I figured this would be easy to carry out here. I know you love subs."

"I do love subs."

I unwrapped my sandwich and dug right into it. He almost nailed my order with turkey, roast beef, and cheese. It had plenty of meat, plus the olive oil and herb mix, which was my favorite thing to add. The only thing I picked out were the tomatoes. He got both of us lemon muffins on the side. I passed on it. Lemon muffins were not my thing.

Once we were done, he threw away our trash and walked us over to the rental booth at the edge of the pond. The teenager working the booth had us sign several waivers before bringing the kayak to us.

"You're actually going to get in the water?" I teased Richard.

"I'm trying something new," he smiled. "A pretty girl once told me to try it."

His dark eyes were peaceful around the water, but his nervous smile reminded me that this wasn't his idea of a good time. I appreciated his willingness to try but felt bad for forcing him into it.

After maneuvering ourselves into the water without getting wet, we moved around in a comforting silence. The water rippled every time we took the paddle out. I stared at the ripples as they got further and further from the center. He splashed me lightly in a moment of childishness, making me believe he was enjoying this as much as I was.

It wasn't particularly crowded today, which was odd for a Friday night. There were a few other people in the water and some walking around. The restaurants were the only places full of life. Laughter and the faint clinking of silverware crowded the air.

I turned to Richard. The light from one of the restaurants behind him gave him a glow. We returned to the shore and returned the kayak to the bored teenager.

"That wasn't nearly as unpleasant as I thought it would be," Richard admitted.

"We don't have to do things you don't enjoy," I laughed, swinging our joint hands.

"I wanted to try something new. You were right. I did have fun."

"I appreciate the creativity, for sure. I've always loved the water. Growing up, I probably spent half of my time in it."

"The only water I grew up around was a river. I always hated being wet. But I admit, I'm not giving it a fair chance now. Maybe it's time to try it again."

Richard stopped walking in front of my building. I was pulled back by his hand, firmly grasping mine. He slipped his arm around my waist and pulled me in, dipping me into a kiss. It sent a flutter of feelings through me.

"What was that for?" I smiled.

"Just being grateful for you."

He rendered me speechless with today's actions. Something that rarely happened to me. He held the lobby door open, and we got in the elevator. I would have let him into the apartment if it wasn't because we had work tomorrow.

"Goodnight, Blake," he leaned in and kissed me. Soft. Kind. Almost loving.

"Goodnight, Richard."

I returned his kiss, feeling a reinvigorated connection with him. I felt for the first time that maybe we could be more than casual dates and fancy restaurants. He had planned something for us, for me, without any expectation of liking it. We ate subs and moved around in a kayak. I could get used to these nights with him quicker than I cared to admit.

I closed the door behind me, still slightly shocked at the night. I was sure this wouldn't help my already befuddled feelings.

As I climbed into bed, I got a text. A mug with the words 'recovering workaholic' came on my screen.

Parker: Saw this today, and I just had to get it for you! I'll bring it into the office tomorrow.

Me: You should've gotten two, and we'd have matching mugs to remind us to enjoy life.

Parker: I'm definitely enjoying it with you.

I stared at the mug and ran my finger over the screen. A slight guilt crept into my heart. Tears pooled in my eyes.

This would all be over soon.

Chapter Twenty-Three

WEDNESDAY AFTERNOON.
Twenty-four days left.

Unofficially, I was exhausted. Officially, I had to put away my feelings and deal with the countdown in front of me. We were running out of time to select the last portion of phase one of Project Porcelain. A decision had to be made today.

Amelia and her team piled into the conference room at the end of the day. Erik and I were each presenting a final idea that we had brainstormed. I had to pivot my team to work on other projects for which the deadlines were quickly approaching, so I had been on my own for this one. The guilt of presenting something that I wasn't proud of made me question how I had let myself even put together this presentation. I planned to propose a tried-and-true idea while, from what I understood, Erik was going with a more untested idea.

My presentation was stale. The idea was overused. We all knew the research; we knew that mailed samples worked. They worked well enough, but it was predictable. We all knew it, but I still had to sit there and pretend that I believed in what I was pitching.

Erik thoroughly presented his research. The kind of experience he was pitching had seldom been done with cosmetics in this way before, but there was no reason why it couldn't be. It would appeal to a younger demographic and would not be a bad idea for the older crowd without social media.

We debated the ideas, and Erik's presentation was clearly better. It was the kind of idea I would have expected me to pitch. However, I had been so focused on helping Lainee juggle the projects we offloaded on her that my thinking capacity for this had been stretched. I was happy that Erik had come up with a good idea and angry at myself for not giving this more attention.

Almost everyone seemed to agree that Erik's idea was the way to go, except for Parker and the more conservative side of Amanda. I stayed quieter than I should have during the debate. It ate away at me that I didn't just encourage using Erik's idea, but my pride wouldn't let me.

Parker claimed that implementing the mailed samples idea that was proven to work with older generations would help increase market share with them. That was a particular struggle for their brand. Social media had been incredible for the younger clientele but somewhat excluded older women from the narrative.

The looks around the room did not agree, but Amelia cracked under Parker's skillful pressure. He was used to getting people reduced jail sentences and sparing them from prison time, so persuasion was one of his well-honed skills. She gave Parker's defense the benefit of the doubt and decided to go with it. Nick was surprised, and Erik was miffed.

My only contribution was that if the mailed sample didn't reach the desired result, the pop-up experience during the second phase was always a possibility.

As they walked out of the room, I felt ashamed. I didn't earn Amelia's decision based on my ideas. The conversation mulled over loudly in my brain, making me angry at Parker for defending me like that. I didn't deserve it, and we both knew it. He had broken one of our rules, and I had let it happen.

Parker and I had plans to get a drink after work at our usual booth in the back of The Boathouse. We never walked there together, so I had time to think as I walked.

The more I thought about it, the more I regretted giving a pitch. I should have told Amelia it wasn't my best week and had Erik pitch his alone. Pride got the better of me. I know she would have understood.

I debated whether I should admit to Amelia that Erik's idea would be the best course of action. I had never had an idea shut down before since I typically didn't present them unless I was fully confident about them. I had also never withdrawn an idea before. This was new territory for me. Apparently, most of what I had done over the last two months was proving to be new territory.

I perused the menu for no reason since I already knew what I wanted. Parker slipped into my side of the booth. We had become same side of the booth people. My leg bounced up and down, slightly shaking our bench. Anger was not a feeling I usually had around or about him, so I didn't know how to handle it.

"All right, what's wrong?" he moved his hand up and down my leg, dragging his fingertips over the fabric of my pants.

"I'm mad at you."

He almost spit out his drink. "What? Why?"

"You broke a rule!"

The sweet caressing stopped, and he clutched my thigh. It stopped my leg from bouncing. "What are you talking about?"

"You treated me differently at work. You went to bat for me with Amelia today."

"Oh..." His eyes darkened. "Look, I think it's a good idea, so technically, no. I didn't break any rules."

"It's a decent idea at best, Parker. We both know it wasn't the better idea of the two."

He didn't bother denying it. I turned slightly away from him. Parker let me stew in silence for a few minutes. The air was tense and heavy, but his grip on my thigh never eased.

"Okay, I'm sorry. But I wouldn't have defended your idea if I didn't think it would work. It might not be the better of the two, but it's not a bad idea."

"That's not the point, Parker. You let your relationship with me affect how you behaved with Amelia and strongarmed her into choosing my idea."

"I trust you, and the research supports that it would work within the demographic that it tries to target. I didn't defend your idea because you let me kiss you on the weekends. I defended your idea because it wasn't bad. Also, I don't like Erik, but that's more of a personal issue."

"There you go, see! You're letting your personal feelings interfere at work. The only reason you don't like Erik is because of me. I'm mad at you. You forced Amelia into it."

"You're cute when you're mad, but I don't like it when it's me you're mad at."

I rolled my eyes at him and looked away. His comment elicited a smile, and I didn't want him to think I wasn't mad anymore. Although it was getting harder to stay mad the more his expression was apologetic.

"Do you want me to tell Amelia I changed my mind?" he asked. "I can backtrack, and we can pivot. I will do whatever I need to if it means that you'll stop glaring at me. Is that what you want?"

I shook my head. I was not going to condone him going to Amelia on my behalf. I had to tell Amelia that we should follow Erik's plan myself.

"I don't support your idea because I like your pretty face," his fingers gripped my chin and turned my face to look at him. "I support whatever you do because you're incredible at what you do, princess. I admit I overstepped. I didn't mean to break a rule. I'm sorry."

I stared at his eyes, trying not to break into a smile.

"Okay...I forgive you. But you need to promise you won't do it again. I want to earn her decisions on my own, not because you and Amelia have a personal relationship and you have a soft spot for me."

"I have more than a soft spot for you," he cupped my face and leaned to plant a kiss on me.

"Parker!" I exclaimed against his lips. "Promise me!"

"I promise, princess."

He laughed before drawing me in for that kiss.

Chapter Twenty-Four

FRIDAY MORNING.

Twenty-two days left.

The week had battered me. Three more weeks of Project Porcelain. Everything was wrapping up, and we were preparing for the final release. The only kink in my plan was that Amelia had not been at the office since Wednesday, and I wanted to back out of the mailed samples in person. They would be in on Monday, and I intended to tell her then.

Gabby, Nathaniel, and I had a late dinner last night after Nathaniel, and I had been up late preparing a presentation for a potential client he was visiting next week. I was also hogging all the time I could living with Gabby before she moved in with him. We had spent almost every afternoon together, watching movies and hanging out like we used to.

I was taking today off since it was the only day I refused to work every year. Sometimes, I still found myself on my laptop, but I intended to watch movies alone while everyone was at work. The blinds in my room were open, and the sunlight started seeping into my room. I rubbed my eyes. My mascara from yesterday came off on the side of my hand.

I loved getting the natural light in my room first thing in the morning, but I didn't appreciate it much today. It was still early, but there was no chance I would be going back to bed, so I finished opening up my drapes.

Suddenly, part of the world came alive in front of me.

I blinked more times than I could count before convincing myself that this wasn't a dream. The view outside my window never seemed as lively and vibrant as it was right now. The few bright white clouds contrasting against the sky made my eyes tear up.

I ran to Gabby's bedroom door. Typically, I would burst in, but I knew Nathaniel was in there, and that was an image I didn't need.

"Gabby!" I pounded on the door. "Gabby! Open the door!"

I heard stirring on the other side, and her door flew open. She ran out in Nathaniel's t-shirt, panic written on her face.

"What happened?! Are you okay!?"

I wrapped my hand around her bony wrist and pulled her towards our balcony. I shoved the sliding door open, and we stepped outside. The day had already started heating up. She looked at me, confused and concerned that I had lost my mind. Nathaniel dragged behind us in pajama pants, trying to wake up.

"It's not even eight, and you have the day off. You better be dying," he rubbed his eyes.

"I've always been told that the sky is blue, right?" I turned towards them. They nodded, confused. "The sky is blue!"

"Okay?" Nathaniel asked slowly. Gabby cocked her head.

"The car parked by the pharmacy downstairs is blue!" I pointed at the car across the street. It was a dark blue minivan.

"Wait..." Gabby started to catch on.

I ran inside. I rummaged through our basket of blankets. Surely one of them was blue.

"This blanket is blue!" I held up the plush blanket in the air.

"No way!"

I picked up my mug from last night's hot chocolate sitting on the table. "The handle of this mug is blue. It's hideous, and we should get rid of it, but it's blue!"

"You can see blue!" Gabby screamed. "You can see a color!"

"I can see blue!"

Gabby hugged me, forcing me to jump with her while she blew out my eardrum with her screams. A soft smile spread across Nathaniel's face as he processed what happened in front of him. He joined our hug and squeezed us both.

"Congratulations, kid," he yawned. "Shit, I need to get ready for work."

Nathaniel frantically disappeared into Gabby's bedroom to get ready.

"I can't believe it! And on your birthday!" Gabby pulled me toward the couch. She set both hands on my knee as I faced her. She gasped. The excitement was wiped from her face almost completely. The same thought I had earlier had just occurred to her.

"Wait! Who is it? You've been on so many dates lately. Oh my god, how can we know? It's got to be Parker. I know it."

"Richard and I went kayaking a bit ago. It was actually a really nice date. I felt a real connection with him. It was nice to see him try to do something else. It could be him."

"Oh gross, no. It can't be Richie. It has to be Parker."

"It can't be Parker."

"Why not? Was the day at the beach not everything your dreams were made of?"

"It was, but it can't be him. I can even use your theory of choice to make sense of it. I can't choose Parker. He's leaving in three weeks."

Based on Gabby's rationale alone, Parker wouldn't have caused the color I was seeing. I couldn't fall in love with him. I couldn't choose to be with him.

"I could be wrong," Gabby muttered, not convincing enough for me or her.

"Try again."

"I could be wrong," she said more definitively.

"Let's talk about the fact that it could be Erik. I felt something...different...when he walked me home the other night," I tried to think about every feeling I had experienced over the last two months. Before all of this, I could have counted the instances of strong feelings I had experienced in three years on one hand. My brain was overrun, thinking about the three men I brought into my mind. "It could also be Richard. It could be Erik. Oh my gosh. What if you are wrong, and it can be Parker? No, no –"

"Blake," Gabby's voice was low.

"It has to be Richard. It has to be him. Or Erik. Erik is okay. I left him once and survived. He could leave, and I would –"

"Blake, you're spiraling," she shook me slightly.

My heart rate increased.

"Oh goodness, Gabby, what did I get myself into?"

I buried my face in my hands as Gabby ran to the kitchen. She came back with some reheated muffins.

"It seemed a little early for wine," she laughed.

Gabby was adamant that Parker had caused the color, which was a possibility I refused to accept. My brain is jumbled. My heart is puzzled. My hands are clammy.

"Gabby, let's be real..."

"Blake, he makes you so happy! I don't see how you can ignore that."

"Gabby, he's leaving."

My breathing stalled. My lungs weren't getting enough oxygen.

Gabby started listing the different ways to make Parker and me work. She pitched that he could stay in Virginia, but his entire family was in Texas, which meant everything to him. Not to mention, he would never abandon Amelia with how fast the company was growing. She suggested I could follow him to Texas, but my life and career were here. I had made a point to prioritize my professional goals after leaving Erik. I didn't think I could give everything up again. Long distance was always doomed to fail, so that wasn't an option.

"You said it yourself," she said, her voice becoming more muffled in my brain. "Erik feels like a memory. He might have gotten better, but people don't change. You have to remember how he made you feel in the moments that mattered the most."

My body started trembling. I recognized the signs but couldn't stop it from happening. Gabby paced in front of me.

Erik held the spot for some of the best moments of my life, but he also held the spot for some of the worst. Even though I couldn't forget about the things he said that night, we might be able to learn from them.

Maybe having Erik around was bringing up old feelings that I had resigned myself to ignoring. Erik was comfortable and reminded me of home. Just because he was a part of my past didn't mean he couldn't be a part of my future. There was the option that Mason had been right from the start, and we were meant to find each other again.

I lost control of my thoughts, trying to rein them back.

Richard would be the safe choice. He had a promising future at Capital Media, came from a normal family, and was a good person. A nice guy. He had plans to grow. We always had a nice time together, and now that I had seen a glimpse of a different side of him, I saw what we could maybe be one day. Richard would be the easy choice.

My skin grew hot, and my eyes started tearing up. I had lost track of what Gabby was saying. My brain wasn't processing her words anymore.

She rambled on about Parker. He certainly had turned my life upside down. I had started to crave his food when he wasn't around. I know I would miss the consistent happy hour drinks. The fun we had every weekend breathed new life into me.

I liked Parker. I liked him a lot more than I should or expected.

But he was leaving in three weeks.

"Blake?" Nathaniel's voice cut through the mumbling. "Hey, hey, come back to us."

Gabby had stopped talking. She had probably stopped a while ago, but I was lost in my head. They brought my attention back to them.

"I'm so sorry," Gabby apologized. "I didn't realize I was inducing a panic attack in you. I'm so sorry."

"It's okay," I managed to catch my breath again. Nathaniel handed me a glass of water. "It's a lot of information. A lot of feelings."

"I have to leave, Gabs," Nathaniel looked at her. "Make sure she eats and stays seated for the next ten minutes."

He leaned closer to her and whispered something into her ear. She nodded along with him, and concern was splattered on her face.

"We tried to talk them out of it," Gabby shrugged. She wasn't great about whispering.

"Let's make sure we watch for the signs and get her out of there if we need to."

I had no idea what they were talking about. At the moment, I didn't care.

"You know what," Gabby brought my attention back to her. "Let's not worry about it right now. Let's spend the morning together and enjoy the new things you can see."

I nodded. She smiled at me. Her smile hid concern.

Gabby made me a cup of coffee, and we stared at the sky. It was my least favorite day of the year, but at least today, I could look at the bright blue sky and feel some semblance of joy.

Chapter Twenty-Five

Friday afternoon.
Twenty-two days left.

Nathaniel impatiently tapped his foot while we waited for Gabby to finish getting ready. I was ready but didn't want to go anywhere, especially after this morning. They insisted on going for drinks at The Boathouse, but I didn't feel the need to celebrate other than just going outside and enjoying the color of the sky some more.

I hated my birthday, so I didn't see the point.

My birthday had a carefully crafted itinerary, a yearly ritual of sorts. Every year, after taking the day off, I binged movies and hid from the world all day. I would finish my day with more bad romance movies and a pizza topped with olives and basil. Sometimes, the only person I saw all day was the pizza delivery guy.

If I wasn't at work, no one could congratulate me, no one could bring me a cake. If I didn't answer the phone, no one could speak to me. I always ignored all texts and phone calls until the next day. I never went out to celebrate and had not had a party since I was thirteen. That was the last year I celebrated my birthday.

My thirteenth birthday was one of the worst days of my life.

•••••●•●••••

Hushed arguing came from inside the house as everyone gathered around me to start opening presents. They must have thought that no one could hear their fight.

My parents had argued this morning about the excessive number of cups my mom had bought. They argued about the fact that my dad hadn't mowed the yard and that it made them look unkept to everyone who came to the party and to the neighbors. Right now, they could have been arguing about the height of the cake or the temperature.

During the last few hours, they had put on an impeccable façade of happiness. They portrayed the image of the perfectly happy family having the perfect thirteenth birthday party for their only child. But I was sure they would argue about something else later when I was in my room, and they thought I couldn't hear them.

Their preferred method of communication for the last six months had been screaming.

I had grown accustomed to it and would either tune it out or go to Erik's house. Today, he stood by the table with the presents, helping his dad move them right in front of my feet. He knew about all the arguments and didn't know what to do to help me, but I found his gaze comforting, even at thirteen. They were the eyes of my best friend. The person who would be there when I cried about it later.

My aunt developed an uncomfortable smile as we waited for my parents. All the adults knew what had been decided and showered me with pitiful looks. This wasn't anything new for me, but I was sure they knew something I didn't. Adults often did.

My aunt opened the back door to bring them out for presents. My mom's voice clearly came through.

"Just because you suddenly decided to divorce me and tell me I wasn't good enough for you doesn't give you the right to treat me like crap!" she screamed at my dad.

A soft but collective gasp took the air out of my lungs. My parents were getting a divorce?

My heart rate quickened.

"That's not what I said! Stop twisting my words around you –"

My hands were clammy.

"Stanley!" my aunt yelled, stopping my dad's voice.

I couldn't breathe with all the eyes on me. I shoved everything aside and ran to the opposite side of the house, straight to my bedroom. I locked myself in my room and sat in my closet.

My body was trembling – an experience I had never had before. I stayed in my wet swimsuit. My hair dripped on my back, mimicking the tears running down my sun-kissed cheeks.

My parents and aunt chased me to my room, but I refused to unlock the door. I was shaking and crying and couldn't breathe.

"Leave me alone!" I screamed for the fifth time.

"Okay, okay," my dad's quivering voice came through the door. "We'll be out here when you're ready to talk, Blake."

I tried to steady my breath. The closet door creaked open, which should have been impossible. I would have heard my parents if they had managed to get the door open. A scrawny Erik stood in front of me.

"I used the window," he explained with a casual shrug.

He took a seat next to me and enveloped me in a hug. We were both still wet from the pool, and the A/C made our swimsuits cold to the touch. I stayed in Erik's arms for who knows how long until my breath steadied, and I could breathe again.

•••••●•●••••

I had been old enough to understand what divorce meant, and my parents told me a million times that it wasn't my fault. After seeing the look on my face that day, they stopped arguing as much. The divorce was quick and painless, as much as one can be. My mom kept the house, and my dad moved just a few houses down.

I still saw him almost every day and maintained a good relationship. Any hint of anger and resentment between them dissipated over the years. Neither of them ever remarried, and life went on.

However, I never celebrated my birthday anymore and hated getting presents for it. It had been marred in my brain as the day that I found out my family was falling apart. I wasn't surprised, but I was heartbroken.

The presents that never got unwrapped sat in the garage for months until I could look at them without crying. My parents tried to introduce a counteracting happy memory about my birthday every year for five years, but I never engaged. They encouraged me to celebrate and bought me presents, but I just wanted to move on with my day.

Today was no different. Except, I had been roped into going to The Boathouse. At least I would finally be able to see the blue that existed in the restaurant.

"Why can't I just keep watching movies and eat my pizza?" I groaned as they ushered me out the door.

"Because you just can't," Gabby said. Even though they were the ones who wanted me to go, they did not seem all that excited about it. I tried to make a run for it, but they wouldn't let me leave their sight.

Nathaniel sighed and reluctantly opened the door to the restaurant. I had a sinking feeling in my chest. We weren't just here for dinner and a drink. In the back room, balloons blocked most of the windows, and I could see Lainee's smiling face.

"No, no, no. Please tell me that you didn't," I turned to Gabby. Nathaniel grabbed my shoulders to stop me from walking out.

"I didn't, no. Richard had the idea. Erik and Lainee helped him pull it off."

"And no one tried to talk them out of it?"

"I tried," Nathaniel raised his hand. "So did Gabby, and so did Parker."

Parker had asked me what I wanted to do to celebrate my birthday a few days ago. He had some ideas of things I would like, but he stopped asking when I told him about my ritual and its reason. I appreciated it.

"Parker saying anything about you did not go over well with either of them," Nathaniel scoffed. "So, here we are."

It was too late to walk away. Everyone was already in the room, and I didn't want to disappoint or upset them. As uncomfortable as I felt, I walked into the room full of smiling faces.

"Happy birthday!" everyone yelled in unison.

I forced a smile and hoped my eyes didn't betray my discomfort. Greeting people was hard when you had to lie about how you felt. I tried to employ the same strategy as I often did at work and hid my feelings in a box deep inside.

The room was set up with multiple tables to accommodate everyone and had a small bar in the corner. Everyone from work was standing around chatting, even Connor and his family. Gabby invited a few friends from college that I hadn't seen in a long time. Mason was already chatting up the bartender.

"What do you think?" Richard walked up to me. He brushed his fingertips across my back before stepping back from me. A small gesture that said a lot.

His eyes pleaded for a kind of approval I couldn't truthfully give him. He had also asked a couple of weeks ago what my plans for my birthday were, and I had told him. I made it clear that I don't celebrate my birthday, so I was confused as to why he thought this would be a good idea.

"This is kind of you," I smiled. I turned to the rest of the room.

Erik stood by the gift table, organizing the bags around. Deja-vu. I looked at him and saw thirteen-year-old Erik. On that day, he wore polka-dotted swimming trunks and stood at the edge of the gift table, much like he was doing now, as I put down my aunt's present. His dark eyes had been wide that day, but today, there was no trace of that memory in his mind. Even though he was the person who had seen me through my first panic attack that day. As well as he claimed to know me, he had disregarded one of the most hurtful memories of my childhood.

He had forgotten.

The speckles of blue throughout the room drew my attention, bringing a silver lining to the situation. The margarita glasses had a blue rim. I never would have guessed that. Connor and Mason had blue eyes, although they were different shades. The tables had scattered blue tiles with designs on them.

With every happy birthday wish, I felt more and more uncomfortable. More alone in a room filled with people. I hoped I was good at concealing my feelings, but given Gabby's constant reminders to smile, I doubted it. Finally, I got to Amelia and her team. She hugged me and reiterated that she didn't even know my birthday was coming up. I rarely told anyone about it.

I turned to Parker. His eyes were apologetic but had a newfound beauty to them. They were light. The color of the sky. The color of our blanket from earlier.

Parker had blue eyes.

He quickly excused himself to talk to Nathaniel, and I chatted with Amelia and Amanda about football season. Well…they did most of the talking while I tried to learn. Parker talked about football a lot, and I never understood what was so captivating about it. As much as it confused me, it was one of his favorite things. He wouldn't be around to explain it, but maybe one day, I would understand his fascination with it.

Nathaniel tried to talk Richard out of making a big fuzz with presents. I tried not to overhear their conversation, but they weren't hiding it well. I was trying not to be ungrateful, but this was not me. It had been fifteen years since I had celebrated, and I was ready to go home.

"Richard, you have no respect for me, and I have no respect for you," Nathaniel almost growled. "I tried to talk you out of this. Blake hates her birthday, but she likes you for some weird reason. If you try to get her to make a big deal about presents, I promise she will walk out of here."

"You're right. I don't respect you."

"I don't give a shit how you feel about me, but Blake is like a little sister to me, and I will protect her. I haven't told her about what you did, but if you insist on the gift thing, I will walk her out here myself."

"She doesn't know?"

"No. It's not my story to tell."

What didn't I know?

At the end of the party, everyone seemed happy enough. Richard asked me to hang behind for a minute. Gabby enlisted Nathaniel and Parker to carry presents back to the apartment and loaded their arms.

I had to assure them I was fine before they would leave. The conversation I had overheard made me uneasy. I always figured that Gabby didn't like Richard for a random reason and that Nathaniel didn't like him because Gabby didn't like him. It bothered me that there was more than that.

Richard walked up to me with a smile.

"I have something for you," he pulled out a small box from his pocket.

The top of it was velvety. It wasn't heavy and fit on the palm of my hand perfectly. I opened it, revealing a shiny, small, sparking 'B' necklace adorned with shiny rocks. It caught the light just right, sending a twinkle into my eyes. It was captivating.

"This is beautiful, Richard. But I can't accept it."

"Please, Blake. Stop resisting me spoiling you. It's for your birthday."

"I just...I don't know what to say..."

"Just say you'll wear it."

"Okay...thank you."

He pulled me in for a hug, and I hugged him back. Erik was hanging by the back of the room, eyes burning a hole through Richard's back.

"I'd kiss you, but Erik is hanging behind to help me clean up," Richard whispered.

"It's okay," I pulled away from him, relieved, pretending that Erik being here was the only cause to stop his kiss.

My feelings for Richard were conflicted. We had an incredible time the other night, and he even stepped out of his comfort zone for me. But right now, I was annoyed with him. He threw me a nice party, but I wasn't shy about sharing why I didn't celebrate my birthday with him. He had ignored me.

I walked out of the restaurant. My lungs cleared out the air in them. My eyes felt heavy. My smile was tired of pretending.

"Button!" Erik called after me. He jogged toward me, a small bag in his hands. I turned to face him, scowling. "What did I do? You have that angry look on your face."

"You helped throw a party...for me...for the birthday I don't celebrate!"

I groaned, hoping the memory would click in his mind. It took him a few seconds longer than it should have, but the recognition flashed in his mind, and his eyes darkened. A frown quickly replaced his smile. So much for never forgetting anything about me.

"Your parents' divorce..." he whispered to himself. He took a step forward and grabbed my hand from my side. "Button, I'm so sorry. I completely spaced. Richard suggested the party since you've been working so hard, and I just...I just wanted to help."

"It is what it is, Erik."

"Well, here," he handed me the bag. "Not a birthday present. It's a peace offering for you to forgive me. I just happen to have hurt you and be begging for forgiveness on the day of your birth."

"That's not the loophole you think it is," I said, taking the bag and rummaging through the tissue paper. My hand touched the pointy end of a box. I grabbed it and pulled it out. Erik tapped his fingers together, seeking approval on my face.

"I know you hate necklaces because it feels like they'll choke you, but I hope you like this."

I opened the box, and a glistening circular piece of metal caught the sun. There was a knot in my throat as I immediately recognized the item in front of me. It was a newer version, yet it almost matched the bracelet I gifted him for his college graduation. The one he still wore every day.

It had a little dome at the top of a flat button, and I was sure I would find an outdated picture of us in the middle.

Erik watched me intently, studying my reaction. The tears pooled in my eyes, and I was on the verge of losing control of my emotions for the millionth time since he came back into my life. I brought the dome to my eye and peeked to see which picture he chose.

When I gave him the bracelet, I had chosen our prom picture. It had been the only nice picture we had taken in years, and it felt fitting to reminisce about a chapter of our life that had closed.

He chose our college graduation. We stood next to each other with wide smiles, smiles that didn't know what kind of future awaited us. If only twenty-two-year-old Blake had known that only two years after that, she would make a decision that would break her. My mom had taken the picture. We had decided to give our relationship a real chance just a couple of weeks before this was taken. Our parents were ecstatic.

It turns out that our graduation gowns had been dark blue.

Feelings that I was trying to suppress were coming to the surface. Erik pulled me closer to him. His thumb pushed away the tear that was rolling down my cheek.

"I'm sorry that I helped throw you a party," he whispered, reaching for the bracelet. He gingerly grabbed it and clasped it around my wrist. "I'm sorry I got you a gift, but I hope you like it."

His own tattered bracelet glimmered in the light.

"Thank you," I managed to mutter as I pulled away from him. I climbed on my toes and planted a soft kiss on his cheek.

I didn't say anything else and left him standing behind me. I took a peek back at him before I turned the corner. He looked at me longingly. Full of hope. The nostalgic part of me wanted my heart to see what he saw. He optimistically saw a future in which we could make us work again.

Walking home, I got more flashes of when I was younger. My mom cried for weeks during the proceedings, and my dad's temper was even shorter. Yet, even with everything going on, I never doubted that they loved me. The main lasting impact was my birthday hatred, which I think broke my mom's heart every year.

When I got home, the only noise in the apartment was the TV. I looked around. Parker was sitting on the couch, the smell of pizza coming from the kitchen. Gabby's door was wide open, but her lights were off, so she was gone.

"I don't want to do any more celebrating. I just wanted to spend my birthday like I usually do."

"I tried, princess," Parker took me in his arms. I wrapped my arms around his waist. He circled his finger on my shoulder. "They wouldn't listen to anyone that you didn't want a party. Erik told me he knows you better than anyone and knows what you like and don't like. Richard looked at me like he might have swung if I kept talking. So, I just let it go and let them dig their own graves."

"They should've known better," I rested my cheek on his chest, using his breath to settle me. "Especially Erik."

"Well, I do have something for you. It's a gift, but not really."

I looked at him skeptically, resisting the urge to roll my eyes at him trying to fix my birthday. There was no fix.

He walked to the kitchen and took out a pizza box from the oven. He opened it to the beautiful sight of a pizza with black olives and basil.

"You didn't eat at the party, so I had this delivered. I figured there was still some of the day left, and you could sit here with your pizza and watch movies."

"This is exactly what I've wanted all day," I jumped up and landed a soft kiss on his lips. He caught me and held me against him. I stared at his eyes. His beautiful blue eyes. "Thank you, Parker."

"Anything for you, princess. I'll leave you to enjoy the rest of the day in solitude. Happy birthday."

He grabbed his keys on the island and walked to the door. My heart begged for me to ask him to stay. Maybe a small break in tradition was okay. After all, he did buy the pizza.

"Wait!" I blurted out. He turned, a small smile slowly spreading through his face. "Stay."

"Wouldn't that break your carefully crafted ritual?" he teased. His eyes lightened, a spark across them. I couldn't tear away from his eyes. They were mesmerizingly blue.

"Maybe a small change isn't such a bad thing. But in moderation."

I walked over to the couch and fell back on it, holding the pizza box tightly. I patted the seat next to me.

"Well, I'm honored that you're letting me spend the rest of your birthday with you."

"Do you want any pizza?"

"I'm okay. Olives are gross."

I feigned offense at his comment, and he quickly snuck a kiss on my cheek.

He looked up the trashiest romance movies of all time and started our marathon. I laid my head on his shoulder, his cologne mixing with the smell of my pizza. I didn't know what heaven looked like, sounded like, or felt like, but I was sure this is what it smelled like.

Then, the thought crept into my mind.

Our time together was almost out.

Chapter Twenty-Six

MONDAY MORNING.

Nineteen days left.

Amelia lightly tapped on my door, her smiling face coming through the glass. I looked up from my computer and waved her in.

She looked so incredibly put together, as always. I liked her style. She always wore a black or white pantsuit with what I assumed to be various colorful shirts and heels that matched.

"Do you mind if we chat for a minute?" Her voice was quiet, sweet, but stern.

"Sure. I was about to email you to see if you had a minute today," I turned to her. I sipped my second coffee from my new favorite mug. I never knew a person could have a favorite mug. "What's on your mind?"

"Look, Blake. I respect you, what you do, and how you do it, so I don't want this to come across as a lack of faith in you. You have come up with great ideas so far, but I don't believe the mailed samples are the way we'd like to go. I'd like to switch gears and pursue the pop-ups instead. I know we might have to shift the timeline slightly to make it work, and that's okay. I know Parker doesn't agree, but the rest of the team isn't convinced about the samples, and neither am I."

"Oh...yeah...absolutely!" I swallowed my feelings. "Thank you for being honest with me. I always want you to feel comfortable with our direction, so never be afraid to express your opinion. Feedback is how we learn and grow at the end of the day."

I had crafted the art of the fake smile more than was healthy in the last few months. My heart was erratic again.

"I knew you'd understand. I love the direction you guys are taking my brand so far. It's just this one idea I don't think fits."

"Thank you. But yeah, I completely understand."

"I love your mug, by the way," she gave me a soft smile and walked out.

Even though I considered withdrawing my idea from her, she had beaten me to it. Making the decision had been harder than expected. I should have been honest that this plan was not my best idea, but I didn't want that to reflect poorly on Parker's defense of me either.

I sat back on my chair, finding my hands clammy and harder to breathe. My ideas had never been shut down by a client before. It wasn't that I didn't have bad ideas – I had plenty of them – but they usually didn't make it past a fleeting thought or my team's feedback. I kept my emotions isolated from my job and always tried to be objective, but my feelings had gone haywire in the last few months. I was struggling to keep everything separate.

I couldn't be on the verge of another panic attack at work. I had to get outside.

I rushed out of my office and told Lainee I would return in a few minutes. I was sure I just needed a breath of fresh air to get my thoughts together, tell Erik we were changing direction, and get on with my day. I ran my hand through my hair and pushed it back, leaning against the cold metal of the back of the elevator. My eyes closed, and I took deep breaths, mimicking what Nathaniel had taught me to do.

"Blake?" Parker's concerned voice traveled down the hall as he walked out of the restroom. The metal doors of the elevator shut in front of me.

Once on the ground floor, I hurried outside. All I needed was air. All I needed was some sunlight, and I would be okay. Nathaniel was getting some muffins from Gabby's with Erik, so I had to walk this myself. I could do it. I could do it alone.

I paced in front of the building before sitting on the edge of the stairs. I pressed my back against one of the pillars of the building. It was hot from the sun and the warm weather. I looked up at the blue sky to calm me. The peaceful blue helped steady my breathing. I watched the clouds move. The last few months of dealing with a jumble of emotions had made me soft.

"Blake!" Parker called after me.

I stood up and tried to walk away. I didn't want him to see me like this anymore. I had cried in front of him enough times, but he didn't know about this side of me. He caught up to me, wrapped his hand around my wrist, and pulled me into him. I almost slammed against his chest.

"I just need a minute, Parker. Please!" my jagged breathing was getting more erratic.

"Hey, hey," he said. I shoved my hands against his chest, and he let me step back from him but did not let go of my wrist. "Blake, what's wrong?"

"Nothing. Nothing."

"Blake, you're about to cry."

"I'm fine...I'll be fine. I'm just...I'm..." I didn't even know how to explain it to him. My breath was labored.

"Princess," he whispered. "You're not fine. Come on, it's just me and you. Tell me what's wrong."

"I'm having a panic attack, okay?!" I hit the side of my hand against his chest, trying to push him further away, but he wasn't letting me go. The knot in my throat grew, and I couldn't stop the tears from flowing.

"A panic attack?"

"Yeah, I have those...sometimes...more often recently. Nathaniel is really good at...helping me stop them...before they progress...but he's at Gabby's getting food. I'm not...so good at it...I just need to...breathe..."

"Okay, okay. Hey, let's breathe together."

He led me over to a bench, holding tightly to me. He sat next to me, his body angled toward me. One arm was draped behind me on the back of the bench, the other hand on my knee. His thumb caressed me as I breathed and stopped the spiral.

"Okay...okay..." I caught my breath. "I'm fine. I shouldn't run a mile for the next few hours, but I'm fine."

I stood up, intending to go back upstairs. He followed me as we walked back toward the building.

"What happened? Like what caused it?"

"Amelia backtracked on my idea, but don't worry, it's not a big deal. It wasn't a good idea anyway. I've had an... interesting... three months, so I've had a harder time than usual regulating my emotions."

"She did?" he stopped walking.

"Yeah, literally minutes ago."

"I'm sorry. I didn't know. I would've told you if I did."

This was news to him. I was surprised she hadn't told him. Although, it was probably better that he didn't know.

"Parker," I ran my fingertips down his other arm, landing at his hand. I encouraged us to break my rules, but I needed to assure him it was fine. He interlocked his fingers with mine, and I felt the tension in my shoulders ease. "Really, it's okay. I need clients to be honest with me. That is the only way that I'll learn and get better. Please, let me learn."

"Okay," his thumb caressed the top of my hand. I pressed my forehead against his blue shirt. He ran his fingers down my hair. "Okay."

It wouldn't be the last time a client rejected an idea, so I had to learn to deal with it. I had to learn to work through it without Parker's calming heart or reassuring presence.

"Feeling a little better?" he whispered, holding me close.

I nodded. "We should probably head back upstairs before anyone –"

"Button?!" Erik's distant voice emerged. "Blake! What the hell is going on here?!"

I ripped myself away from Parker, cursing under my breath. Short of it having been Richard or Connor, who were meeting with some software developers at their site today, Erik was the worst person to have seen this.

Erik angrily walked towards us on the sidewalk. He held his coffee, and Nathaniel walked next to him. I wasn't sure what to call the emotion I saw on Nathaniel's face, but concerned would get pretty close.

"Button?" Parker mumbled under his breath.

"Blake Elena! What the hell did I just see?!"

I turned to face him. He was rapidly tapping his fingers together as he marched toward us. His eyes were almost black, and the bag of food he clutched in his hand started to rip.

"Erik, please calm down," I pleaded, stepping even further from Parker.

"Explain. What. I. Just. Saw."

He crossed his arms in front of us. I tried to say something to him, but no sound came out.

"Is this what you've been doing on the weekends that I can't get ahold of you?! Him?!"

"No!" I tried to defend myself. "We're friends! I just had a –"

"The way you and I were just friends?! Because I'll remind you how that ended!"

"It's not like that!"

"What is it like then?! Why were his hands on you?!"

Erik demanded answers, but I didn't have any he would accept or that would explain this. I didn't know what it was like. I had no idea what was happening to me. My brain struggled to find words to explain what I couldn't explain or admit to myself.

"Is this why we're going through with your idea?" he stared into me.

"What?"

"This is why we're moving forward with your idea! Oh, this explains so much. They only accepted your shitty idea because you're sleeping with him. This explains everything!"

"What are you talking about?!"

"The mailed samples over my pop-up experience. I mean, what kind of choice is that? Mine was clearly better!"

"Erik, I –"

"Tell me, Button," he uttered my nickname with disdain. "Did you sleep with him to win us the contract too?"

Rounds of objections came from Parker and Nathaniel.

"Erik!" Nathaniel called out. "That is uncalled for!"

"I'm not sleeping with him!" my voice broke, but the anger brewing within me replaced any other feelings trying to claw their way out.

"What happens between Blake and me outside of work is of no concern to you," Parker growled.

Erik gritted his teeth. The tapping of his fingers hastened.

"This conversation doesn't concern either of you," Erik walked forward. He clutched my arm and yanked me toward him. "This is between Blake and me."

"I'm not going to stand here and let you disrespect her," Parker shoved him backward as I broke out of his grip. "Don't fucking put your hands on her."

I hurried between them. Erik wasn't much of a fighter, but I didn't want anything happening in front of the building. The familiar snapping of the rubber band filled the brief silence. Both men looked at each other with anger. Time felt like it stood still while I figured out what to do.

Something snapped within me, bringing me back from the last three months, bringing me back to reality. My perfectly crafted shell of perfect Blake was cracked but not broken. This was not what I did. I didn't let people speak for me, and I wasn't known for baking down when there was conflict. I needed to take control of the situation.

I had become careless. I had let my emotions get the better of me at work. I needed to take control of myself.

"Parker. Nathaniel," I regained my composure. "Can I have a moment with Erik? Alone, please."

"Pr – Blake, I'm not sure that – you just had a panic attack."

"You had one?" Nathaniel looked at me concerned.

"I'm fine."

"Blake, I kind of agree –"

I stopped Nathaniel mid-sentence. "I am a grown woman. I am fine. Now, I will not ask again. Let Erik and me have a minute. Alone."

Parker resisted, but Nathaniel forced him to walk back into the lobby. He knew when it was useless to fight me. The wall was all windows, so I could see them as they took a seat on the couch in the waiting area. Parker shook his head; Nathaniel was trying to calm him down.

"That was absolutely uncalled for, and you know it!" I turned to Erik. "You know I would never sleep with someone to further my career!"

Erik shook his head. The shell of himself that he had developed over the last few months was splintering, and his old self was showing. The one that made wild accusations based on what he was feeling.

"Then please, please explain to me what I saw! Because from where I'm standing, it looks like you're sleeping with the chief counsel of the company that just gave us our largest contract!"

Out of the corner of my eye, I saw Parker's eyes fixed on Erik. His hand was curled into a fist, and he rhythmically snapped the rubber band. If looks could kill, Erik would have been six feet under already.

I crossed my arms. Anger consumed me, but I knew I had brought this upon myself.

I had meant what I said to Gabby about my date with Erik. There had been a feeling of comfort, a feeling of home that had yet to be replicated anywhere else. Good memories flooded my brain, trying to wash out the bad that came along with them. When it came to Erik, I had allowed those memories to fool me into considering that we could work again.

I allowed myself to review the past in a true honesty moment. In reality, Erik and I hadn't been good for a long time before I left. I looked into his dark eyes, and I knew. I knew I could never choose him again. I could never choose to be with, to love, someone like him. Someone who accused me of anything that came to mind when he was angry and brought out the worst in me.

"Let's get one thing clear, Erik. I am not sleeping with Parker, nor would I ever do so to get a professional advantage. I am offended, angry, and hurt that you would ever consider that. Two, Parker and I have become... friends...over the last three months, and I had a panic attack. My emotions got the best of me, and he was comforting me. Three, you and I are not together. What I do in my personal life is none of your business."

"Come on, Button! We had such a great time the other night, and we've been getting along so great. I saw in your eyes the spark that was there when we were younger. I thought I was on my way to winning you back!"

"I'm so sorry, Erik. But no. No. I can't. I won't let myself fall for you again."

"Why not?! We were so good together."

"How about you have an honesty moment yourself, Erik! We hadn't been happy together for a long time by the time I left. You wanted me to give up my career, my life. I couldn't do that. We argued all the time and fought over everything. It's been three years. We're not the people we used to be. We don't want the same things."

"Is it because of...him?"

I didn't answer immediately, and his anger flared.

"Button, please don't lie to me. Did he give you colors? Is he the reason that you won't be with me?"

I looked up at the blue sky and sighed. My eyes watered. I pictured Parker's blue eyes and the way they shined. The logic in my brain and the feelings in my heart agreed for once and knew the real, truthful answer. But there was also no truth to Parker being the barrier keeping us apart. Just like Erik, he was leaving.

"He's leaving at the end of the week."

"So, it is him. You're screwing him."

"I'm not screwing him."

"The Blake I knew wasn't a liar!" he screamed.

"I'm not lying!" I yelled back.

Nathaniel and Parker heard my scream and perked up their heads. Parker almost got up, but Nathaniel stopped him, shoving him back onto the couch. I was done playing defense. This needed to end, and it needed to end now.

"You know," I tried to calm my quivering voice. "There was a time when I thought you and I would get married and live a fairytale happily ever after. In fact, I believed that most of my life. We were what movies were based on. A pair of best friends who grew up together in a small town, whose parents were best friends, and who were destined for each other. But the moment I found success and started having an identity and something I loved outside of my life with you, you resented me for it. You became cold and distant every time I was excited about work. You guilted me for going on business trips that were the building blocks of the career I wanted. You accosted me when I was selected for the promotion over you and told me I didn't deserve it. I can't be with you, Erik. You don't support nor respect me."

"I do respect and support you, Button! I'm so sorry that I hurt you. I said things I didn't mean that night. Please...forgive me."

He reached for my hand, and I let him. This time, I knew it would be the last time I would feel his skin against mine.

"Do you remember the night we broke up?" I asked, his thumb caressing the top of my hand. "You accused me of abandoning our dreams when I tried my hardest to salvage them, just in a new place. All I wanted was for us to take a leap of faith together. But you refused. Instead, you wanted me to abandon the career that I loved. You were so angry after we fought that you didn't even come to say goodbye."

"This job changed you, Button. I missed the girl I grew up with."

"This job didn't change me. I grew up. I grew into my own person. I didn't need you anymore, but I certainly wanted you. Yet, you couldn't understand that. You said a lot of really hurtful things that day, Erik. Those things don't just disappear because you say you didn't mean them. I'm sorry, but that's not how it works. As much as I've debated a future for us over the last three months, I can't."

"Please, Button. There's so much history between us. You can't just be so willing to forget it."

"I don't intend to," I sniffled, trying to keep the tears at bay. "I will never forget anything about you. I will never forget everything I learned from and with you. We learned how to ride bikes together, and you learned how bad at balancing I was. I learned to love with you. You helped me through my parents' divorce, through my first heartbreak, through my first panic attack. We learned to compromise when we moved in together. But I also learned that I need more. I need someone who supports me and doesn't let anger speak for them. I need someone who doesn't guilt me for pouring myself into my job. All the history between us doesn't make up for the fact that you are not that man."

I stared into his dark eyes and knew he was holding back tears. Even if, by some unlikely and unfair twist of fate, the time we had spent together over the last few months had convinced my heart to see blue, I knew I couldn't choose him.

I had grown a lot over our time apart, and time away allowed me to see the toxicity of our relationship. He robbed me of a lot of happiness and peace and replaced it with guilt and pain. After leaving him, I promised myself I would never be fooled into thinking I was happy again when I wasn't. That is what I would be doing if I went back to him.

I would be fooling myself into happiness with help from past memories. I would be trapped in a cycle of yesterday promising a better tomorrow.

"I've loved you since we were kids, Button. But I see that means nothing to you anymore."

Tears rolled down my cheeks. "I will always love you. I just don't love you the way you want me to. At one point, your love was all that meant anything to me. At one point, my life with you was everything to me. But a lot has happened to show me that's not the future I want. I will not stand here and let you guilt me into trying to love you again. A lot has changed, and I would rather live in a world without color than in one with you."

My heart broke as I uttered the words that I knew I meant. I was no longer ten-year-old Blake, who depended on her best friend for everything. Fifteen-year-old Blake, who held Erik on a pedestal, had left me long ago. Twenty-two-year-old Blake, who thought she loved Erik more than life itself and would have done anything for him, was gone.

Twenty-eight-year-old Blake knew and accepted that things were different. Whatever spark had burned brightly between us had burnt out, and I had no intention of relighting it.

I pulled out the bracelet he gave me out of my pocket. I couldn't put it on this morning, but I couldn't leave it behind. He looked at my hand quietly as I pressed the bracelet to his palm.

"Please prepare to implement your idea for the campaign," I transitioned back into the protection of work mode. "Amelia decided to go with your plan. Congratulations. I'm going home. Call me if the building burns down. Otherwise, I trust you can all handle everything until tomorrow."

Erik stared at me. The Blake he once knew was gone.

"If you love and respect me as much as you say you do, you'll do me a favor of keeping this to yourself. I'll pretend this never happened, and we'll continue working as we were. I respect you as a colleague. Nothing more."

"Blake..." Erik whispered as I turned and walked away.

Chapter Twenty-Seven

MONDAY MIDDAY.
Nineteen days left.

I slammed the front door so hard that the framed caricature of Gabby and I fell to the ground. I collapsed against the door, and a series of expletives escaped my mouth at full volume as my back ran down the door. My sobs echoed on the cold hardwood floor. Smudges of mascara covered my hands and cheeks.

With my back pressed to the ground, I let myself feel the emotions. I allowed the heartbreak to tear me apart again. I screamed and shouted, the misery shuddering my entire body. Once I had shattered, I could put myself back together.

My phone rang repeatedly with calls from Nathaniel and Parker. I didn't answer. Once I moved to the couch, I took a peek at my text messages.

Gabby: Nathaniel called and told me what happened. Say the word if you need me.

Me: I'm fine. I just need to be alone.

Gabby: I'll stay with Nathaniel tonight. We'll talk about it tomorrow.

Me: Thank you.

I smiled at my kind best friend and reveled in the silence until Parker's latest message came through.

Parker: At least tell me you made it to the apartment, princess.

Me: I'm home.

I turned my phone off. I changed into an oversized t-shirt, pulled my hair up, and glued my butt to the couch. No matter how hard I tried, the interaction replayed in my head like a scratched CD.

I wanted to be angry at Parker, but I wasn't blameless. I should have backed away. I should have objected when he ran his fingers through my hair. But I didn't. I encouraged it, and now, I was sitting here, feeling the heartbreak I had felt as I drove to Virginia three years ago.

Around seven, someone knocked on my door. I dragged my feet to open it, not knowing who would be on the other side. My phone had been off all day.

I opened it to see Parker holding my purse and a bouquet of flowers. There were blue daisies in his hands, mixed in with what I assumed were other colors. His bright blue eyes were dimmed. He looked at me with a mixture of sadness and pity. I hated the look of pity.

"I could have just gotten my stuff tomorrow," I grabbed it from him and threw it on the island.

"I wanted to check on you," he walked in behind me. "I got concerned when I didn't hear from you all afternoon."

"My phone is off," I collapsed on the couch.

"I noticed when I called, and it went straight to voicemail."

He slowly walked to the couch and kneeled in front of me. He cupped my face with his hands. I hadn't cleaned off my mascara yet after I had done several rounds of crying. My arms stayed on my side, and I didn't meet his warm hands. "I broke one of your rules, so I came to beg for forgiveness on my knees. Apparently, quite literally. This whole thing is my fault, and I don't like it when you're angry at me."

"I'm not mad."

"You're not?"

I shook my head. "I wasn't exactly blameless when I grabbed your hand. I have no right to be mad at you for something I let happen too. You were comforting me. It just feels like I've broken up with Erik all over again, and we weren't even together. Plus, you brought me daisies, so how could I be mad at you? They're my favorite. I just wish I could see what colors they are."

He pulled me into his chest, and his scent took over me. He was still wearing work clothes, so there was a black smudge on his shirt when I pulled away. The shirt highlighted his eyes. I could stare at them forever, but I only had days to memorize every shade of blue they could be.

"Have you had dinner yet?" he asked.

I shook my head.

"When was the last time you ate?"

"Yesterday. I think. Nathaniel was bringing me breakfast from Gabby's. I know...I know...I'm sorry."

"It's okay. You don't have to apologize. I'll take care of you, princess."

He walked over to the back of the kitchen and rummaged through the pantry and the fridge. He started pulling out ingredients. I didn't recognize what they made together. I stared at him while he got organized, memorizing how his nose scrunched when he counted the containers. I walked to the kitchen and leaned on the island, staring at his muscular forearms as he rolled up his sleeves.

He caged me into the island and ran his knuckle over one of the mascara streaks that ran down my cheek. He easily lifted me and set me on the counter. The kitchen towel draped over his shoulder found its corner under the faucet as he soaked with warm water. He took the waffle fabric to my cheeks and the mascara that stained them.

"What are you doing?" I wrapped my hand around his wrist, stopping him.

He pried my fingers away and kept wiping. "Helping," he sighed.

He maintained his saddened gaze on my eyes as he wiped away my smudged mascara. This moment was oddly intimate. The lump in my throat grew tenfold with his touch, and I swallowed the new set of tears threatening to undo his work.

"I lied to you," he said.

My heart dropped. "About what?"

"My fears." The confusion on my face must have been obvious. "I told you weeks ago that my only fear was not living life. Well, I lied."

"What's your other fear?"

"Being like my dad."

Parker always spoke highly about his family, but as I ran the conversations in my head, his father was seldom mentioned as more than a passing character in a story.

"When I was a kid, he was angry all the time. Our house was a constant battlefield of arguing and fighting between my parents, between my sisters and him, and eventually, between him and me. He got it together when my mom threatened to leave him and take us with her. He's a great dad and a good man, don't get me wrong, but he's not the most pleasant when he gets into one of his moods. Every time I get angry, which happens quite often, I'm worried that I'll end up like him."

"Oh, Parker. You're not him."

"I know. But I wanted to tell you about him after what happened today. That's why I have the rubber band. I know you've never really asked much about it, but I've seen the look in your eyes when I snap it."

I ran my finger over the rubber sitting flush against his skin.

"I'll apologize to Erik for shoving him tomorrow once the mere sight of him doesn't make me want to throw him out the window. But I needed to apologize to you first. I know you care about him, regardless of my burning desire for him to fall into a volcano. But I couldn't contain myself when he yanked you. I wanted to kill him. You deserve much better than that, both from me and him. I'm sorry, princess."

"Thanks, I appreciate you not killing him. That would be hard to explain to his mom," I chuckled slightly. "I wanted to believe that he had changed, but he hasn't. I loved him once, and he will always be a part of me, but I don't feel the way I used to for him. Now, I just feel like an idiot for even considering that things could be different."

"No, Blake," he pulled me toward him until our chests were merely inches from each other. He stood between my legs. "You're not an idiot. Far from it. Feelings just make us do crazy things."

I rested my head on his chest. His heartbeat was pounding.

He was right. Feelings make us do crazy and stupid stuff. They have us believe that things can radically change. They give us the power to face our fears and jump off cliffs. They encourage us to pursue something, even if it involves signing up for a painful ending.

He pulled back from me and finished wiping off the mascara in silence.

"What are you making?" I asked when I was no longer mesmerized by how intensely he looked at my face while he brushed the makeup away.

"Comfort food."

Like the first day he cooked for me, he moved seamlessly within the kitchen. My parents were not great chefs, so the bar wasn't set high, but his food was the best.

I watched him season some chicken and bread it. He covered a pan in oil to fry it. While the chicken cooked, he mixed ingredients and pulled out Gabby's waffle maker. He was making chicken and waffles. The smell of fried chicken crowded the apartment once he was done and set the plates on the table. He pulled the syrup out.

"It's my favorite comfort food, so I brought you a taste of Texas today."

"Thank you," I mumbled through a mouthful of fluffy waffles.

We had been ignoring the elephant in the room. We were set to expire in a couple of weeks. I didn't know whether we should talk about it or just let it happen, but every time I thought about it, I knew it was a conversation I didn't want to have.

I looked at him again. I tried to memorize the proud blue of his eyes as he savored his waffle.

Chapter Twenty-Eight

WEDNESDAY MIDDAY.
Ten days left.

Richard cleared his throat behind me while my lunch spun in the microwave. Almost everyone was gone for lunch. The pizza place down the street was having a ridiculously cheap deal, and everyone jumped on it. The floor was quiet.

Amelia and Parker sat at one of the tables in the corner of the break area. She wasn't happy with him, and he wasn't happy with her, but unlike Gabby, they were good at whispering. Lainee and Nathaniel ate at the table across from the microwaves. Lainee told Nathaniel a story I thought would have him rolling on the floor laughing.

Richard wore navy blue slacks with a white button-down. He stood closer than usual. A faint smell of soap emanated from him. He seemed taller than usual. He was almost imposing.

"Hey Blake, can we talk?" his quiet voice asked.

"What's up? Is there something wrong with the numbers I sent you?"

"No, no. I haven't looked at them yet, if I'm being honest. I just wanted to apologize."

"Apologize?" my heart rate increased.

This had all the markings of being a personal interaction and not one I wanted to have in the break area. I looked around. Lainee was hooked on her story. Nathaniel was paying attention, but his eyes occasionally darted toward us. Amelia huffed at Parker and stomped to the conference room, muttering under her breath. Parker stayed on the table, pretending he wasn't trying to listen to Richard and me.

"About the party. I know you told me what happened, but I mistakenly thought it had been a long time ago, so it wouldn't be such a big deal. Erik and I talked, and now I just feel terrible."

"It's okay. Now you know."

"Yeah, but you told me what you wanted to do, and I ignored it," he took a step closer, taking my hand into his. "I'm sorry."

"Can we talk about this later?" I tore my hand away from his. I didn't want to be touched at work. The faint snapping of rubber against skin came from Parker's table.

"You've been ignoring my texts, so no."

I cleared my throat.

"Look, Blake," he kept his voice low and slow. "I care so much about you, and I like you a lot. I feel happy around you and want to make this official."

"Richard, this is not –"

He suddenly stepped forward, and his cold lips cut me off.

His hands cupped my face and pulled me into him before I knew what happened. I wanted to slap or punch him, but I was conscious of the fact that we were in the office. Yet, that didn't seem to matter as much right now.

"What the fuck?!" I shoved him off and took a step back. My back hit the edge of the counter, and a stinging pain shot through it.

Lainee was taken aback. Neither of the boys reacted, although they both wanted to. Lainee's eyes were wide, staring right at us. She gasped slightly and brought her hands to her mouth.

I switched to Parker. His jaw twitched, and his blue eyes were the color of the deep ocean. Dark and scary. His hand tightly gripped the cup he drank his coffee from. The veins in his hands were popping. His other hand held onto the table as if that was the only thing stopping him from coming over here. The rubber band sat torn on it.

Nathaniel looked between Parker and I. Lainee looked to him for an explanation, an idea of what was happening, but he was waiting to see how it played out. I could read in his eyes that he was assessing whether he should walk Parker out or step in to help me. I nudged him toward Parker. I could take care of myself.

He told Lainee to give Richard and me some privacy. She nodded and walked away. Nathaniel gripped Parker's bicep and dragged him away.

"This was not the time nor the place!" I said through gritted teeth.

Richard's eyes went angry as what he thought would be a romantic gesture was rejected. It was the exact thing I had asked him not to do. I was mortified. Embarrassed. "What the hell was that?!"

"Blake, I didn't want to wait any longer. We don't have to keep our relationship a secret. I don't want it to be a secret anymore."

"Kissing me here, at work, in full view of other people, is not the way to ask for that!"

"Blake, I –"

"No, Richard. No. I asked to keep our relationship under wraps, especially as we work on this project, and you blatantly disregarded me. We're not together in any official capacity, even in private. You made clear that you wanted the option to date other people when we started seeing each other, and I made it clear in our rules that something like this was completely inappropriate!"

"The rules you set were stupid, Blake. I was wrong to ask that of you, not realizing how incredible you are and how much I like you. I see how Erik looks at you. I hear how he talks about you. I'm not stupid. I can see the regret in his eyes for letting you walk away from him. It made me realize that I don't like the thought of you with anyone else. I can't let anyone else have you. And I won't make the same mistake Erik made!"

"Excuse me? I'm not property to be had! You can't even respect one of my basic boundaries!"

"You're seeing other people, aren't you?"

Hiding things had gotten me into this mess. I wasn't going to let it drag me even further in.

"You know what? Yes, I am! Like we agreed we were allowed to do. But that's completely irrelevant. What you did was completely unacceptable, and you knew it wouldn't be welcome."

"I'm sorry, Blake. But what I said was true. I like you so much, and I think we could have something special. I...acknowledge...it wasn't the best way to go about it, but you had been ignoring me."

"I can't right now. I don't know, Richard. We need to put a pin in this. I need some time away from you."

"Okay, okay," his eyes were shameful but angry. "I'm sorry. I can wait for you. Erik made the mistake of letting you go once. I'm sure he'll do it again, and we'll have all the time in the world to figure us out after he's gone."

I turned around and left him standing in the break area. There would be no us after this. He had crossed a line I was sure we could not come back from. His disregard for the most basic ask was telling. If he ignored these boundaries, what else would he ignore later on?

If, by some cruel joke of the universe, the brief happiness I felt with him was the cause for the blue, I would be happy with just seeing the sky for the rest of my life.

Chapter Twenty-Nine

FRIDAY NIGHT.

Eight days left.

I burrowed myself into the blue blanket, shielding my body from the fan. I was battered. Exhausted. Absolutely done with the week. My brain and body had been trampled by elephants, run over by a train, and tossed off the side of a mountain. I would eventually recover, but I needed this to be over.

"What a hell of a week."

"Are you doing okay though?" Gabby walked over with the pizza that had just been dropped off at our door.

"No," I laughed, somewhat maniacally.

"I'll drink to that."

We tapped our plastic cups filled to the brim with wine.

Gabby didn't force me to talk about anything. She sat beside me and played my favorite movie until I was ready. I wanted to keep it all in, but I needed answers to at least one question. My mind was plagued with all sorts of thoughts.

Erik would be out of the picture of my personal life for good. Once next Sunday rolled around, he would be on a flight back to California. I would keep the memories of the laughter, the love, and the hurt forever. They were a part of who I was, but that's all I wanted from him.

Parker would be on a flight back to Texas next Saturday morning. Just as quickly and abruptly as he entered my life, he would exit. I was bracing myself to say goodbye to any more colors and to say goodbye to him. I braced myself for a kind of heartbreak I didn't understand was possible.

Then, there was Richard.

"Honesty moment. Can I ask you something?" I turned to Gabby.

"No, I'm not an alien. Yes, you can have the leftover muffins in the fridge."

"Debatable. Thank you. But that's not it," I hesitated on my phrasing, but I needed to be straight to the point. "The only people in this world you hate are people who hurt animals and the guy that left the café without paying that one time. Why do you hate Richard so much?"

"You're just angry at him, Blake. I don't want to ruin your image of him or whatever you guys have."

"We won't have anything anymore. Even after Parker and Erik leave, I can't build a life with him."

Her chest rose with a deep breath and then collapsed. She looked at me with a sincere yet regretful look in her eyes. "Where did Richard tell you he grew up?"

"He never did...He just said he grew up near a river. In hindsight, I probably should have asked more."

"He grew up in Mississippi, but his family moved here when he was a junior in high school." I turned to her, confused. "Richard and I have known each other since high school. He was a junior, and I was a freshman when things got complicated..."

"Gabby...what happened?"

"Nothing bad like what you're probably thinking. It was actually kind of stupid. I had a schoolgirl crush on him. He thought it would be funny to lead me on for months. I mean, I thought the guy had created the sun back then. He just saw me as an annoying little girl when he broke my heart."

"Oh, Gabby," I set my hand on her shoulder.

"It was a long time ago, but it shot my confidence in love. It made me an easy target for people like Jackson and continually messes with my relationship with Nathaniel. But I'm working through it. It's crazy that what someone does to you at fourteen can follow you for a long time."

"Why didn't you tell me?"

"You seemed to like him, and he was also a kid back then. We all make mistakes, and this was a childish one. People grow up, and they change. I didn't want to ruin what he could be for you."

I hugged my best friend tightly. "You are too sweet for your own good."

"I'm sorry about everything, Blake. Him. Erik. Parker. You're set to be hurt, and it's all my fault."

"What do you mean it's your fault?"

"I was the one that pushed you to go out with Parker. I was the one who kept pushing you to enjoy life more, and it's about to destroy you. I'm so sorry."

Gabby never cried, so the sight of tears in her eyes was foreign, and I didn't know how to comfort her. On one hand, she was right. Every risk I had taken in the last three months was thanks to her advice. But she was completely wrong if she thought I believed it to have been a mistake. Everything I did was my choice, and I would do it all over again regardless of how much it hurts.

"Gabby, no. Please, no. You have no reason to feel bad about anything. I chose to do all of this. I could have stopped it at any point, but I didn't. I knew what I was signing up for. And guess what? Now, I have three months of wonderful memories and learning experiences I wouldn't have had otherwise. No matter how I feel or what happens, this does not go in my regret column. I have felt more in the last three months than in the last three years, and I would rather have the memories than nothing at all."

There was a beat of pensive silence between us. Tears rolled down both of our cheeks.

"You love him, don't you?"

I sighed. "Unfortunately."

Chapter Thirty

THURSDAY NIGHT.
Two days left.

The smiling faces in the private event room in the back of the restaurant stared at Connor as he got ready to start his speech. We were celebrating the launch of Project Porcelain as a team. His wife stood proudly next to him, holding their daughter's hand and ready to pop with their son any day now.

Everyone involved in the project was invited, including the rest of the leadership team from Capital Media. Hugh, Connor's right-hand man, flew in from California for it. Amelia's wife Kate flew in from Texas to celebrate. She was the complete opposite of Amelia, according to Parker. They must balance each other well because they seem as happy as I have seen anyone be. Kate and Parker were just as close as he and Amelia were. The three of them kept making little bets along with Amanda.

I bet you Parker will order a lemonade and not a Coke. He did.

I bet you Amelia will trip over the ledge at least once if she goes to the bathroom. She did not.

It was interesting.

Connor clinked his glass, and we all took our seats.

Stephen was joined by his carbon copy daughter. She and Desha were chatting about the Barbie movie and how her dad was awesome for taking her. Jamie's boyfriend was chatting with Nathaniel about their common sales background and making sports jokes. I had a feeling that Nathaniel had his eye on him as the next member of their softball league.

Gabby didn't leave my side all night, which might have been the only thing keeping me from falling apart. I avoided talking to anyone as much as I could, afraid I wouldn't be able to contain myself.

"All right, everyone," Connor cleared his throat. "Thank you all for coming tonight and celebrating the successful launch of Project Porcelain with us. On behalf of Capital Media, I want to extend our most sincere thank you to the Truly You team for the faith and confidence you placed in us to handle this. I am very proud of what our teams have accomplished and look forward to a continued productive relationship between our two companies."

Claps around the room.

"Over the last few months, a lot of hours have been poured into making this project a success, and I want everyone to know that it does not go unnoticed. Now that it's official, I also have a big announcement to make. Capital Media will be opening two new locations in the US to serve our Midwest and Southern customers better."

Cheers spread across the room. Parker made eye contact with me, pride emanating from him. I knew Richard had already been assigned as the Finance Director. Erik was as surprised as everyone else.

"We will have dedicated teams for each region of the country and look forward to placing a more personalized focus on all our customers. Now, you might be wondering how this will work. The details will be announced in a company-wide communication, but we have three representatives of our national leadership team in this room who have all accepted their new roles. Overseeing our national salesforce, none other than one of the individuals who made all of this growth possible – Nathaniel Williams, National Sales Director."

More clapping. Gabby hugged Nathaniel as if she didn't already know. Nick high-fived him across the table.

"In charge of ensuring we don't go broke with wild ideas will be Richard Trenton, Finance Director."

Slower claps.

"Now, I think we all know where this is headed. This last individual is young but motivated and relentless. She will ensure that our standards are met and that we continue to put forth our best efforts for our customers. She has been with us from the very beginning as one of my first hires. None other than Blake Johnson, National Account Management Director. Now, I do believe she has some words for all of us."

Claps and cheers rang in my ears, muddled with congratulations. I knew he planned to announce this today, but I hadn't been ready. The change in my life dragged me out to water like a riptide, but I had enough practice at pretending to be functional to talk for a few minutes.

"Thank you, Connor," I stood and anxiously smoothed my dress.

I looked around the room and took a deep breath. Parker's confident blue eyes roamed my body. His attempt to hide it was laughable. Erik's sad and angry eyes broke my heart again. Richard eyed me skeptically.

"I want to start by thanking every single person in this room. Everyone here has put countless hours of hard work and many brain cells into making this project a success and this expansion possible. I hope you all know how much I appreciate all the work that has been poured into this, and I hope you know that none of this would have been possible without you guys. Jamie was reviewing some initial engagement numbers on our tester posts, and I think we certainly have a great ride ahead of us with many successes. We appreciate you, Amelia, and your entire team for taking a chance on a small company that could take you to a big place. I look forward to continuing to impress you for the duration of the contract and, hopefully, many years of collaboration. Your contract will be moved under the southern regional office umbrella, but I will ensure that whoever heads your account is the best of the best. That is a promise. On a more personal note, I'm going to miss all of you! It has truly been a blast to have some new faces and voices around the office. But it's time to check off Project Porcelain Phase One from my never-ending to-do list!"

Laughter was heard as dinner was served. I sat back down and sighed. Gabby sat to my right. She threw her arm around me as a congratulation, but I knew she meant it more as a comforting gesture. The feelings of this ending weighed heavily on my heart.

I was incredibly proud of everything I had accomplished over the last three months. My team had been great, and we successfully managed all our projects. We all deserved some time off. I intended to take a few days off to decompress, which was a new thought in my head.

I was also proud of letting myself have fun for three months. Incredible experiences, facing fears, and finally seeing the ocean again. My habit of working late had almost been squashed, except for a few occasions. I was sleeping better and longer. My eating improved.

On the other hand, this spelled the end of Parker and me. We had actively avoided that topic or addressed him leaving, but we could both feel it. He would go home in a couple of days to continue reading long documents and advising Amelia on legal stuff. I would be here, deciphering my new position and how to grow the company I loved the most. The late-night calls, the incredibly creative dates, the gym encouragement, and the relaxed bad-movie binging sessions would disappear.

I didn't know what my life would look like after Sunday, but I could afford to take a few days to heal.

Chapter Thirty-One

Friday afternoon.

Less than twenty-four hours left.

Amelia rented out a rooftop pool for a few hours to celebrate the rollout of the campaign in a less official capacity. We had all grown as friends over the last three months, and I thought they deserved a proper goodbye. So did the California team.

The place had a beautiful view of the city, nestled deep within the skyline with soaring buildings surrounding us. It was the kind of place where they would shoot movies, so I felt like a celebrity. Part of the wall opened up to a bar inside that had started to get crowded. We only had the pool for another hour before it opened to the public.

I sat at the furthest end of the pool from everyone, taking a few minutes to admire it all and take it all in. Lainee and Amanda sat on the pool chairs, laughing at something on their phones. I would love for her to manage their contract if I could convince Lainee to move to wherever we decided to put the southern office. Nathaniel draped his arm around a content Gabby and chatted with Stephen and Nick. Desha, Jamie, and Melanie were having their own conversation by the stairs of the pool. They reminded me of high schoolers with the way they were laughing. Richard and Erik stood by the bar window, waiting for their drinks.

Amelia sat with Kate at one of the tables off to the side, talking to Parker. She was smiling, but it didn't reach her eyes. Kate had a stern and concerned look. She was pointing something out to him and kept poking the table. Parker's head was down, avoiding eye contact with both of them like a kid in trouble. His shoulders tensed.

They were all flying out in the morning. By lunchtime, they would be gone. The California team was leaving Sunday morning. Erik has asked to have one last meal together, but I declined.

After today, my life would go back to normal. Predictable. Part of me was sad about it, but another was relieved.

My eyes found Amelia scowling at Parker now. Kate was trying to run interference between them at this point. I wished I could read lips to know what they were saying. Parker adamantly shook his head and ran his hands through his hair before pushing his chair away and walking toward me.

I looked up and locked into his blue eyes. I sat up straighter and shared a smile with him, hoping to comfort him. His tattoos were in full display, and his swim trucks were probably a little shorter than they should've been. Almost everyone had been shocked at how much ink covered his body when his shirt came off.

"Honesty moment?" he said, taking a seat next to me. His thigh pressed against mine as his feet met the water next to mine. "I'm going to miss this place."

"This place is going to miss you," I kept my eyes on the movement of the water as I dangled my feet.

"How about you?" he faced the skyline, avoiding eye contact with me. "Are you going to miss me?"

Over the last week, I tried to commit everything about him to memory as best as I could every time I looked at him. I memorized every laugh line that formed on his left cheek with his smile, his sometimes earthy and sometimes smokey scent, the feel of his hand on my waist and how his fingers pressed in every time he pulled me in for a kiss, and the sound of his labored breathing while we jogged. But I especially memorized every shade of blue in his eyes.

After tomorrow, what I memorized would be all that's mine to keep.

"Blake?" he whispered.

"Yes, I will."

He leaned back, putting his hand over mine. It was warm and sent goosebumps up my arm. His touch left like a jolt of electricity on my body.

"I want to spend more time with you before we leave tomorrow."

"Aren't we spending time together right now?"

"Alone."

For the millionth time in the last few months, my brain warned against something that would undoubtedly be a bad idea. I wasn't confused about what I felt for him, but I knew from the beginning that this was temporary. I should say no, but I could never say no to him.

"Okay. Do you want to grab some ice cream tonight? We could go to Scooped."

"How about I come over and make some food?" he countered.

"You know I can't turn that down."

His lips curled into a smile. Laugh lines appeared on his cheek. His gaze was still locked on the buildings in front of us. There was a moment of heavy silence between us. We both knew it was over no matter what happened over the last few months.

"Will you visit me?" he asked.

I saw his gaze move toward me from the corner of my eye. His Adam's apple bobbed hard as he swallowed, waiting. His eyes weren't full of life for the first time in months. They were sad. And it was tearing me apart.

"Do you want me to?" I asked.

"Yes."

"Then, yes."

"Promise?"

I made eye contact with him for the first time since I sat down. This might be the only promise I couldn't keep.

"I promise."

He let out a sad chuckle and put his arm around my shoulder, pulling me into a brief but lingering hug. He hesitantly released me and shifted his body toward me. His hand reached my knee and squeezed it. I laughed as a tickle ran up my leg.

"There's that smile that I love to see," his hand lingered on my knee as I met his eyes.

I looked away and inadvertently met Richard's fiery eyes. Erik was standing too close to him, whispering something in his ear. I knew he was telling him about what he saw outside of the office.

"I knew it!" Richard's anger flared, and his scream distracted everyone in the pool. "I fucking knew it!"

Richard crossed the pavers towards Parker and me. He left his drink at the bar, and his fists were curled into balls at his sides. I tore myself off the edge of the pool and stood up to meet him.

"You are sleeping with him!" he screamed, getting closer to me. "Dammit, Blake, I knew it. I knew I wasn't imagining things when he looked at you. He knew your favorite muffin. He defended an idea that even I knew was pretty bad. I knew it!"

"What are you talking about?"

All the other conversations around us stopped. Amelia had a defeated look about her.

"Don't play stupid, Blake! You know exactly what I'm talking about. You've been sleeping with Parker this entire time!"

Gasps surrounded me. Nathaniel let out an exasperated sigh.

"I'm not sleeping with him. We're friends!"

Calling Parker and me friends was wrong. It felt like it invalidated every feeling and every moment between us. But we also weren't sleeping together, and I would be dammed if I would let Richard believe so.

"Don't lie to me. Erik told me what he saw. This is why you wouldn't commit to me!"

"Richard, you have no idea what you're talking about!"

"So, this is your thing then? You go around, jumping from guy to guy until they've served their purpose to you. Is that why you wouldn't move forward with me? Because I have no contract or promotion to award you?"

"Excuse me!? What the hell are you implying?"

"You were sleeping with Erik when and until you were promoted to your role here. Then, as soon as you got your promotion, you left him."

"You know that's not all that happened with us! Why are you doing this?!"

"Now, you're sleeping with Parker. Tell me, superstar, did that earn us the contract too?!"

"Richard!" Nathaniel warned, wading through the pool toward us.

"Maybe you're sleeping with Braeden since you guys are so buddy-buddy on all your projects!"

My mouth was ready to say something, anything, but my brain wasn't cooperating. Anger clouded every thought I had. I stood there as Richard continued muttering accusations.

"For all I know, Nathaniel chooses you for his projects because you're doing him too!"

"Richard, enough!" Nathaniel demanded. Gabby rolled her eyes.

Erik smugly looked at me and sipped his beer. If his goal was to burn down my life and credibility because of what happened between us, this was certainly a way to do it. I could recover from this; I had to. But it helped solidify that the boy I knew and loved in him was long gone.

Parker's chest rhythmically rose and fell, and his new rubber band snapped at the pace of his breath. His jaw was strained, and the veins in his forearms were protruding. Amelia's eyes were wide. Kate whispered something in her ear that she agreed with. They both moved slowly towards Parker.

"This is so ridiculous!" Richard screamed at the sky. "You are just such a –"

"What the hell has gotten into you?!" I snapped, matching his anger to shut him up. "This is not the time nor the place to vent your frustrations with me about our private, personal relationship. You don't seem to understand that basic concept, regardless of how many times I tell you. I am offended that you genuinely think I would reduce myself to using my body to succeed. I have never slept with anyone to advance my career, and I never will!"

My heartbeat was running wild. I begged my own body not to do this right now.

"It would make sense, though, wouldn't it?!" his voice was slow, enunciating everything. "Maybe that's why superstar Blake has been able to rise so fast!"

"I've been able to rise fast because I work hard! I give my life to my job, and you have the audacity to question me like this? Who the hell do you think you are?!"

My hands were clammy and cold despite the sun beating down on me.

"Apparently, the only guy here who hasn't had the pleasure of screwing you!" he spat. "Maybe you should screw Connor while you're at it; really lock in that promotion."

"Fuck you, Richard!"

"Oh, no, no, I'm not worthy of you! I can't believe I wasted so much time on such a whore!"

A collective gasp emerged from everyone. The air around us lacked for a second. I couldn't breathe.

He had never laid a hand on me, but his words punched a hole through me. I wanted to slap him across the face and make him eat every word he said, but I couldn't move. And doing so would have been another bad idea in a string of bad ideas that led me to this moment.

"What the hell, Richard?!" Parker snapped and got in Richard's face. He wasn't much taller than him, if at all, but his eyes were dark and menacing, and his anger loomed over him. He shoved him back a few steps. "What the hell is wrong with you?!"

Out of the corner of my eye, Nathaniel rushed out of the pool, followed by Gabby. She instantly made her way to me. She set her hand between my shoulder blades and guided my breathing.

"Oh, look! It's big, tough Parker coming to Blake's rescue. Tell me, how does it feel knowing you had nothing but everyone else's left-overs?!"

This time, the punch was real.

Parker dropped Richard to the ground with one punch and would have kept going if Amelia and Kate hadn't pulled him away. They had recognized the signs of his anger, the same way Nathaniel and Gabby recognized the signs of my panic. They were only a couple of feet away from him when they pulled him back.

Richard scooted back on the floor, startled and with a cut on his cheek. Erik helped him back up. I tried to get to Parker, but Gabby held me back, shaking her head.

"I dare you to say that again," Parker threatened Richard. Amelia stood in front of him, both hands on his chest. "Give me a reason."

"Forget it," Richard scoffed. His ego and cheek clearly hurting. "She's not worth it."

Richard walked around Parker somewhat cautiously. Erik followed him. Amelia whispered something to Parker, but he didn't tear his angry gaze from Richard until he disappeared into the watchful crowd inside the bar. Erik slowed down as he passed me. Nathaniel stood next to me.

"Blake, I–" he mumbled, barely audibly.

"Go screw yourself, Erik."

He followed Richard out.

Gabby led me to a chair and breathed with me, the adrenaline of the argument wearing off. It left me with a pang of exhaustion, and my body trembled. Amelia forced Parker onto a nearby chair. He sat on the edge, head hanging down.

"I should go home," I whispered under my breath. We were only five blocks from the apartment.

"We'll walk you home," Nathaniel chimed in.

I shook my head. I needed to be alone. "No, I'll walk myself home."

"Blake, let us walk you home," Gabby insisted. "You're in no state to go by yourself."

I shook my head, and they didn't push me.

"No," Parker stood up. "I'll walk you home."

"No! I will walk my own damn self home!" I almost screamed, leaving everyone stunned. I turned to Gabby. "Will you grab my stuff when you leave, please?"

She nodded and hugged me. I pulled my coverup over my swimsuit and grabbed my keys from the table. I had to leave with whatever shred of dignity I still had left. How I was going to face my team on Monday was now a mystery to me.

I went down to the street and started walking home. I was angry. Embarrassed. The last few months had seen more outbursts and feelings out of me than the last few years. I didn't know how this would impact Connor or our contract, but I'm sure I would find out soon enough.

"Blake!" A woman called after me. The popping of her flip-flops got louder as she ran toward me. "Blake, wait!"

"Amelia?" I turned. "I really don't mean to be rude, especially after what you just witnessed, but what do you need?"

"Just give me five minutes, please."

After the embarrassment I had just suffered, the last thing I wanted to be told was that our contract was pulled. I wouldn't blame her for wanting to. We didn't necessarily give her the best version of us. I wouldn't want someone like me managing my brand, either.

She motioned to the bench off to the side. I followed.

"Are you okay?" she asked.

"No," I cynically chuckled. "No, I'm not."

"Yeah, I figured as much. That was...a lot."

"Tell me about it."

"Men can be unpredictably stupid sometimes, as portrayed by what both Richard and Parker did," she shrugged. "Unfortunately, women are not excluded from that narrative. I have a few things to tell you. First, I wanted to ease your mind that Truly You is more than happy to keep the contract with Capital Media. I knew this would be the forefront thought in your mind. Parker has told me how much your job means to you, and I've observed it first-hand. This was a completely separate and personal issue, so I just wanted to let you know that."

"Oh wow, thank you. I really appreciate it. I am so sorry that you had to witness that. I don't know what got into Richard. He's usually fairly levelheaded."

"Can I talk to you, not as a client, but as a friend? More specifically, as Parker's friend."

"Be my guest. Please."

"I know you're not sleeping with Parker, but I know you're not just friends like you claim to be."

"He told you?"

"Yes and no. I assume that Parker told you we've been friends for the better part of two decades. I knew about you the day he met you. We talked that night to make sure we had everything ready to go, and Parker told me all about his new friend. When I arrived on Sunday, I got more details. It was a woman that he met at the gym. This new friend, according to him, was incredible. She was smart, gorgeous, funny, and a workaholic, just like him. Finally, someone that understood him."

"He said that about me?" Her words warmed and broke my heart at the same time.

"He said a lot more, but I don't think it's my place to tell you what else he said. He can be a little too honest and...descriptive... sometimes."

"Oh God..."

"Anyway, he had one of the most fun weekends of his life and couldn't wait for me to meet her because he was sure I would love her. Then, he shook your hand rather uncomfortably, which is odd for the extrovert in him. Then, he adamantly refused to let me meet this friend with excuse after excuse. She was busy. She was out of town. She had grown a third head. I made that one up, but I really think he considered using it."

"Some days, I felt like I was going to grow a third head for sure," I laughed. She chuckled.

"I saw how he looked at you while you were presenting, but for a minute, I just thought he had a massive crush on you. I mean, you're smart and beautiful. Any man would be lucky to have you. Then, he knew your muffin preference. Blake, he and I grab coffee together three times a week, every week, and he still doesn't know how I take my coffee. But the nail in the coffin of my suspicion was the mug. I was there when he bought it for his 'friend,' and then you had it the day I came into your office. It was kind of easy to put everything together from then."

"Oh, goodness..." I felt stupid for keeping the mug in the office. I should've known that he would be with Amelia when he wasn't with me.

"So, I confronted him a few days ago about it, and he told me everything."

"I do want you to know that neither of us knew we would be working together when we first met."

"I know. He told me it was a shock. I know the man like the back of my hand, Blake. He looked at you differently. He was happy around you. He's been the happiest I have seen him in a long time while we've been here."

"Amelia, I appreciate everything you're saying," I sniffled. "But it doesn't matter. You guys are leaving tomorrow, and I'll be here. It's over."

"I know, but you deserve all the information before we board that plane."

She stood up and hugged me.

I appreciated her words and the 'information,' but I had to accept the harsh reality. As much as I didn't want him to, Parker was leaving in the morning. I repeated in my mind that this was never supposed to be permanent, just fun. No strings. No commitments.

It had been the most fun three months of my life, but that's all it was. Three months of fun. He was going home to continue his own life. I would stay behind and try to salvage the pieces of my life after the bomb that fell on me.

Nathaniel was right. I got bold and reckless. I should have been more careful.

I aimlessly walked back to the apartment, watching the lights come on as the sun set behind the buildings. The apartment felt empty with most of the décor that Gabby took down, and it would soon be emptier once she was gone. She owned most of the furniture, so I had to start thinking about how to decorate. I considered downsizing since it would just be me.

I stepped into the shower and sat on the floor. My tears joined the water dripping down my face. I sobbed into my knees and repeatedly tried to catch my breath. The echo of the bathroom made it even harder to calm down. The warm water ran out, and I resigned myself to finish showering with cold water. I deserved this anyway.

At some point, Nathaniel and Gabby came back. I could hear their hushed voices in her room while they packed. They were trying to give me space, but movers were coming for Gabby's stuff on Monday, and they hadn't finished packing. But I also knew they were trying to keep an eye on me.

I put on a zip-up blanket over my underwear and watched TV on the couch. I would be lying if I said I was paying attention.

This whole time, I knew the end of the project would spell pain for me. But this was a kind of pain I wasn't expecting. Heartbreak was not the only emotion taking residence in my heart today.

The pain of losing Parker was searing, making it feel like my chest was on fire. The thought of him not being there on Monday morning was devastating. I thought back to the waterfall and how I had also lied to him. Going back to a world he wasn't in scared me. It terrified me more than anything else I had told him combined.

But amidst the pain, I felt Erik's betrayal. He was a speak or act before you think person, and it had consequences for me. I should have expected people to find out eventually, but I didn't expect it to be like this.

Humiliation was also on the docket. Richard's explosion in front of everyone was beyond reproach. On Monday, I would pull my team into the conference room and have an honesty moment with them about what happened. I would need to work to earn their respect back, but I was determined. I could only hope they didn't judge me based on my terrible non-work-related decisions.

It was almost nine o'clock when there was a knock on the door. I looked at the door, hoping it was a 'wrong apartment' mistake and they would disappear. After a few seconds, there was a louder knock. When it was clear that Gabby and Nathaniel weren't coming to open the door, I opened it.

Parker was on the other side. My outfit was embarrassing compared to his jeans and blue shirt, so let's add one more bad thing to today's column. The long top of his hair was wet and messy. There was a bruise on his hand.

"Hi," he whispered.

"Hi," I let him in. "Look, Parker..." I started before I was even sure of what I would say.

"No talking, princess."

His lips rushed to silence my words. My heart rate rose as I got on my toes, eager to be in his grasp. He pulled away for a split second to get a good grip on me. He lifted me up and slipped his arm under my butt. I wrapped my legs around him and clutched his hair.

His lips met mine again with all the pent-up emotion of the last few months. Lustful. Uncontrolled. I parted my lips to let him in, and he took the invitation. He bit my bottom lip for a second as he dug his fingers into my back, ensuring no space was left between our bodies. His kiss was minty, sweet, yet harsh.

He pulled away and nestled his face into the crook of my shoulder, squeezing me tighter. My arms wrapped around his neck as I breathed him in. The world stopped moving as we both caught our breath.

After however long I was locked into his embrace, he gingerly set me down, and my legs buckled. My breath was ragged in a totally different way than before. He dug his hand into my hair and pressed my face to his chest.

"Now we can talk," he whispered. "I'll start."

He cleared his throat and gathered the words in his mind. We still stood in the middle of the living room, but he took two steps back to give us space.

"I'm sorry about what happened today. I should not have lost my temper like that and taken the shot at Richard. That was way out of line. I know you can fight your own battles, and my anger did not help the situation. I am sorry about the punching part, and that part only, but I want to make it very clear that I am not sorry for defending you. I would not stand there and let him say all those horrible things about you without consequence."

"Thank you," I muttered.

"There's a lot I need to say, and I need to say it without you stopping me," he sighed. I nodded. "I just need you to listen. I've had the best time over the last few months. We explored so much, tried delicious food, and shared a lot of laughs. I've been lucky enough to steal many kisses from your sweet lips. Neither one of us was used to living in a world where the workday actually ended, but we managed it. We ran every other day, went out for drinks, and weren't glued to our laptops every weekend. Every day, I've had to remind myself that our time together is short and temporary. I've repeated that to myself every time I stared into your sparking and hopeful eyes, every time I heard your sweet, melodious giggles, and every single time you blew me away with your brain. I needed to stop myself from feeling the way I do..."

He took my hand into his. His body was trembling as I stared at his eyes. A wistful look enveloped them.

"We've succeeded a lot over the last few months. We had succeeded in keeping our...relationship...under wraps. We succeeded by launching what I know will be a successful campaign for companies we both love, and we tackled our goal to work less. But where I would have failed is if I boarded that plane without being honest with you. I am hopelessly and irrefutably in love with you. I don't expect you to leave your life behind any more than you'd expect me to leave mine, but I needed you to know. It scared me to board that plane without you knowing. You are the most brilliant, funniest, most dedicated, and most gorgeous woman I have ever met. I know you have started to believe that love is a choice and not a magical feeling that reveals the colors of the world. And as much as I respect that, I think you're wrong. There is absolutely something magical in the way that I feel about you. I love you, Blake Elena Johnson, and if I had the opportunity, I would choose to make you feel the magic that I do every second of every day."

He didn't let me get a word in before he pulled me into a kiss that felt like goodbye. He pulled back and rested his forehead on mine, giving me one more chance to memorize his blue eyes. They were tearful as he ran his fingertips down the side of my cheek. I stared at him, lost in his ocean eyes. My voice failed me.

My feelings about him were clear, but my choices were a little more complicated. I didn't know if I could love him the way I wanted to, the way he deserved, and be true to who I was.

Could I leave a man for my job? Yes.

Could I leave my life behind for Parker? I didn't know.

"I understand," he placed a kiss on my forehead. "I love you, princess. I'm going to miss you so much."

My breath was gone with him. My feet bolted to the ground. I stared at the white wooden door, feeling my heart shatter as I heard the elevator door close.

I didn't chase after him.

Chapter Thirty-Two

Saturday morning.

Out of time.

I poured myself a third cup of coffee with vanilla creamer as I stood in the kitchen. Sleep had been more than elusive last night. My body felt like it had been awake for a week.

On a typical Saturday, I would be sipping on a cup of Mr. Alder's coffee while browsing through the white tents. James and Adam would be cracking a joke at my expense over my love for their food while giving me a discount for it. Ms. Mabel would be showing me more pictures of her adorable grandchildren. Parker would be there with me like he had been every weekend for three months.

Except, he wasn't and wouldn't be anymore. My eyes shifted between the clock above our TV and my coffee. Parker should be in the air, on his way home now. His flight left a few hours ago, so he was likely closer to landing.

He was gone.

Gabby walked out of her bedroom. I gulped down the rest of my coffee and reached for a fourth. She looked at me, horrified that I was standing in our kitchen. Her palm went to her forehead, creating a loud smacking sound, and she let out a frustrated groan.

"What are you doing here!?" she almost screamed.

"What do you mean? Drinking coffee? Evaluating all of my life decisions?"

"Why aren't you with Parker?!" she stood across from me. I looked at her in confusion. Her face morphed from shock to horror. "Oh...my... goodness. Blake!"

"Is she still here?!" Nathaniel called out, hurrying out of Gabby's room. He sloppily closed his robe, hiding his heart-covered boxers.

"Yeah!"

"Do you guys know something that I don't?!"

"Let me put it this way," Gabby paced in front of me. "A man, who is gorgeous and perfect for you in every single way, comes and professes his love to you, and you just let him walk away?!"

"What was I supposed to do?" I asked, knowing what her answer would be.

"Ask him to stay?! I don't know! Go with him! Literally, anything else except go to bed and let him walk out of the apartment."

"Gabby, it's not like that. We were never supposed to end up together, remember? It was all temporary."

"You also didn't expect to fall in love with him, but then you did!" she yelled at me. "Yes, this started as some pact with a virtual stranger to go sightseeing and explore the city you live in, but Blake, it's so much more than that. You fell in love with the man!"

"Yes, Gabby, I know! So what?!" my voice broke. Tears started pooling in my eyes again. I thought I had a handle on it after crying all night, but apparently, my emotions and eyes had a mind of their own. "I don't live in a fantasy world! I don't live in a romance movie! Love is not enough! I have my job here, and I've always put my career first. He puts his career first. We live in different cities. It doesn't matter that I've had the best few months of my life. It doesn't matter that I fell in love with him. It doesn't matter because he's already boarded that plane. What am I supposed to do, Gabby?"

The daisies that Parker brought were dying. Petals dropped every time I slammed my hands on the counter. I would never get to see what color they were. I was stuck with just blue for the rest of my life, but I had made my bed. Now, I had to lie on it.

The room was starting to spin under my feet. I slowly collapsed on the floor against the kitchen cabinets and buried my face in my hands. I sobbed loudly. "What am I supposed to do, Gabby?"

A burly presence sat next to me, followed by a much more delicate figure in front of me. Nathaniel threw his arm around me, and I leaned into him, sobbing.

"Blake," his voice was soft. "We know each other well, right? We probably know more about each other than we should."

I nodded.

"Honesty moment. Do you trust me?"

"Almost more than anyone."

"Then hear me when I tell you this," he sighed. "I've seen a side of you over the last few months I hadn't seen in a long time. Since we left California. Maybe even ever. You've always been incredible at your job and fun to spend time with, but I had never seen you allow yourself to fully enjoy life outside of work after Erik. Parker helped you do that. He got you out of the office, and you were relaxed. You were happy. He tapped into a part of the old Blake that was hidden, afraid. When you came into work each morning, you were in such a great mood that it radiated to everyone else. It showed in your work. You've had some of your best ideas while not working yourself to the bone. I knew you when you were with Erik, and I know you now, and I can confidently tell you that Parker brought out a different Blake. A Blake who finally found a little bit of balance in her unbalanced world. A little bit of light and a little bit of color. He loves you, Blake, and you love him. Take it from me, don't wait to tell the person you love how much you love them."

He looked at Gabby. She crouched in front of me.

"Blake," her voice was kind. "I know you love Capital Media. I mean, how could you not after everything you've given to it? But there are similar jobs out there. I know you don't want to think it, but you can be incredibly successful elsewhere. There are other things that you can do for other companies, but there isn't another Parker. He makes you so happy, Blake. Please, for once in your life, choose to be happy."

The tears in my eyes blurred her face. My brain worked overtime to compensate for the hindrance my heart was causing. The montage of the last few months played in my head, just like it had last night when I stared at my ceiling. I imagined every ending possible, but I only looked forward to one. And it wasn't the one I had chosen.

I thought I had been happy with Erik, but if the last three months had taught me anything was that I wasn't as happy as I could have been. He had been my rock at one time, but he had been sinking me.

I thought I could be happy with Richard, but that had also blown up in my face. There was only so much steak and fancy wine that I could stand. He had been stable but boring. And, it turns out, a calmer version of Erik.

I looked between Gabby and Nathaniel. They looked at me with sad smiles and hopeful eyes. After watching them for two years and silently wishing for a sliver of what they had, I finally had that opportunity. And I had let it go.

Parker's face flashed in my mind, and all my senses were overwhelmed.

The picture of the strange but handsome man at the gym, with sweaty hair struggling with the lockers, brought a sad laugh out of me. The memory of feeling his hands on me as he carried me up the rock to face my fears and how he held my hand as we jumped sent shivers through me. The sound of the pounding music when we glided through the dance floor and of his confident voice booming across the conference room rang in my ears. The smell of the food I had grown accustomed to him cooking in my kitchen opened the pit in my stomach.

His tearful eyes from last night were burned into my memory. They were a beautiful ocean blue as he held back tears. My heart shattered, and the pieces attacked me like shrapnel. I wasn't sure what he expected or wanted me to say last night, but I didn't say the one thing I should have.

I didn't tell him I loved him.

"I didn't say it back," I whispered.

Gabby turned to me, stunned.

"Gabby, I didn't say it back!"

"What do you mean?" Nathaniel asked.

"He gave me a whole speech about how much he loved me, and I just stared at him. He left and boarded that plane without me telling him I loved him!"

"So, what are you going to do about it?" Gabby asked, almost in a taunting tone.

"What can I do about it?" I racked my brain. "He's gone."

"Planes go both ways, Blake!" Gabby jumped with her idea. She pulled out her phone and started looking for a flight. Within seconds, she had a solution.

"There's a flight that leaves in a few hours. If you pack and leave now, we can drive you to the airport, and you can make it."

"You think?"

"Yes!" Nathaniel lifted me from the ground and ushered me toward my room. "Gabby, buy the ticket. Blake, change and pack. I'm parked out on the street, so that'll be the easiest car to take."

I did exactly how I was told. I grabbed a backpack from under my bed and started packing. I threw in a couple of changes of clothes, my toothbrush, contacts, and my laptop. I changed out of my pajamas and into more appropriate public clothes.

Gabby booked me the flight and called out that we had to go if I had any chance at making it. We locked the apartment door and almost ran to Nathaniel's car. He risked a traffic ticket to get me there.

"Wait!" I turned back to Gabby's open window at the drop-off point. "I don't know where he lives."

"Call Amelia!" they both yelled back.

"Right! I love you both. I could never thank you guys for this."

"Blake, go!" Nathaniel yelled.

"We love you too!" Gabby called out as I ran through the doors to the terminal.

Chapter Thirty-Three

SATURDAY MIDDAY.

Six hours left.

The never-ending ring of the call echoed in my ears as I sat at the gate to catch my breath. She usually picked up the phone immediately. Maybe she didn't want to talk to me after I broke her best friend's heart.

"Blake?" Amelia questioned. "Sorry, I was in the yard. Is everything okay?"

There was a clattering of dishes in the background. Her voice was a combination of panic and expectancy.

"Yes, I just need a major personal favor. It's about Parker."

"What is it?" I heard her smile on the other end.

"I need you to send me Parker's address."

Amelia started laughing on the other end of the line, and Kate asked who she was talking to. She explained, and I could hear Kate laughing in the background.

"What's so funny?" I demanded, slightly hurt and annoyed at their amusement.

"Kate and I were taking bets with Amanda on how long it would take one of you guys to crack. I think Amanda wins with less than a day."

"You were taking bets on Parker and me?"

"It's what we do. Kate and I also had a bet about how long it would take Parker to admit he was in love with you. She won that one. I was surprised it took him as long as it did. Parker told me on the flight back what happened last night. When we saw him this morning, he was pretty broken up about it."

"Oh no."

"Oh, no is right. He left your apartment last night, convinced he would never see you again."

"I promised I would visit."

"It might have more to do with not telling him you loved him back. You do love him, don't you?"

"I do. I love him, Amelia. I was wrong to let him walk away. I should've told him. I didn't know what to do. Can you please give me his address?"

The flight attendant called for group one to start boarding.

"Wait, are you at the airport? What time do you land?"

"Around four."

"Send me all your flight details ASAP. Kate will go pick you up. Parker and his oldest sister are coming here for dinner. It took some convincing to get him out of his apartment, but otherwise, he would be sad and wallow with his body weight in pizza and beer."

"You're a good friend, Amelia."

Telling him I loved him, asking for forgiveness, and meeting his sister all on the same day. Wow.

"I'm glad you're choosing him, Blake. He loves you in a way I've never seen him love anyone. But I might have to momentarily hate you for breaking his heart."

"I promise I will never hurt him again if he doesn't hate me yet."

"Oh, Blake, he could never hate you. I'll see you in a bit."

I hung up the phone and joined the line to get on my flight. I absolutely hated flying since it poked at one of my biggest fears, but hey, I've jumped off the side of a small cliff; I could ride on one of the safest forms of transportation. I had Parker to thank for that.

I squeezed through the two women sitting on the aisle and the middle seat to get to the window. I settled in for the relatively short flight. My heart rate skipped again upon take off, but I distracted myself by thinking of what I would say to Parker when I saw him. It wasn't much of a distraction since my brain was stumped on any words.

"Why are you headed to Texas?" the woman in the middle seat asked while we were in the middle of the air. "Sorry, I like to ask questions on flights. It keeps me distracted."

"No worries," I laughed, appreciating the distraction. "I'm going to tell the man I love that I love him. It's a really long story."

"No way! It's like you're part of a Hallmark movie. Can you see color?"

"It sure feels that way right now. I can only see blue. How about you? Why are you headed there?"

"I can see color. I got married a few years ago," she explained. "I'm actually coming home. I was at a conference in Boston and just had a layover here. How did you meet your guy? If you don't mind me asking."

"I met him at the gym, but we worked together," I smiled at the kind stranger. "How about you?"

"College, classic class story. The more time we spent together over our first year, the more colors I could see, but I knew from day one that he was mine. We've been together for over ten years."

"Wow. Congratulations."

"So, if you can only see blue, how are you sure he's the one you love?"

Momentary doubt entered me. Everything lined up with Erik and Richard, and no more colors had developed since my fights with them. What was clear before was momentarily muddled in my brain. But the momentary doubt quickly dissipated. If, by some cruel twist of fate, Parker hadn't been the cause for the colors, I didn't care.

I wanted it to be him.

"I guess I don't, but he's the one that I choose to be with. Long story short, I spent the last handful of months having the best time of my life with him, and I can't imagine sharing those memories with anyone else. I would rather live in a world without color than in a world without him."

"That is so sweet! He's a lucky guy."

"No," I shook my head. "I'm the one that's lucky."

She put her hand over mine and gave me a reassuring pat. I blinked several times before I realized what was happening. The kind smile across her lips gradually became colorful in front of me. The color that once was just another shade of grey was now vibrant. Powerful. A hint of warning accompanied by passion. It highlighted how white her teeth were.

"I'm sorry, are you wearing lipstick?"

"Yeah, I am," she questioned me with her eyes and brought her fingers to her lips. "Why?"

"What color is it?"

"Red...Oh my goodness! OMG! You can see it."

"I can see it," I whispered. "I can see red."

"Can you see this too? They usually go together!" she rummaged through the pocket in the seat in front of her and held up the brochure to the airline.

The cover was a different shade than her lips. It was lighter and more of a subtle shade. It was almost a mixture of red and something else. It was an optimistic color.

I nodded.

"This is orange!" she smiled at me.

I returned her smile and looked around, taking in the new things that were now colorful. The seat in front of me had little speckles of orange spread through the fuzzy fabric. Gabby had done my nails in red a few days ago.

When we were about to land, I took a deep breath and opened the window. Seeing the tiny world below us gradually get closer made me nervous, but today was a day for facing my fears. I closed my eyes and walked myself through some deep breathing. When I opened them again, more of the world was alive in front of me.

The tops of the growing trees were vibrant. The greens of the world brightened, and I realized how much nature there was in the city.

The world was becoming more beautiful as the minutes went on, and I hoped to be able to appreciate it all one day. But what I said remained true. I would rather live in a world where Parker makes me smile every day than in one that's full of color without him.

Chapter Thirty-Four

Saturday afternoon.
Two hours left.

The air outside was heavy with moisture and heat. The sun was out, and I was sure you could fry an egg on the sidewalk. Tons of cars were waiting in the airport's arrivals parking lot. Amelia told me that Kate would be in a white truck waiting for me as soon as I walked out. My subsequent text was from Kate telling me to look up.

"Blake!" she called from across the street. I nodded and ran toward her. She pulled me into a hug as I finished climbing into the truck. "Amelia is so excited that you came. I want it on record that I thought it would be Parker who broke and rushed back to you. When we saw him at the airport this morning, we knew it hadn't ended well after he went to your apartment. Outside of, you know, what happened at the pool."

"Yeah, that was embarrassing," I felt my cheeks redden.

"I don't know. The idea of the person I love knocking down someone insulting me with one punch is romantic, don't you think?"

"I guess," I laughed as we drove out of the confusing airport. "It's just embarrassing when it happens in front of your coworkers and people that you have to face on Monday."

"Well, in the decade that I've known Parker, I've never seen him as much as threaten to hit someone. It's not something he typically lets himself do, but Richard really got under his skin."

Almost an hour later, Kate pulled up in front of a plantation-style red brick house surrounded by trees. I had no idea where I was, but the landscape formed a beautiful picture.

The house was nestled in through tall trees that rustled in the hot, hairdryer-like wind. They had red flowers lining the sidewalk to their opaque glass front door. The white window trims contrasted against the brick. I could see Amelia and Kate's personalities on full display.

I grabbed my backpack from the back seat and took a deep breath before entering their house. It was beautiful.

The floor underneath me was a dark shade of wood that I couldn't see yet. Immediately to the left, there was an office that was cluttered with papers. Books were on the ground, and boxes were lined against the walls. Then, I remembered they had just remodeled it.

To my left, there was a perfectly designed living room. They had a white couch that faced a flat-screen TV. Their house reminded me of a TLC show.

"You're here, you're here!" Amelia came around the corner screaming, throwing her arms around me. "You'll never believe what happened."

Amelia recounted the last twenty minutes that she spent on the phone with Parker. He had called to tell her that he was going to go back to Virginia tonight, even though there were no more direct flights anywhere near New Windsor. She had talked him out of it by reminding him that his sister would be coming tonight and that he needed another night to think about what he was going to do more thoroughly.

"It was tough to convince him and so hard to keep my voice still. He's going to die once he sees you!"

Amelia hugged me tightly and shook me like a rag doll. Kate joined in the hug, and I could feel their love for Parker. I helped them set up dinner while we waited for seven to roll around.

There was a light knock at the front door as I set the table. My heart rate raced, and I felt my pulse in my ears. Amelia looked at me to calm down and opened the door. A female voice traveled from the foyer to where I stood in the kitchen. I heard their steps as they made their way to me.

"No way!" the woman from the plane screamed when she saw me. "OMG! OMG! The guy you flew to is my brother! OMG!" The woman tried calming herself down amidst Amelia's confused look. "What are the odds?! You must be gym girl! Man, you're so much prettier than Parker said. I literally can't believe this."

"Wait, what?" Amelia looked between the woman and me. The scream brought Kate in from the backyard, who looked just as confused as Amelia.

Parker had told his family about me.

"We met on the plane!" Parker's sister jumped up and down, shaking Amelia by the shoulders. "She sat next to me and said some really sweet things about my baby brother. This really is like a movie!"

I was sure my face was bright red by now.

"Well," Amelia laughed. "Blake Johnson, meet Ciara Stanford – formerly Robinson. This is Parker's oldest sister. He didn't show you guys any pictures either, huh?"

"No! Mom was annoyed because she didn't understand why he was so secretive. I mean, he's usually so forthcoming with everything!"

"That makes sense," Amelia laughed. "He was trying to hide their relationship because of the whole work thing, and I'm sure his mom would have forwarded me a picture."

"It's nice to officially meet you," my voice quivered as I shook her hand.

"I'm so excited for Parker to get here!" Ciara squealed before putting her dish in the oven to heat up. "And yeah. Mom was always asking for a picture, but he adamantly refused. He also wouldn't tell us your name. He just referenced you as gym girl."

"I know!" Amelia agreed. "Your mom called me multiple times, asking me to figure it out, but Parker was really good at keeping this secret."

Parker knew his family would immediately run to Amelia and tell her everything. He wanted to uphold our agreement to keep us a secret so much that he kept identifying details about me from his family. The family that knew everything about him.

"What are the odds that he's totally gonna cry when he sees her?" Ciara asked. "I would bet my life savings on that."

"What is it with you all and bets?" I laughed.

I looked at Amelia and Ciara as they moved around the kitchen. I tapped my foot on the floor, waiting for Parker. Every minute that went by was one more beat per minute that my heart rate would increase. My hands started shaking, but I still couldn't think of what to say when I saw him.

Someone tried to open the door before ringing the doorbell. My heart rate was officially in dangerous territory.

"I usually keep the door unlocked, so he just walks in," Amelia explained. "I locked it so we would have a warning that he was here."

"That's so genius," Ciara praised. "I'll go outside with Kate and give you guys some privacy."

There was a second, third, and fourth ring of the doorbell. Parker was getting impatient. My hands got clammy.

"Are you ready?" Amelia asked before walking to the foyer.

"No, but I'm as ready as I'll ever be."

Amelia gave me a reassuring hug before she disappeared to the foyer. The house was big but open, so he would see me standing by the island as soon as he turned the corner. I gripped the edge, worried I would fall to the ground if I let go. I heard Parker's voice greeting Amelia. It was stiff and forced.

"Kate is going to be so excited that you made peach cobbler," Amelia said.

"Yeah, whatever."

"Don't be short with me, Park. You know I was right to tell you to wait. You can't go around making impulsive decisions."

"I don't need a lecture, Ame. I need Blake. I burnt the cobbler just a little, but I needed something to keep me occupied until dinner. Especially after you–"

They both materialized around the corner. He wore a black shirt with jeans, which seemed to be his staple outfit. His voice trailed off and went quiet. His blue eyes were wide, and his mouth parted open. I started at his hair; it was not what I expected.

He was a redhead.

"Blake," he finished softly. Amelia bowed out of the kitchen and went out to the patio with Kate and Ciara.

He stood in the middle of the living room, looking at me in the kitchen. I felt naked under his gaze. Vulnerable. He took unsure steps toward me, wondering if his imagination was making me up. Once he was close enough, I could smell his cologne again.

"Blake," he repeated under his breath.

He was inches from me, trapping me between his body and the island. He ran his bruised knuckles down my cheek, another check that I wasn't a figment of his imagination.

"I promised I would visit," I breathed out, shivering under his touch.

"What? But how? When?"

"I boarded a plane here about an hour after you landed. Look, Parker, I need to apologize."

His head cocked slightly, and he narrowed his gaze. His confusion was genuine. I took a deep breath in and out.

"I need to apologize for letting you walk out of my apartment last night and letting you board that plane without being honest. Parker, you are intimidatingly smart and annoyingly funny. You push me to try new things, even things that terrify me, like jumping off a cliff. You have given me the incredible gift of color. But, regardless of it, you have given me the gift of a magical feeling I now understand as love. I am irrationally and unequivocally in love with you, Parker Scott Robinson. I don't care if love is a feeling or a choice because I'm ready to choose to feel this way for you every day. I am so sorry for letting you leave the apartment last night thinking that I wasn't."

Tears crowded my vision again, and his face became blurry. He grabbed my waist with one of his hands, leaving the other on the island, and pulled me until my body was against his. His familiar fingers dug into my spine. He was breathing heavily and staring down at me. I needed him to say something, but he quietly looked at me as if I was speaking a different language.

"Parker, please say something," I begged. I lifted my hand and lightly placed it on his cheek, not knowing what his reaction would be. He closed his eyes and leaned into my touch as I ran my fingers over his cheekbone.

"You're here," he muttered, finally convincing himself that I was real and standing in front of him. "And you love me."

"I love you," I repeated.

He kept his hand firmly on my waist and brought the other one to my face. He pushed back the strands that lay on my face and tucked them behind my ear. His thumb ran under my eyes, wiping away the tears running down my cheek.

"I told you I don't like to see you cry," he pressed his forehead against mine. "Please don't cry, princess."

"I'm sorry," I sniffled and chuckled. "I never expected to fall in love with you, and now I know that I don't want to live in a world without you. I won't stand here and promise that everything will be sunshine and rainbows because it will never be, but I'm willing to figure it out with you. You've shown me a life with balance, a life where I go home at a normal time and have something to look forward to. A life where I can work and excel at my career but also enjoy it outside of that. Good times or bad times, if you still want me, I will choose you every day. I'm not going to ask you to give up your career or your life here, but if this is what you want, I'm ready to leave Virginia and give us a shot."

"Blake, I can't ask you for that. Your career means everything to you."

"You're not asking me to. My career has meant everything to me, but I've realized there's much more to life than working a ridiculous number of hours a day. There are other jobs out here. I don't care what it is as long as I can be with you. But after last night, I understand if you don't want to be with me."

"Don't you ever think that. I want nothing more than to wake up next to you every morning and cook gumbo for you every Sunday. I just want to make sure that this is what you want."

"We don't have to have all the answers right now, but I'm sure," I threw my arms around his neck. "As long as you'll still have me."

He took my face in his hands, and his bright smile returned for the first time since he walked around the corner. He needily closed the space between us, and I felt his smile as he kissed me like it was the first time all over again. He sent a shiver down my spine and laughed when I wriggled against him. He kissed me like he would never let me go, like his life depended on it.

"We can figure it out," he whispered into my lips. "I don't care if we live in Virginia or here or in Timbuktu. I don't care if we have to harvest corn for a living. I love you, Blake."

I pulled him into me and ran my hands through his bright head of red hair. It was an unexpected color, but I loved it.

"I love you," I whispered into his lips.

"I'll never get tired of hearing that."

I pulled away from him and smiled. I didn't have to memorize his face anymore.

"There is something that I haven't figured out."

"What is that?" he kissed my neck.

"Can you see color?" I pushed him back slightly.

In all the time Parker and I spent together, I assumed he couldn't see color, just like me. He never talked about colors and never referenced being able to see them. But I didn't know if that was true. Did he know he loved me because the colors appeared for him too?

He chuckled. "I've always been able to see color, but I don't need my eyes to tell me how I feel about you."

"Wait, so you've been able to see color this entire time?"

"Yeah," he sheepishly smiled. "I've been committing everything about you to memory since we met because I thought we had an expiration date. I'm not sure how much you can see right now, but I've been falling in love with all of it. I love seeing your brown eyes in the sunlight, your blonde hair swinging back and forth as you run, and the way your cheeks turn pink almost immediately in the sunlight. I should confess something, though."

"What?"

"I've known you can see blue. You started staring at the sky more, and I saw the glimmer of recognition in your eyes every time you saw blue things. You kept staring at me every time I wore something blue, so I went shopping and bought more blue clothes than anything else I owned. I guess now I'll have to expand my closet."

"You are perfect, Parker." I clutched his shirt and pulled him in for a kiss.

Out of the corner of my eye, I saw Amelia, Kate, and Ciara with their faces pressed against the glass. They rapidly pretended not to be looking when we turned toward them.

"They're so nosy," Parker shook his head. "Sorry."

"Nothing to be sorry about having people like them in your life. Oh, you'll never believe how I met your sister."

I recounted to Parker my encounter with his sister on the plane. He revealed his plans to go back to Virginia tomorrow. We would have to talk about how exactly this would work, but for now, I was happy enjoying the moment.

Ciara almost tackled Parker to the ground when she came back inside, and we all stood in the middle of the kitchen for a minute, wrapped in a tight hug. Kate announced that the steaks were ready, and we all piled out to the patio for dinner. The food was delicious, and the view of the trees in the back was even better. The heat and humidity would take a while to get used to, but that was a sacrifice I was willing to make.

My stomach was full, and my heart mended from last night. I looked at the smiling faces around me. Parker's hand was firmly planted on my thigh as he chatted with his sister. I was feeling at home already.

I know I had made the right decision. But on Monday, I had to tell Connor I was leaving Virginia.

Chapter Thirty-Five

MONDAY MORNING.
A lifetime left.

Gabby and Nathaniel picked Parker and me up from the airport late on Sunday night. We caught them up on all the decisions made in the last twenty-four hours.

Nathaniel wasn't thrilled with my decision to leave since the dream of the power duo would be over, but he supported us wholeheartedly. Gabby threw back in my face how resistant I had been the first night she strongarmed me into dancing with Parker. I gladly gave her the credit.

Parker and I had many discussions over the last day while I stayed at his apartment. He offered to leave Truly You and settle in Virginia, but I couldn't let him do that. He was a big part of what made Truly You special, and Amelia needed him. Not to mention, most of his family was in Texas, and that was important to him.

I decided I would resign and look for a new job. There were plenty of jobs available and, with my resume, I would surely find something. I was worried about telling Connor, but at the end of the day, I was replaceable, and I would gladly train whomever he chose to replace me before leaving.

I shook in my flats as I walked into the building. Parker was going to wait downstairs for me. After this, we would grab breakfast and go get boxes to pack up my life.

"Are you completely sure this is what you want?" his eyes studied me, concerned.

"Yes," I confirmed. "I'm not going to lie and say that it's easy, but this is what I want."

"I just don't want you to regret it."

"Parker, I will never regret choosing you."

"Promise?"

"I promise."

He gave me a soft kiss, and I walked into the lobby. I didn't bother going to my office before I headed to Connor's. It was almost nine, so I knew he'd already be sitting at his desk. I knocked on his door, and he called me to come in.

"I was wondering when I'd be seeing you," Connor stood up from his chair, motioning for me to sit. I recognized his tone. He wasn't having a good morning, and I was about to make it worse.

I sat on the chair while he leaned back on his desk in front of me. He grabbed three pieces of paper from his desk and slightly waved them in my face. His arms were strained against his shirt, and his blue eyes were dark.

"We need to talk," I said.

"Oh, I would say so," he scoffed. The news of what happened probably had gotten to him before I could. He sorted the papers in his hand. "One of these is Richard's request to work out of the California office. One of these is an email from Amelia praising your work over the last few months but requesting that Erik and Richard be removed from any future projects involving Truly You. The last one is Erik's surprising resignation letter."

"Did you really print an email?" I tried to diffuse some of the palpable tension.

"I printed three. All of these came by email. Don't try to change the subject, Blake. What the hell happened?"

I let out a big sigh and looked up at him. He was angry but concerned.

I didn't know where to start, so I started at the very beginning. I told Connor everything he had not been privy to over the last three months. I began with meeting Parker at the gym. I gave him more detail than necessary, but I wanted him to know the whole story.

He listened intently and nodded along with my explanation. I walked him through my thought process years ago when I left Erik for Virginia. I told him about the beginning of Richard and me. Finally, I told him about Parker and our relationship. I was very clear that it started before we knew who each other was, but I admitted to it not being the best idea.

His face winced when I told him about what happened at the pool. He didn't seem as angry as I thought he would be but was clearly disappointed with our behavior. I had spent five years learning from him, and seeing the disappointment on his face was painful. If I wasn't planning to resign, I would understand if he fired me immediately.

Finally, I got to the end of the story.

"I have decided to move to Texas," I couldn't face him, so I stared at the ground. "I understand this isn't easy staffing-wise, so I can train whomever you choose to replace me with. I'm sorry that my decisions put your company's reputation at risk." I took a deep breath. "If I can speak candidly, and I will, I have realized that there is more to life than being holed up in the conference room for hours on end. I know that my relationship with Parker was...inappropriate...but it's one of the best things that has ever happened to me. I have loved working here every minute, and my job has always been the number one priority in my life, but I need to choose to be happy outside of these walls for once."

"Well," his gaze softened, and a small smile spread across his face. Almost paternal. "When I came in this morning, this was about the last thing I expected, but after reading the three emails, I knew you'd be by to explain. I've had time to think, and I don't accept your resignation. I would like to counteroffer."

"I'm sorry, Connor, but I've made up my mind," I stood up to stop him from trying to convince me. "As much as growing this company and working here has meant and done for me, no amount of money could make me stay."

"I'm not going to offer you money outside of the raise you were due for with the promotion anyway. Please, Blake, hear me out."

I slowly sat back down, questioning him.

"You are one of the greatest assets this company has, and I cannot let you walk out of that door knowing the growth we are facing. I have been impressed with you every day, starting with your class presentation. Over the last handful of years, you have been able to help me grow this company beyond what I imagined would be possible. I would be doing my company a disservice if I let you go."

"But I won't stay in Virginia."

"And you don't have to. There is no reason why my directors can't work from one of the other regions. After all, Hugh works out in California."

"Wait, what?"

"You know we're expanding into the South, and it seems we have just selected Texas as the new office location. It was on the shortlist anyway. I trust no one more than you to build a team because you have built a great one before. You can move there, find us a space, and grow a team there. It won't be easy, but I think you can do it. I've tried to discourage you from overworking but failed, so having Parker around will help you keep a balance. I want you to stay with us, Blake, and I think this is the best way to do it. Please tell me you'll consider it."

"I'll talk to Parker tonight and let you know first thing in the morning."

"I can live with that. Please take the day off. Hell, take the week if that's what you need."

I nodded and stood up again. "Thank you, Connor."

"No. You're the one that deserves a thank you, Blake. I am happy for you. I've seen you grow and develop personally and professionally, and I support your decision to choose yourself. I just hope you choose Capital Media too."

I left his office feeling better than when I had walked in. I had decided to take the opportunity, but I wanted to run it by Parker before agreeing to it.

I didn't have to choose between Parker and my job.

I could have both.

"How did it go?" he held out his hand for me to grab. We started walking to Gabby's for breakfast.

I told him everything.

"You're going to take it, right?"

"Absolutely. Whoever said you can't have it all was wrong."

"I'm so proud of you, princess."

He kissed the top of my head, and for once, I wasn't afraid that someone would see.

"We never finished the joke," I gasped, recalling back to our first night together. Parker stopped walking in front of the café, looking at me with a puzzled look.

"Two workaholics got together and started to enjoy life more..." I repeated. Recognition flashed in his eyes.

"...and they fell in love."

Epilogue

Almost A Year Later

MY LAPTOP CLAPPED SHUT in my empty, echoey office. It was just before four in the afternoon, and it was time to go home. My start time today was earlier than usual so I could get home earlier.

I walked out to the disaster of a bullpen. Boxes of records, packages of computers yet to be installed, bags of decorations, and mountains of supplies were scattered throughout the floor. Paintings and framed articles sat up against the wall of windows that allowed everyone to see into my office.

"I'll see you guys on Monday," I waved at my team.

Zach, our market researcher, was also packing up. He was my first hire for the southern office. He was headed to the lake with his wife for the weekend. They had invited us along, but Parker and I had a different kind of eventful weekend waiting for us.

Tilly, our new graphic designer, was chugging the last three ounces of her water bottle to hit her goal before leaving work. She was running a marathon this weekend. I wished her luck.

Jane, our executive assistant, was staring at the wall with a painting in her hands. We had bought some decorations yesterday, and I had tasked her with deciding where things went. She loved it and was great at it.

Lainee, our southern region manager, was writing in her planner. She had moved down a few weeks ago and would be spending the weekend setting up her new apartment. She had been promoted months ago but was finishing projects in Virginia and helping train the new northeast region manager.

I admired the new office, feeling proud of what I had accomplished. I had almost complete control over hiring decisions for the office, except for the sales team. Nathaniel controlled that part, but I knew he would hire an incredible few people for the South.

We had been in our new office for over six months, but we were finally getting around to decorating it. I had managed to hire the first four people, but there were still a couple of open positions. We were missing an on-site IT specialist and a financial analyst.

Connor had filled Erik's position as the west manager with an incredibly capable guy, Jerry. He reminded me of myself when I was his age. I could tell he was going places. I was working on training him, as well as developing what my new role would look like.

Connor decided to establish the Midwest office in Chicago. The Midwest manager, Erin, had started a few weeks ago, so we were still in the learning phase. But she was already impressing me as well.

I walked out to the car, and the weather felt nice for a change. It was my first spring in Texas, and it hadn't stopped raining in weeks. But today, the sun was bright, and I wasn't boiling to death. It was slightly chilly.

The end of summer had been challenging. The heat and humidity were killer. But the winter had been pleasant. No snow.

I pulled into our new driveway. The garage door was open, and Parker had beaten me home. He was already working on pulling stuff out of boxes.

From the car, I admired the beautiful house we had closed on last week. I always wanted to live in the city, but the more we looked at a place to live, the more the outskirts, like where Amelia and Kate lived, called us. We built our own house in the middle of a couple of acres of land but stayed within fifteen minutes of a grocery store.

"There's my beautiful fiancée," Parker smiled at me as I got out of the car.

I couldn't help but smile at the handsome man I was going to marry. A cloud of sweaty and messy red hair. Charming, deep blue eyes. Black wickaway long sleeve that hugged his toned arms.

My engagement ring still felt new and heavy on my finger as I kissed him. The beautiful princess-cut diamond glimmered with the sun.

I assessed the mess in the garage. Brown cardboard boxes, half still closed and half perfectly broken down. The black shelving was already assembled, and Parker's tools were hanging on the wall.

"Let me change, and I'll help you," I pulled away from him and walked into our home.

I was greeted by an intense lemon smell spreading throughout the living room. Parker had cleaned the entire main area of the house. The white marble counter was short of sparkling, and all of the appliances that previously crowded the counter were neatly put away in the walk-in pantry.

"I think we did good," Parker threw his arm around me and kissed my head.

"I agree," I smiled at the mostly empty house. "We still need a couch big enough for the living room, though."

After I moved down, I moved in with Parker. He had a small, one-bedroom apartment downtown, making learning the city easier. I was moving states for him, so why not go all the way and just move in together?

Six months later, he proposed. I screamed yes. Four months later, we bought a house.

With the growth of Truly You, Parker had been knee-deep in paperwork and reviewing all of their contracts. He had also reviewed every word of our house-buying paperwork. He worked a lot, but we kept our promise to enjoy life.

On the Capital Media side, Lainee was the sole manager for the Truly You contract while she trained as the southern regional manager. I stepped away from managing their contract almost completely, except for the general updates I received from my team.

I walked out to the backyard and looked at the land I now called home. We had enough room for a pool and had planned to start building one after we had furnished the house. Parker walked out behind me.

"Honesty moment?" he looked into my watery eyes and pulled me in. I got on my toes and pressed my lips to his.

"I'm really glad I chose the bad locker at the gym."

Acknowledgements

There are so many people to thank for helping us bring Blake's story to life. This story has been swirling in our minds and has been a work in progress for what feels like years. So, thank you to everyone who helped us bring it out of our brains and into the page.

To our beta readers – Emma, Taylor, Sierra, and Liana – thank you for your invaluable feedback and love that you gave the story. This kind of support is invaluable to us as we try to bring our best book forward (hah, get it?). Your comments and reactions to our words as we take this journey provide great encouragement to continue.

To Aliyah from @kylahdesigns – thank you for creating the beautiful cover and helping our readers get a first impression. We absolutely love it, and it was a pleasure to work with you on it.

To the internet, thank you for all the research you provided us with regarding various topics in this book. We owe you one. If you're curious about some of the Google searches, head over to Instagram (@author-bellapursell) to see some of the random things we looked up while writing the book.

To our readers and reviewers, none of this would be possible without you. Your reactions and encouragement are paramount to our success and ability to continue telling these stories.

Don't Forget To Review!

Reviews are critical for authors. Please consider taking a minute to review **Love Me In Color** on GoodReads, Amazon & any other platform you wish to use!

Scan the QR code below for the links!

About The Authors

Bella Pursell was born in Venezuela and moved to the US at ten years old. She began writing at 13 and has always loved to tell stories. As an avid reader herself, she hopes to create worlds to which readers can escape. She has a degree in Supply Chain Management from Texas A&M University (Whoop!) and lives in Houston, TX, with her husband, Nick, and dog, Penny.

Find her on all social media as @authorbellapursell !

Reba Toledo was born in Mexico and moved to the US at eight years old. She fell in love with books very young and is a dedicated reader, reading as many as 47 books in a month. She has a degree in Forensic Science from Eastern New Mexico University and currently lives in Dundee, Scotland.

Other Works

Charlotte's Blank Page
A sweet, found family romance
June 2023

Love Me In Color
A secret/workplace relationship romance
November 2023

A Witchy Situation
A best friends to lovers Halloween novella
October 2024

<u>The Frederick Hill Series</u>

Nice To Meet You (Book #1)
Ana & Wyatt
May 2024

GTSY (Book #2)
Hayden & Sadie
Est. Spring 2025

Title TBD (Book #3)
Bennett & Kennedy
Est. December 2025

Made in the USA
Columbia, SC
01 February 2025

52597670R00155